B.C.
for Free
(and Almost Free)

B.C.
for Free
(and Almost Free)

Pat Kramer

WHITECAP BOOKS
Vancouver / Toronto

Edited by Elaine Jones
Cover design and illustration by Warren Clark
Interior design by Carolyn Deby
Maps by John Kramer
Typography by CompuType, Vancouver, B.C.

Printed and bound in Canada by
    D.W. Friesen and Sons Ltd., Altona, Manitoba

Canadian Cataloguing in Publication Data

Kramer, Pat
    BC for free

    Includes index.
    ISBN 1-55110-020-7

    1. British Columbia—Description and travel—1981
—Guide-books. I. Title.
FC3807.K72 1992   917.1104′4   C92-091019-X
F1087.K72 1992

Table of Contents

Introduction 1

Chapter One: Greater Vancouver 13

    City of Vancouver 15

    North Shore 32

    Richmond 39

    Burnaby.................................. 42

    New Westminster 47

    Coquitlam, Port Coquitlam, and Port Moody 49

    Surrey and White Rock 51

    Delta, Ladner, and Tsawwassen 55

    Langley and Fort Langley 57

    Maple Ridge and Pitt Meadows 59

Chapter Two: Short Trips from Vancouver 65

    ■ *Sea to Sky Country—Highway 99* 67

        Squamish and Area 67

        Whistler 71

        Pemberton and Area 76

        Lillooet 77

    ■ *The Sunshine Coast* 80

        Langdale to Earl's Cove 80

        Powell River to Lund....................... 83

    ■ *Heritage and Rainbow Country—The Fraser Valley and Canyon* 88

        Abbotsford and Matsqui 88

Mission 91
Chilliwack 94
Agassiz and Harrison Hot Springs 98
Hope and Area 103
Manning Park 106
The Fraser Canyon 108

Chapter Three: Victoria and Area 113
Greater Victoria 115
Saanich Peninsula 125
West of Victoria 128

Chapter Four: Vancouver Island 131
■ *South Vancouver Island* 134
Salt Spring Island 134
Other Southern Gulf Islands 135
Duncan and Area 136
Side Trip to Lake Cowichan 138
Chemainus 140
Ladysmith 140
■ *Central Vancouver Island* 142
Nanaimo 142
Parksville and Area 147
Port Alberni 151
Ucluelet 154
Pacific Rim National Park 155
Tofino 158
Qualicum Beach 159
Denman and Hornby Islands 161
Comox Valley Area 161
Campbell River 165
Quadra Island 168
■ *North Vancouver Island* 170
Side Trip to Strathcona Park, Gold River 170
Sayward 173
Port McNeill and Area 173
Alert Bay and Sointula 176

Port Hardy and Area 179

Chapter Five: The Okanagan 183

■ *The Similkameen* 186

    Princeton and Area 186
    Keremeos 189

■ *The Okanagan* 191

    Osoyoos 191
    Oliver 194
    Okanagan Falls ("O.K." Falls) 197
    Penticton and Area 199
    Summerland and Peachland 203
    Westbank 207
    Kelowna 208
    Vernon and Lumby 214

■ *The Spallumcheen* 218

    Armstrong 218
    Enderby 219

Chapter Six: Mountain Highs 223

■ *East to the Rockies—Shuswap Lakes to the Rocky Mountains* 225

    North Shuswap—Chase and Sorrento 226
    Salmon Arm and Area 228
    Sicamous and Area 230
    Revelstoke 232
    Glacier National Park 234
    Yoho National Park 235

■ *The Rocky Mountain Trench—Golden to Fernie* . . . 236

    Golden 236
    Kootenay National Park 237
    Radium Hot Springs 238
    Invermere and Windermere 239
    Fairmont Hot Springs Area 240
    Kimberley 240
    Cranbrook and Area 242
    Fort Steele 244

Fernie and Area............................245
Sparwood 248
■ *The Kootenays—Wandering Mountain Valleys*.....249
Midway, Greenwood and Area................249
Grand Forks...............................253
Rossland and Area.........................255
Trail.......................................257
Castlegar..................................259
Slocan, New Denver and Area...............264
Nakusp 264
Nelson and Area...........................266
Kaslo and the West Shore..................270
Creston and the East Shore................271

Chapter Seven: The Cariboo-Chilcotin............275
Merritt and Area..........................278
Kamloops and Area.........................280
Cache Creek and Ashcroft..................283
Clinton 285
100 Mile House and Area...................287
Williams Lake and Area....................289
The Chilcotin—Side Trip on Highway 20.......292
Quesnel and District......................295
Barkerville and Wells.....................297

Chapter Eight: The Yellowhead Highway..........301
Mount Robson Provincial Park..............304
Prince George and Area....................305
Side Trip to Mackenzie, Chetwynd, and
    Hudson's Hope..........................308
Vanderhoof.................................311
Side Trip to Fort St. James...............311
Fraser Lake...............................313
Burns Lake and Area.......................313
Houston and Side Trip to Babine Lake..........316
Smithers and Area.........................317
Villages of New Hazelton and K'san..........319
Terrace and Area..........................321

Kitimat 324
Prince Rupert 327
The Queen Charlotte Islands, or Haida Gwaii 331

Index 336

■ Introduction ■

Beginners to the concept of free travel experiences may be as surprised at the number, quality, and variety of free experiences available in British Columbia as I was during the compilation of this book. The generosity of industry, individuals, and governments in providing free services in B.C. should indeed be the envy of many other regions. During the research that went into these pages, each discovery of a free service or attraction was like uncovering a new treasure. What fun to discover another place to pan for gold, to watch native dancing, to search the horizon for migrating whales, to sample wines, or to soak in an undeveloped hot springs. That wonder and sense of discovery is now passed on to you.

This book will prove indispensable to anyone who has a crowd of house guests bearing down on them, group organizers called upon to arrange an appropriate outing, instructors looking for low-cost educational experiences, those with a pressing need to avoid yet another boring weekend, and vacationers with a heartfelt curiosity to discover more about what makes British Columbia tick.

Those who search for a deeper meaning through their journeys, may also be surprised to discover the hidden benefits of many of these experiences: they often bring travellers into contact with local residents, open doors to knowledge, and tell about an area's culture and natural wonders. If you truly love meeting new people on their own turf and exploring off-beat places, if the idea of learning about the forest first-hand and plodding around backroads looking for ghosts thrills you, these experiences may be the very ones you are looking for.

The suggested activities in this book will add to your enjoyment of British Columbia at a price that is affordable to us all—absolutely free or almost free. The information in this guide is current at the time of printing; however, changes may occur after this writing—facilities may alter admission arrangements or change their visiting conditions. Always phone ahead, and be prepared to have a more flexible attitude than is generally required for paid attractions.

Before browsing through this book, take a few minutes to read the following few pages. They explain what certain phrases mean, give valuable pointers about accessing free experiences, and outline how the book is organized. Then go out and discover all that's free in B.C.

Terms Used in this Book

No mention of cost: If the entry makes no mention of cost, readers may assume the service or activity is provided free of charge.

Token admission: A charge of $2, $1 or even less.

Small admission: A charge of under $3 to $4. This is the "almost free" part of the book. The benchmark used to establish a small admission is the price of a return public transit fare in a major city. Free activities in this book outnumber those requiring any admission.

Outstanding Value: A few entries represent an extraordinary value. Admission is more than the "small" category and is marked on each entry. Why include them? Because the attraction is of exceptional merit and deserves to be included for the proportion of value it represents. It may be a heritage site of special significance, a special presentation which is little advertised, or an 8-hour ferry ride up the coast. Activities that require monetary outlay were carefully considered and the few that are included—just over a dozen—are clearly marked.

Guided tours are available: Either tours are scheduled on a regular basis or the facility is familiar with scheduling conducted tours whenever they receive notice.

Guided tours may be available: The facility has expressed a willingness to conduct guided tours, subject to the availability of volunteers or staff and their own internal organizational constraints.

What's a guided tour? Guided tours include the services of a tour leader who points out interesting details and provides background information. Always take a guided tour whenever one is available; they add immeasurably to the quality of an experience. The guided tours in this book are free of charge unless otherwise stated.

What's a presentation? A presentation can take three forms: instruction in a classroom setting, such as making raspberry vinegar; a set of exhibits, paintings, or displays that change on a periodic basis; a re-enactment of an historical event or a special celebratory game, such as a "pioneer-style firehose-reeling contest." The presentations in this book are free of charge, or included in the small admission.

What's a visit or a demonstration? The public is allowed to enter a facility, but a tour leader is not necessarily provided. The public can see the workers, look around in non-restricted areas, and occasionally taste a few samples.

What's an interpretive program? Paid guides or trained volunteers explain nature through a mini-lecture, using displays of plant or animal materials, or they take a group on a walk to see living examples of nature's works. These programs are frequently held during the summer in provincial or regional parks. Interpretive programs are free of charge.

What's a Visitor Centre? Drop-in facilities for the public are designed to explain the details of an operation and feature permanent displays of photographs or educational material; others have audio-visual rooms for educational presentations. All are staffed and are free of charge.

What's a nature walk and how does it differ from an interpretive walk? A nature walk is a designated trail, usually upgraded for easy access, that meanders through an area of visual beauty, verdant foliage, and abundant wildlife. There are no explanatory signs, but the trail is designed to take advantage of the beauty of an area. An interpretive walk is an educational, as well as a visual, experience. Signs are set into patches of wildflowers, pointers give the details of tree growth, or explanatory pamphlets are available. Nature walks and interpretive walks are free of charge.

Groups only: In these cases, the tour is offered only when numbers warrant it. Group leaders, club organizers, committee chairs, and teachers will find these activities suitable, but groups need not be registered to qualify. A family grouping, a few friends and neighbours, may also qualify as a group. Each facility has a different idea about group size. For some, a group is 3 or 4 people; for others, minimums are 10 or 20 people. Phone ahead to determine group policy.

Valuable Tips

Free activities require more planning than paid attractions. This is the tricky bit. Opening hours may be restricted; guided tours take place at odd intervals; groups or individuals may be asked to book in advance. Unlike paid attractions, free tours and services do not always receive priority and they can be abruptly cancelled. Persist in obtaining information. Be assured that the extra effort required to phone ahead is more than repaid in the final experience. Free activities are a bit more trouble and require a sense of humour at times, but are worth it in the end. Timing your visit is crucial.

Many festivals are listed, but not all elements of an event are free. Festivals, celebrations, public parties, and contests may feature some free opportunities. For example: big-name festivals sponsor sample performances for free; community festivals feature fireworks, parades, community picnics, and heritage activities such as old-time machinery demonstrations; multicultural festivals offer dancing exhibitions, entertainment, and crafts from many nations; competitions, such as sand-castle building, are free for spectators; heritage sites stage free history recreations. Smart festival-goers seek out the free elements surrounding a festival; phone ahead.

Opening hours and opening seasons for free activities change without warning. Facilities that offer free experiences are sometimes run by volunteers. Since their services are free, administrators have few qualms about switching days, or changing opening hours. Some are closed in winter one year and open a month longer the following year. No matter what hours or seasonal openings this book might list, readers may find a change. Museums may close, park workers remove "interpretive" signs from nature trails, and guided tours shut down for the season. The best plan is a quick phone check before you visit any facility.

All groups should phone ahead for an appointment. Groups of more than 5 persons may require more chairs, extra samples, an additional tour leader, special attention, clean-up staff, and additional security for the building. As a courtesy, groups should always make prior arrangements, and then a second confirmation call shortly before arrival.

Who answers the listed phone numbers? When you call a Travel InfoCentre (shortened to InfoCentre in the listings), particularly in outlying areas, it may be answered with "Chamber of Commerce," "Business Information Centre," "Business Development Centre," "Tourist Information" or even "Hello." Many communities in British Columbia combine their tourist information depots with municipal functions. No matter how the phone is answered, the people on the other end should help you.

Always double check directions with a Travel InfoCentre. The directions here have been taken from public sources and confirmed independently. But directions to places without addresses can be a confusing business and subject to misinterpretation. Particularly important before leaving any main road is to get a diagram in advance.

Maps. The maps in this book are simply intended for readers to orient themselves. Always have a good road map before setting out.

How This Book is Organized

Not included: Serious hiking trails, expedition routes, canoe routes, white-water rivers, fishing lakes, and those experiences that require specialty know-how, physical conditioning, or extensive preparation are covered in other guide books.

Only a few provincial parks are listed. Each of the more than 300 provincial parks in British Columbia has been set aside for some sort of natural wonder. For the purposes of this book, only those parks that offer something extra qualify for inclusion: park naturalist guided programs, a discovery experience such as the ability to pick up industrial grade rubies, examples of our native heritage, recreational panning for gold, or opportunities for viewing abundant wildlife.

Categories in each section: The items under each main entry are grouped in the following general categories.

■ **Parks, Gardens, and Nature:** Nature is the prime attraction. Places and activities noted for wildlife, flowers, greenery, or natural phenomena, such as salmon enhancement facilities or interesting geology, are listed here. Plan your visit when conditions are at their best—usually summer or autumn.

■ **Museums, Notable Buildings, and Structures:** Man-made things are the prime attraction. Artifacts, collections, historical buildings, museums, art galleries, old train stations, abandoned sites, heritage sites, and bridges are listed. Always phone ahead to determine open seasons or opening hours.

■ **Tours, Visits, and Demonstrations:** A special information experience is the prime attraction. Tours focus on nature, industry, the forest, and B.C.'s history. Two kinds of tours are covered: guided tours include a leader who takes participants around a site; the self-guided tour may consist of interpretive signs that lead the participant around a site or a walking or driving tour of historic buildings or wildlife preserves. For self-guided tours, you may need to obtain a map or brochure in advance.

■ **Cultural Appreciation:** Customs, arts, and music are featured. Listings with an emphasis on native people, multicultural enrichment, or artistic performances are found here. Determining the exact dates and locations of these activities may take some additional research.

■ **Join in the Fun:** An element of fun is found just in "doing it" or "being there." Festivals, contests, celebrations, competitions, mini-adventures, as well as those activities that defy classification in other sections, are listed here. Most have free elements or are free. The challenge in this category is to get the timing right and to find out what's free surrounding an event.

To Obtain More Information

Area codes are (604) unless otherwise stated.

Tourism British Columbia Information: toll free, 1-800-663-6000.

Accommodations Guide: Ministry of Tourism, Parliament Buildings, Victoria B.C., V8V 1X4. Phone: 387-1642.

Archaeology and Outdoor Recreation in B.C.: Director of Archaeology and Outdoor Recreation, 5th Floor, 800 Johnson St., Victoria, V8V 1X4; phone: 356-1045, FAX: 387-4429. Archaeological Society of B.C., P.O. Box 520, Station A, Vancouver, V6C 2N3.

B.C. Ferries: B.C. Ferry Corporation, 1112 Fort St., Victoria, V8V 4V2. Phone: 669-1211 or 386-3431; from Seattle: (206) 624-6663; for the phone numbers of small regional ferries, such as those that cross rivers or lakes, phone Centrex, 660-2421.

B.C. Hydro Recreation Areas: B.C. Hydro, Environmental Resources, Corporate and Environmental Affairs, 970 Burrard St., Vancouver, V6Z 1T3.

Bed and Breakfast Establishments: See Accommodations Guide.

Campgrounds in National Parks: Inquiry Centre, Main Floor, Vincent Massey Bldg., 351 St. Joseph Blvd., Hull, Quebec, K1A 0H3. Phone: (819) 997-2800.

Campgrounds in B.C.: See Accommodations Guide and the official B.C. road map; or ask for the booklet "Super Camping" from the Ministry of Tourism, Parliament Buildings, Victoria, V8V 1X4. Phone: 387-1642.

Campsites that are Remote: See Forestry Backroads Maps.

Caves: B.C. Speleological Federation, Box 993, Gold River, V0P 1G0. Phone: 283-7144, FAX: 284-2461.

City Parks: Phone City Hall in the municipality and ask for the Parks Department.

Charter Boats: Western Canada Charter Boat Association, P.O. Box 1010, Station A, Vancouver, V6P 2P1. Phone: 681-2129.

Demonstration Forests: Contact each area's InfoCentre separately.

Ecological Reserves: Friends of Ecological Reserves, Room 420, 620 View St., Victoria, V8W 1J6.

Elderhostel: Write for catalogue of 60 sites. Elderhostel Canada, 300-33 Prince Arthur Ave., Toronto, M5R 1B2.

Festivals and Special Events: Contact each area's InfoCentre separately. B.C. Association of Agricultural Fairs and Exhibitions, Box 39, Lantzville, V0R 2H0. Ministry of Tourism, Parliament Buildings, Victoria, V8V 1X4. Phone: 387-1642, 1-800-663-6000.

Fishing, Fresh Water: B.C. Fishing Resorts and Outfitters' Association, P.O. Box 3301, Kamloops, V2C 6B9; phone: 828-1553. Ministry of Tourism, Parliament Buildings, Victoria, V8V 1X4; phone: 387-1642, 1-800-663-6000.

Fishing, Salt Water: Sport Fishing Institute of British Columbia, #270 - 1075 West Georgia St., Vancouver, V6G 2G3. Phone: 669-3788. Ministry of Tourism, Parliament Buildings, Victoria, V8V 1X4. Phone: 387-1642, 1-800-663-6000.

Forestry Backroads Maps: Contact each area's Forest District; for assistance in sorting out the Forest Districts, contact the InfoCentre in each area or the Recreation Division, Ministry of Forests, 2nd Floor, 610 Johnson St., Victoria, V8W 3E7. Phone: 387-8480.

Forestry Tours and Resource Materials: British Columbia Forestry Association, 9800A - 140th St., Surrey, V3T 4M5. Phone: 582-0100, FAX: 582-0101. Summer Tour Brochures - Northern Sector, Council of Forest Industries, 400 - 1488 4th Ave., Prince George, V2L 4Y2.

Ghost Towns: Contact each area's InfoCentre separately or see Heritage Information.

Gold Panning: Serious hobbyists should contact the Gold Commissioner in each area of the province. Casual recreational panners can contact the InfoCentre in the area. Public Information Unit of Energy, Mines and Petroleum Resources, phone: 356-2824.

Guest Ranches: Cariboo Tourist Association, P.O. Box 4900, 190 Yorkston St., Williams Lake, V2G 2V8. Phone: 392-2226, FAX: 392-2832.

Guide-Outfitters: Guide Outfitter's Association of B.C., Box 759, 100 Mile House, V0K 2E0. Phone: 395-2438, FAX: 395-2410. Northwest Guides and Outfitters Association, P.O. Box 2489, Smithers.

Heritage Information: Recreation and Culture Library, Librarian, Room 101, 800 Johnson St., Victoria, V8V 1X4; phone: 356-1440. Heritage Society of B.C., 411 Dunsmuir St., Vancouver, V6B 1X4. B.C. Historical Federation, P.O. Box 35326, Station E, Vancouver, V6M 4G5; phone: 748-8397.

Heritage Sites and Attractions: Heritage Properties Branch, 5th Floor, 800 Johnson St., Victoria, V8V 1X4; phone: 387-1619. Heritage site information, 1-800-663-6000.

Hiking: See Outdoor Activities.

Hydroelectric Dam Tours: Public Relations Department, B.C. Hydro, 970 Burrard St., Vancouver, V6Z 1Y3. Phone: 663-2212.

Map of Highways and Parks: Ministry of Tourism, Parliament Buildings, Victoria, V8V 1X4. Phone: 387-1642 or 1-800-663-6000.

Museums: British Columbia Museums Association, Secretariat Office, 514 Government St., Victoria, V8V 4X4. Phone: 387-3315.

Native Festivals: Contact each Tribal Council separately. For assistance with names of Bands, contact Indian and Northern Affairs, British Columbia Regional Office, 300 - 1550 Alberni St., Vancouver, V6G 3C5. Phone: 666-5121.

Nature Information: Federation of B.C. Naturalists, Room 321, 1367 W. Broadway, Vancouver, V6H 4A9. Phone: 737-3057, FAX: 738-7175.

Outdoor Activities: For assistance in sorting out the 48 associations that sponsor outdoor activities, contact The Outdoor Recreation Council of British Columbia, Suite 334, 1367 W. Broadway, Vancouver, V6H 4A9; phone: 737-3058. Call Sport B.C., 737-3000, for information on outdoor activities. Ask for "Outdoor and Adventure Guide" booklet from Ministry of Tourism, Parliament Buildings, Victoria, V8V 1X4; phone: 387-1642.

Parks, Maps and Information, Provincial: B.C. Parks, 2nd Floor, 800 Johnson St., Victoria, V8V 1X5. Phone: 387-5002, FAX: 387-5757. Ministry of Lands and Parks, Parks and Outdoor Recreation Division, 1019 Wharf St., Victoria, V8W 2Y9.

Parks, Maps and Information, Federal: Visitor Services, Canadian Parks Services, P.O. Box 2989, Station M, Calgary, Alberta, T2P 3H8. Phone: (403) 292-4401, FAX: (403) 292-4746.

River Rafting: See Outdoor Activities.

Rock Hounding: Lapidary Rock and Mineral Society of British Columbia, 941 Wavertree Rd., North Vancouver, V7R 1S4. Minfile Unit, Ministry of Energy, Mines, and Petroleum Resources, Room 201, 553 Superior St., Victoria, V8V 1X4; phone: 356-2824.

Salmon Enhancement Facilities: Salmonid Enhancement Program. Department of Fisheries and Oceans, 555 West Hastings St., Vancouver, V6B 5G3. Phone: 666-3545.

Ski and Summer Resorts: See Accommodations Guide.

Skiing: See Outdoor Activities; or ask for "Skiing in B.C." booklet from Ministry of Tourism, Parliament Buildings, Victoria, V8V 1X4. Phone: 387-1642.

Topographic Maps: Maps B.C., Surveys and Mapping Branch, Ministry of the Environment, Parliament Buildings, Victoria, V8W 1X4.

Tourist Information on B.C. from London, England: Tourism B.C., 1 Regent St., London, England. Phone: (01) 930-6857, FAX: Call operator 7-2121, then 930-2021.

Tourist Information on B.C. from Los Angeles: Tourism B.C., Suite 1050, 2600 Michelson St., Irvine, CA, 92715. Phone: (714) 852-1054, FAX: (714) 852-0168.

Tourist Information on B.C. from San Francisco: Tourism B.C., #400, 100 Bush St., San Francisco, CA, 94104. Phone: (415) 981-4780, FAX: (415) 981-0223.

Tourist Information on B.C. from Seattle: Tourism B.C., #930, 720 Olive Way, Seattle, WA, 98101. Phone: (206) 623-5937, FAX: (206) 447-9004.

Trail Riding: See Outdoor Activities.

Travel InfoCentres: All InfoCentres are listed in the "Accommodations Guide," available from Ministry of Tourism, Parliament Buildings, Victoria, V8V 1X4. Phone: 387-1642.

Wilderness Fishing: North by Northwest Tourism Association, 3840 Alfred Ave., Box 1030, Smithers, V0J 2N0. Phone: 847-5227, FAX: 847-7585. Ask for the "Sport Fishing Guide."

Wilderness Preservation: Western Canada Wilderness Committee, 20 Water St., Vancouver, V6B 1A4; phone: 683-8220. Sierra Club of Western Canada, Room 314, 620 View St., Victoria, V8W 1J4; phone: 386-5255.

Wildlife Viewing Areas in B.C.: B.C. Environment Wildlife Branch, 780 Blanchard St., Victoria, V8V 1X5. Phone: 387-9767, FAX: 356-9145. Ask for the "Wildlife Watch" pamphlet.

• • (1) • •

GREATER VANCOUVER

Vancouver rightly deserves its repu-
tation as a vibrant, beautiful city
pushing up against a relatively unex-
plored wilderness, a place where the mountains romance the sea. With an abundance
of timber, minerals, farms, fish, and hydroelectric power all around, beautiful Vancouver
is a city that faraway visitors often long for,
and residents surprisingly take for granted.

"It rains," grumble the locals.

"We haven't had rain for two years. This
is so refreshing," marvels the visiting California fruit grower.

Visitors find that the city has several notable qualities: it is greener than expected, rains

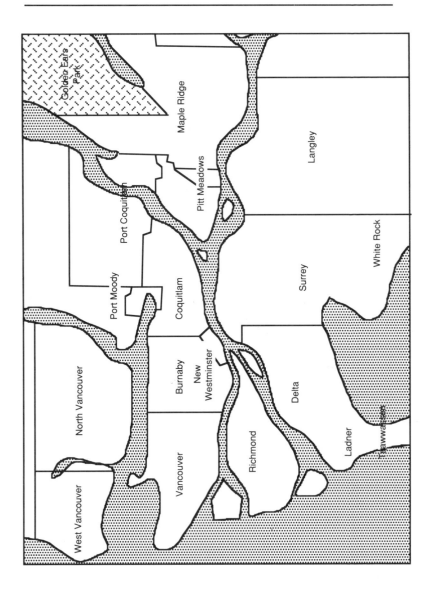

less than they had been led to believe, has many more worthwhile activities than they have allowed for in their timing, is located in a beautiful setting, has wonderful gardens, is full of hospitable people. And it's expensive. It is the last point that is addressed in the pages of this book. Greater Vancouver, like the rest of British Columbia, has a multitude of free experiences available to those who scratch beneath the surface. Armed with a little knowledge, anyone can take advantage of a variety of activities, while keeping one's wallet neatly pocketed.

This chapter is divided into listings for each municipality and district as far east as Fort Langley, as far north as the districts of North Vancouver and West Vancouver, and as far south as White Rock on the border with the U.S.A. These civic centres combine to form Greater Vancouver, also known as the Lower Mainland.

General Information

Information on the attractions and festivals of Greater Vancouver: Tourism Association of Southwestern British Columbia, #304 - 828 West 8th Ave., Vancouver, V5Z 1E2. Phone: 739-9011, 1-800-667-3306.

Information and maps on B.C. parks in the Lower Mainland: Ministry of Parks, 1610 Mount Seymour Road, North Vancouver, V7G 1L3. Phone: 929-1291, FAX: 929-2425.

Information on programs, tours, and educational publications on south coast forests: British Columbia Forestry Association, 9800-140th St., Surrey, V3T 4M5. Phone: 583-0040, FAX: 582-0050.

City of Vancouver

Transit Information: 261-5100.

Events, Recorded Info Line: 661-7373.

Talking Yellow Pages Events Line: 299-9000.

Arts Hotline: 684-ARTS.

Information on the attractions and festivals of Vancouver: Vancouver InfoCentre, Waterfront Centre, 200 Burrard St.,

Vancouver, B.C. V6C 3L6. Phone: 683-2000, 1-800-888-8835,
FAX: 683-2601.

■ **Pacific Spirit Regional Park:** Old-growth fir and
cedar forests are found along the 50 km (31 mi.) of trails
set aside for walking or cycling. At Camosun Bog, plant
remnants from the last Ice Age, such as the arctic starflower, cloud-
berry, and carnivorous sundew, survive in a soggy environment.
The Visitors' Centre has pamphlets and sponsors a volunteer program for regular park users. Periodic interpretive programs are
available; phone ahead.
Location: University Endowment Lands, next to UBC Campus;
Visitor's Centre at 16th Ave. and Blanca St.
Information: 224-5739 for general information; 432-6350 to book
group tours.

■ **Queen Elizabeth Park:** An old basalt rock quarry converted into meticulously maintained flower gardens is the basis of
Little Mountain's park. Technically the geographic centre of Vancouver and the highest point within the city limits, a well-used
lookout features views of downtown Vancouver and Mount Baker
in the distance. A geodesic-domed conservatory houses an exotic
plant collection; a small admission fee is charged.
Location: Cambie at 33rd Ave.
Information: Bloedel Conservatory, 872-5513.

■ **Stanley Park:** Occupying a peninsula in the heart of downtown Vancouver, this 400-ha (1000-ac.) park is considered to be
one of the premier city parks in North America. Some of its many
features include gardens and forests, Beaver Lake, the Hollow Tree,
a children's water-park, Lost Lagoon, a collection of totem poles,
and a formal Rose Garden. A small zoo houses a collection of mon-
keys, otters, and bears. On Saturdays and Sundays, weather
permitting, outdoor artists display their wares. A dip in the saltwater pool at Second Beach can be a prelude for a walk to Siwash
Rock or around the 9-km (5.5-mi.) SeaWall. Events are held here
throughout the year, and guided walking tours may be sponsored

in summer by the Vancouver Parks Board; phone ahead. Allow 1 hour for the nature tour.
Location: In downtown Vancouver at the west end of Georgia St.
Information: Vancouver Parks and Recreation. Nature House, 685-7314, for guided walking tours.

■ **Stargazing:** Two observatories in Vancouver, staffed by volunteers, are open periodically. Visitors can take turns viewing the sun, moon, planets, and the stars through large telescopes. Special activities, such as nights for amateur photographers, are held from time to time; phone ahead.
Location: Gordon Southam Observatory, Vanier Park, near 1100 Chestnut St.; UBC Observatory, UBC Campus. Phone for exact directions.
Information: Gordon Southam, 738-2855, for astronomical events of note and to confirm that staff is present; UBC Observatory, 822-6186, to confirm that staff is present.

■ **UBC Botanical Gardens, Nitobe Memorial Gardens:** Free on Wednesdays and from November 1 to the end of February. The 47-ha (116-ac.) botanical garden consists of five main parts, including a collection of native plants, a re-creation of a medieval herb garden, a food garden, and an alpine garden. Nitobe Memorial Garden, a classical Japanese garden, is outstanding in May, when cherry blossoms emerge. The Japanese Tea Ceremony is performed periodically in a small house on-site; phone to inquire. For a fee, guided tours of the gardens may be available; phone ahead. Two other separate, but smaller, campus gardens are free to visit: a children's garden with educationally designed spaces for youngsters, and a rose garden featuring 300 varieties considered at their best in June and July.
Location: UBC Botanical Gardens, 6804 N.W. Marine Dr.; Nitobe Memorial Gardens, 6500 N.W. Marine Dr., beside the Asian centre; Neville Scarfe Children's Garden, through the main foyer, west side of the UBC Neville Scarfe Education building; Rose Garden, beside the Faculty Club.
Information: UBC gardens, 822-3928; campus security, 822-4721, for directions to the gardens; gardening information, 822-5858.

■ **B.C. and Yukon Chamber of Mines, Mineral Room:** Rock hounds can enjoy a look at minerals, ores, gems, and chunks of gold ore; all are identified in their natural state and set out in glass showcases. No guided tours are available. Opening hours are limited.
Location: 840 West Hastings St.
Information: 681-5328.

■ **B.C. Trade Showcases:** Permanent displays of some of British Columbia's export-ready products and services are featured in this special room set aside to present B.C.'s contributions to the global marketplace. Communications companies, machinery parts manufacturers, food exporters, telecommunications companies, and the emerging electronics industry have collaborated on displays in a maze of glass showcases. Come and be amazed at the variety of products and services that B.C industry and government send around the world. Allow 1 hour. Limited opening hours.
Location: 601 West Cordova, main foyer of the station for SeaBus and SkyTrain.
Information: 775-0374.

■ **Canadian Craft Museum:** Small admission; children under 12 free. Functional art pieces and handicrafts, along with works that are purely artistic and non-functional, are displayed in this stunning museum. Special group activities for a fee are available; phone ahead.
Location: 639 Hornby St., Cathedral Place.
Information: 687-8266, FAX: 684-7174.

■ **Canadian Pacific Railway Cars:** Admission varies. Historic railway cars and examples of vintage rolling stock are on display in changing locales sponsored by the non-profit Railway Association. A restored 100-year-old Canadian Pacific Railway business car finished in Honduran mahogany, leather, plush velour upholstery, etched glass, and brass fixtures is an example of the elegant executive living of a bygone era. Guided tours may be avail-

able; phone ahead.
Location: Various locations. Contact West Coast Railway Association, P.O. Box 2790, Vancouver, V6B 3X2.
Information: Railway Association contact number, 522-9068.

■ **Gobelin Tapestries:** Two masterfully executed tapestries are on display to illustrate a little-understood medical phenomenon. The unfortunate weaver suffered a cerebral hemorrhage and recovered. The neatly executed design he had been working on then evolved into distorted faces and melting images; the artist maintained that his work had improved.
Location: Woodward Biomedical Library, UBC Campus.
Information: Campus security, 822-4721, for directions; 822-3131 for a campus tour (summer only).

■ **Old Hastings Mill Store:** Admission by donation. This building is the only structure known to have survived the great fire which destroyed Gastown in 1886. Although plain in looks and small in size, it is one of Vancouver's few links to its pioneering past. Before 1858, there were only a few hundred non-native persons in British Columbia, their needs met by fur-trading companies. With the discovery of gold in 1859, a rush of prospectors invaded from the United States and the first general stores were established. Early store-keepers acted as information depots, bankers, outfitters, and developers; many owners became the first mayors and aldermen. The museum is closed part of the year. Limited opening hours.
Location: 1575 Alma St. at Point Grey Rd.
Information: 228-1213.

■ **Museum of Anthropology:** Free on Tuesdays. The masterful yellow cedar carving called *Raven and the First Men*, by Haida carver Bill Reid, is the focal point of the native art collection housed in an award-winning building. Totem poles and an argillite collection representative of B.C.'s rich aboriginal heritage are complemented by a permanent collection of outstanding ceramics donated by the museum's moving force, Walter C. Koerner. The museum is also an active storage centre for cultural artifacts owned by UBC, and assembled by anthropology professors or other

academics during their world travels. The public can use the cross-reference guides to find out more about the storage collection on display. Guided group tours require a fee.
Location: 6393 N.W. Marine Drive, UBC Campus, Point Grey.
Information: 822-3825 for a recorded message; 822-5087 for specific inquiries.

■ **Museum of the Exotic World:** Evidence of unusual tribal customs is on display along with odd keepsakes and thousands of photographs, mounted collections of large insects, butterflies, and a display of stuffed crocodiles. Harold and Barbara Morgan assembled memorabilia during 36 years of world travel. Limited opening hours; phone ahead.
Location: 3561 Main St.
Information: 876-0073.

■ **M. Y. Williams Geological Museum:** Dinosaurs in Vancouver? A 10-metre-long (33-ft.) skeleton of one of these fellows (find out why it's likely not a girl) can be seen here. Rock hounds can view a display of fossils, minerals, ores, and gemstones. Limited opening hours. Guided tours may be available; phone ahead.
Location: UBC Campus. East of the Neville Scarfe Education Building, inside the Geological Sciences Building.
Information: Geological Museum, 822-5586.

■ **Rodde House:** Token admission (may vary depending on tour). The first Victorian house set aside for preservation in Vancouver is now a restored home, especially beautiful at Christmas time. During opening hours, a guide covers the home's architectural and human history. Tea is sometimes available (for a fee). Usually open the second and fourth Sunday of the month; phone ahead.
Location: 1415 Barclay St.
Information: Heritage House, 684-7040.

■ **Rogers Sugar Museum:** Artifacts used in connection with sugar and interpretive displays about the company's historical forays into the Dominican Republic illustrate the importance of the sugar industry to Vancouver from its earliest days. Housed in a heritage structure, the supporting beams of parts of this building are hand-hewn tree trunks. Allow 1 hour. Guided tours may be available; phone ahead. Suggestion: combine this tour with a visit to the nearby Vancouver Port Corporation. **Location:** Foot of Rogers St., off the foot of Clark Dr. **Information:** 253-1131.

■ **Vancouver Art Gallery:** Admission by donation on Thursdays from 5:00 until 9:00 p.m. Vancouver's art collection is housed in a renovated 1934 courthouse building. On permanent display are the works of pioneer B.C. artist Emily Carr, an emerging collection of modern art, and the eclectic collections of earlier Vancouver art committees. Visiting exhibitions add variety to the permanent groupings. For a fee, guided tours may be available; phone ahead. **Location:** 750 Hornby St. **Information:** 682-5621.

■ **Vancouver Centennial Police Museum:** Small admission. On display are a range of artifacts including antique handcuffs, illegal street weapons, contraband from drug seizures, and modern crime prevention devices. Allow 1 hour to read the commentary which accompanies the exhibits. Opening hours are limited. **Location:** 240 East Cordova St. **Information:** 665-3346.

■ **Vancouver Museum:** Free on Tuesdays for seniors; small admission for others. Native artifacts retell the story of the area before white contact, while early British naval artifacts and pioneer exhibits tell the post-contact story. A realistic model of a ship's dark and dank interior simulates the conditions under which many white settlers arrived in this country; various travelling exhibits provide additional interest. **Location:** 1100 Chestnut St. **Information:** 736-4431.

■ **Art-Glass-Making Demonstrations:** Visitors can drop in and watch a demonstration of how hand-blown glass is made at two facilities. Using ancient techniques, glassmakers heat and twirl glass rods, then thrust the pipe into the "tank," a hot furnace containing molten clear glass. The "glory hole" is a furnace used for re-heating in order to prolong the working time of the glass. After blowing and spinning, the glass object solidifies quickly. Most demonstrations take place in the afternoon. **Location:** Robert Held Art Glass, 2130 Pine St. at 6th Ave.; New-Small and Sterling Studio Glass, 1440 Old Bridge St. at Granville Island. **Information:** Robert Held, 737-0020; New-Small and Sterling Studio Glass, 681-6730.

■ **B.C. Place Stadium Tour:** Groups of 10 or more can prearrange a tour for a fee. This stadium is the largest air-supported dome in the world. The Teflon fabric roof is inflated by 2 jet engines and up to 60,000 fans can be seated in various configurations, depending upon the event. Tour participants peek into furnished private boxes, the field area, the dressing rooms of football players and entertainment personalities. Ask which rock star had an entire dressing room filled with wall-to-wall jelly beans. Allow 1 hour. **Location:** Robson St. at Beatty and Pacific Blvd. **Information:** 661-7305 for booking group tours; Recorded Events Hotline, 661-7373.

■ **B.C. Sports Hall of Fame:** The pucks that scored the winning goals, the photos of sporting old-timers, and the jerseys of famous football players are on display. Pictured here is the moment of victory in the "four-minute mile" first accomplished by runner Roger Bannister during the Commonwealth Games in 1954. There are also tributes to cross-Canada runner Terry Fox and wheelchair marathoner Rick Hansen. Allow 1 hour. Limited opening hours. **Location:** Gate A, B.C. Place Stadium, 777 Pacific Blvd. South. **Information:** 687-5523; Infoline, 687-5520.

■ **Brewing Company Tour:** Life cannot promise many free lunches, but it does permit the odd free beer. The products of this cottage brewery adhere to the 1516 Bavarian purity law and the conducted tour covers the brewing process, but there is no examination at the end—only a tasting. Guided tours are available; phone ahead. Allow 1 hour. Start a Bachelor's degree in Brewology at Granville

Island then continue a "spirited" education in the wineries of the Okanagan.
Location: Granville Island Brewing Co., 1441 Cartwright St.
Information: 688-9927.

■ **Canada Place Tour:** This facility was built as a cooperative venture between Tokyo Corporation of Japan and the Federal Government of Canada to create a showcase facility for Vancouver's waterfront. The guided tour covers the cruise ship terminal, the public areas of the luxury hotel, the convention rooms (if not in use), and the World Trade and Convention Centre. Or visitors can take a self-guided stroll along the promenade decks outside the convention centre, where plaques along the railings outline the history of Vancouver. Scheduled tours are available in summer; phone ahead. Groups can book an appointment year-round. Allow 1 hour.
Location: 999 Canada Place.
Information: 688-8687 for tours.

■ **Canadian Memorial Church Tour:** Donations gratefully accepted for ongoing restoration. Nine beautiful stained-glass windows were created in 1920 by Robert Mac Causland to represent the provinces of Canada. Since then, other windows have been added: an "all Canada" scene, the Resurrection, and the "tributes to service" donated by the War Amputees and Nursing Sisters organizations. In addition, the church holds the only copy, outside of the city of Ottawa, of the Book of Remembrance of war casualties. Groups only, by appointment. Allow 1 hour.
Location: 1811 West 16th Ave.
Information: 731-3101.

■ **Chocolate-Art Demonstration:** Greg Hook specializes in the design of chocolate, including emblems for organizations and reproductions of Haida art. He will give demonstrations and estimates on custom-made chocolates. Small groups only, by appointment.
Location: Chocolate Arts, 2037 West 4th Ave.
Information: 739-0475.

■ **Chocolate-Molding Factory Open House:** During the pre-Easter rush, this facility may hold an open house, or present a demonstration on the process of handling and molding chocolate. Phone for current details at least 6 weeks in advance of Easter.
Location: Purdy's Chocolates, 2777 Kingsway.
Information: 430-6444.

■ **Fire-Hall Tour:** Group leaders can organize a fire-hall tour; big fire engines and the thrill of fire fighting continue to delight youngsters. After an initial phone call is made to the number listed below, written permission must be obtained from the Fire Chief. Groups only, over the age of 8 years.
Location: Various fire-halls, as arranged.
Information: 665-6000.

■ **Flag-Sewing Demonstration:** Participants can see the techniques used to produce colourful "hangings" in a manufacturing facility which assembles the flags of various nations and creates festive banners for all occasions. Small groups only, by appointment. Allow 1 hour.
Location: Flag Shop, 1755 W. 4th Ave., near Burrard St.
Information: 736-8161.

■ **Forestry Talks and Tours:** Clubs, groups, and organizations can arrange guided tours of active forestry operations, mills, or seedling facilities. Alternately, an experienced forester will speak about forest management issues at any organization's venue.
Location: Association of Professional Foresters of B.C., #440 - 789 West Pender, Vancouver, V6C 1H2.
Information: 687-8027, FAX: 687-3264.

■ **Granville Island Visitor Centre:** A short audio-visual presentation (available on demand during opening hours) and interpretive display outline the history of Granville Island and how it emerged from a conglomeration of manufacturing plants to become a vibrant assembly of fresh-food stalls, bakeries, theatres, galleries, and shops. Brochures and maps are available. There are several recurring festivals and frequent periods of street entertainment. The on-site Emily Carr College of Art and Design features ongoing displays of art work and several of the Island's art studios combine to offer periodic "art-walk" tours. To tap into all the activities and celebrations at this varied facility, ask for a booklet of seasonal events.

Location: Johnstone St., below the Granville Bridge.

Information: Granville Island InfoCentre, 666-5784.

■ **Gastown Walking Tour:** The oldest portion of Vancouver, once the domain of an eloquent pioneer English saloon owner named "Gassy" Jack, was saved from the wreckers ball in the 1960s. Now a centre of street entertainment and shopping, a walking tour covers architectural features of the area and colourful stories from the past. Brochures are available and guided walking tours may be available in summer; phone ahead. Sponsored by the Gastown Merchants Association. Allow 1 hour.

Location: Water St. Inquire about exact start point.

Information: 683-5650.

■ **Grocery Store Tours:** Grocery shopping may be a rote activity, but an insider's look at bakery and butchering operations can give visitors a new perspective. Groups only, by appointment. While the Safeway company's phone number is listed here, other food chains also offer guided tours. Call any regional headquarters or the store manager.

Location: Various commercial grocery stores.

Information: Safeway Regional Office, 687-4833. Ask for public affairs.

■ **Jade-Works Demonstration:** Drawing from a supply of more than 9 tonnes (10 tons) of jade and marble on-site, craftsmen execute tiny cuts, turning the stone into ornaments, various-sized sculptures, and jewellery. Discuss the value of Canadian jade versus varieties found elsewhere. Demonstrations are available; phone ahead. Allow 30 minutes.

Location: Jade World, 1696 West 1st Ave. Free parking on the side.

Information: 733-7212.

■ **Mastodon Ivory Mini Museum and Studio Visit:** Owning or purchasing elephant ivory has become an ecological issue for which the solution may be a unique Canadian product

formed from the ivory tusks of extinct mastodons. Pitted by centuries of weathering, the tusks are in-filled with semi-precious stones. This small studio will permit participants to browse among examples of jewellery, sculptures, and working tools. Open only by arrangement. Allow 30 minutes.
Location: Manus Enterprises, #320 - 380 West 4th Ave.
Information: 988-1299.

■ **Orpheum Theatre Tour:** This heritage concert hall was saved from destruction to become the longest-surviving grand theatre in Vancouver. The guided tour covers the details of its glittering splendour, the story of its restoration, and a recounting of colourful stories from the theatre's star-studded past. Guided tours are available; phone ahead. Groups can phone year-round for an appointment. Allow 1 hour.
Location: 884 Granville St.
Information: Arts phoneline, 684-2787, for information.

■ **Port of Vancouver Loading Facility Tour:** After an audio-visual presentation in one of two versions, adult or child, visitors move to an elevated viewing area to watch loading and unloading of container ships. Interpretive displays enhance the viewing area. Guided tours are available in summer; phone ahead. Groups can phone year-round for an appointment. Allow 45 minutes to 1 hour. Worth noting are two annual activities sponsored by the Port of Vancouver: a "party" with bands and flag waving for the arrival of the first cruise ship of the season in early May, and Port Day, the last Sunday of May, with rides on the paddlewheeler *Constitution* and visits to Roberts Banks, an enormous coal-shipping facility near the U.S. border. Inquire specifically about special events.
Location: Foot of Clark Dr.
Information: 666-6129.

■ **TRIUMF Tour:** Deep underground, this complex houses a cyclotron, and above-ground experimental devices are designed to explore the smallest particles in the universe. This pioneering physics and medical facility is at the forefront of research into muons and other subatomic marvels and is about to embark on an international venture into kaon, antiproton, and neutrino research. TRIUMF stands for the Tri-University Meson Facility. Guided tours for non-scientists are scheduled year-round; phone ahead. Groups can book guided tours. Technical tours for scientists can also be arranged; phone ahead. Allow 2 hours. **Location:** South end of Westbrook Mall, on the UBC Campus. **Information:** 222-1047. For safety reasons, this tour is unsuitable for people with pacemakers, children under the age of 14, or pregnant women. There are many stairs to climb.

■ **UBC Animal Science Dairy Barn Tour:** Children are particularly impressed with mooing beasts and the demonstration of milking techniques. During a 30-minute tour, milk storage is discussed and participants see the calf barn. Tours are available in summer only; phone ahead. **Location:** 3473 Westbrook Mall, UBC Campus. **Information:** 822-4593.

■ **UBC Campus Tour:** In addition to libraries and faculty buildings, the University of British Columbia includes gardens, galleries, and extensive recreational facilities set on a point of land above the ocean. Guided walking tours are available in summer; phone ahead. Groups can book an appointment year-round. Suggestion: tour the nearby atom-splitting TRIUMF complex. **Location:** Meet at the desk in the Student Union Building, UBC Campus. **Information:** 822-3131 or 822-4319.

■ **Vancouver Stock Exchange Visitor Centre:** A display area with interpretive photographs and signs reveals how a stock transaction takes place, as well as the colourful "gold fever" origins of today's modern stock-trading facility. A video shows recent day-to-day computerized floor trading. Allow 45 minutes to read the commentary which accompanies the exhibits. Guided tours may be available; phone ahead. **Location:** 609 Granville St. **Information:** 643-6590.

■ **Chinatown:** Chinese tea can be sampled at Ten Ren Tea, 550 Main St., located in a district of Asian butcher shops, herbalists, and fishmongers. One block from the China Gate is the Sam Kee Building (8 West Pender St.), listed in the Guiness Book of World Records as the "world's thinnest office building"; it is a bay-windowed structure, 1.8 m (6 ft.) deep and two stories tall. Dr. Sun Yet Sun Gardens, 578 Carrall St., offers an excellent guided tour of a Chinese philosopher's garden, for a fee. Held variably in January or February depending upon the phase of the moon, the Chinese New Year celebrations feature snapping firecrackers, a bazaar, martial arts displays, and a colourful Chinese Lion Dance parade.
Location: Main St. and Pender St. between Gore and Carrall.
Information: Chinese Cultural Centre, 687-0729; Vancouver Multicultural Society, 731-4647, for specifics on festivals.

■ **German Community Events:** While the German community is dispersed throughout Vancouver, it unites to sponsor visits by German performers who come to Vancouver at various intervals throughout the year. Some performances or lectures are free.
Location: Various venues.
Information: Goethe Institute, 732-3966.

■ **Hungarian Open House:** This society sponsors a day in June to discover the food, crafts and culture of Hungary.
Location: Hungarian Cultural Society, 728 Kingsway.
Information: 876-4720.

■ **Japantown(s):** The specialties of Japan are found in widely separated areas. On Powell St., food stores stock serving dishes, as well as rice crackers, fresh mushrooms, fish, and giant daikon radishes; retail outlets offer rice papers and calligraphy supplies. Japanese gift stores are found along 4th Ave. Dedicated to Japanese history, art, and culture, the Powell Street Festival in early August is a celebration of sights and sounds from sumo wrestling demonstrations to origami paper arts.
Location: The old section of Japantown is in the 300- and 400-block of Powell St. The new section of Japantown is scattered inter-

mittently along East Hastings from the 300- to the 700-block. Japanese gift stores are found along 4th Ave. in the 2000-blocks. **Information:** Nitobe Gardens, 822-3825, for periodic tea ceremonies; Powell St. Festival Information, 682-4335; Vancouver Multicultural Society, 731-4647, for specifics on festivals.

■ **Jazz Festival:** Several short sample concerts are held in public venues before and during the annual Du Maurier International Jazz Festival in June. Performers arrive from the southern U.S., South America, Japan, and Africa. Find out about free events surrounding this festival.
Location: Various venues.
Information: Jazz Hotline, 682-0706.

■ **Kitsilano Showboat:** On warm summer evenings amateurs of all ages strut their best dancing steps on an amphitheatre stage resembling a Mississippi River showboat. These performances are a Vancouver summer tradition, weather permitting.
Location: Outdoor Amphitheatre at Kitsilano Beach.
Information: InfoCentre, 683-2000.

■ **Little Greece:** Bouzouki music, Greek crafts or a selection of little girl's dresses, the delights of Greek restaurants, baklava and Greek coffee, are found in the local concentration of Greek businesses. A festival celebrating Greek food is held in early March. St. George's Orthodox Church welcomes visitors to Easter services.
Location: West Broadway near the intersection with MacDonald.
Information: Hellenic Community and St. George's Orthodox Church, 266-7148; Vancouver Multicultural Society, 731-4647, for specifics on festivals.

■ **Little Italy:** Fresh pasta and home-made ice cream, bakeries, jewellers, and grocery stores alternate with coffee houses serving the best cappuccino in Vancouver. During the first week in July, Italian Week Celebrations feature Italian dancing, games, cultural activities, and a parade.
Location: Fourteen blocks along Commercial Drive from 6th Ave. to Venables. Concentrated Italian services between 3rd and Kitchener.

Information: Vancouver Multicultural Society, 731-4647, for specifics on festivals.

■ **Medieval Re-enactments:** Sometimes free, the location varies. The public is invited to behold the pageantry of life in the Middle Ages through exhibitions of period music, costumes, dancing, and mock battles as presented by the Society for Creative Anachronism. Phone ahead.
Location: Various venues.
Information: 988-0304.

■ **Performing Artists at UBC:** Recitals are performed by UBC students and there are periodic visits from out-of-town musical artists; phone ahead.
Location: Various performing venues, UBC Campus.
Information: Communications and Concerts Division, 822-5574, for visiting artists; Music Department, 822-3113, for student recitals.

■ **Punjabi Market:** Within this two-block area, officially dubbed "Punjabi Market," a rich mosaic of East Indian culture can be found. Admire beautifully embroidered silks, savour the scents of hundreds of exotic spices, or browse through inexpensive trinkets or costly gold jewellery. The staff of the Bombay Sweet store (6556 Main St.) will sometimes allow visitors to taste a few samples before buying.
Location: Main Street where it intersects with 49th Ave.
Information: Vancouver Multicultural Society, 731-4647, for specifics on festivals.

■ **Quebecoise Festival:** A late June festival with games, street performers, and Quebec cuisine is a celebration of francophone culture. Music is performed by artists from across Canada.
Location: Various venues, but mainly in front of La Maison de la Francophone, 1555 West 7th. The block between Granville and Fir is usually closed to traffic.
Information: 736-9806.

■ **Robson Square Media Centre and Court House Complex:** Ongoing demonstrations, symposiums, noon-hour lectures, concerts, trade fairs, visiting lecturers, and travel films are

sometimes free to the public; phone ahead.
Location: 800 Robson St.
Information: Recorded events, 661-7373; Conference Centre, 60-2830, FAX: 685-9407.

■ **Celebrations:** Yearly events include Polar Bear Swim on January 1; Chinese New Year Celebrations in February; Greek Food Festival in early March; First Arrival of a Cruise Ship Public Party, Port Day Celebrations, Children's Festival in May; Asia Pacific Festival, Dragon Boat Races, Quebecoise Festival in June; Canada Day Fireworks on July 1; Italian Celebrations, Folk Music Festival, Vancouver Chamber Music Festival, Bathtub Races and Sea Festival, Symphony of Fire in July; Powell St. Japanese Festival, International Comedy Festival Week, B.C. Salmon Derby, Pacific National Exhibition Agricultural Parade and Fair Week in August; Vancouver Fringe Festival, Terry Fox Annual Run, Octoberfest Bavarian Celebrations in September; International Film Festival September through October; Writers' and Readers' Festival on Granville Island in October; Hadassah Bazaar in November; Christmas Carol Ships in December.
Location: Various venues in Vancouver.
Information: InfoCentre, 683-2000, 1-800-888-8835, FAX: 683-2601.

■ **Fireworks Displays:** During late July, an annual international competition features five nights of pyrotechnic displays, as various nations compete for the best fireworks. A second smaller local celebration of fireworks is held on Canada Day, July 1.
Location: Benson and Hedges Symphony of Fire, presented from a barge in English Bay; Canada Day fireworks, best viewed from Canada Place.
Information: InfoCentre, 683-2000, 1-800-888-8835, FAX: 683-2601.

■ **SeaBus to the North Shore:** Fare of under $2, one way. Riders can enjoy a view of Burrard Inlet from water level on the

SeaBus, a public transit ferry. The 12-minute ride terminates at Lonsdale Quay, a fresh-food market with several retail outlets. **Location:** The Seabus crosses from Waterfront Station, on Cordova St. to Lonsdale Quay, North Vancouver. **Information:** Seabus, 986-1501; Transit Info, 261-5100, for fares and schedules.

■ **Vancouver International Comedy Festival:** In early August, free hourly demonstrations by festival performers are held in two open-air venues at Granville Island; performances range from acrobats to stand-up comedians; phone ahead for a program. **Location:** Granville Island Market, Johnstone St. **Information:** Comedy Festival, 683-0883.

North Shore

Information on the attractions and festivals of North Vancouver: InfoCentre, 131 East 2nd St., North Vancouver, V7L 1C2. Phone: 987-4488, FAX: 987-8272.

Information on the attractions and festivals of West Vancouver: InfoCentre, 1563 Marine Dr., West Vancouver, V7V 1H9. Phone: 926-6614, FAX: 926-6436.

Information and maps on walks and hikes on the North Shore: Map of trails, North Shore Tourism, 131 East 2nd Ave., North Vancouver. Phone: 987-4488, FAX: 987-8272.

■ **Capilano Fish Hatchery and the Cleveland Dam:** Adult salmon return from their ocean sojourn to this location. Visitors can see models and maps, a fish ladder and holding tanks, or join in summer guided tours; phone ahead. Best viewing times: July through October. A short distance up Capilano Rd., the Cleveland Dam offers picturesque views of the watershed and Capilano Canyon 100 m (330 ft.) below. **Location:** Drive north on Capilano Rd. and turn left to 4500 Capilano Park Rd. Continue northward to the Cleveland Dam. **Information:** Fish Hatchery, 666-1790.

■ **Lynn Canyon Suspension Bridge and Ecology Centre:** After crossing over a heart-stopping pedestrian-only cable bridge suspended 50 m (165 ft.) over narrow Lynn Canyon, turn left at the end of the bridge and take a short walk through the woods. The thickly forested area was selectively logged in 1912 and the holes made to insert loggers' buckboards are still visible in some cedar stumps. On-site is a small nature house which presents interpretive nature programs, guided walking tours, ongoing displays, and film showings; phone ahead.
Location: 3663 Park Rd., North Vancouver.
Information: Ecology Centre, 987-5922.

■ **Lighthouse Park and Point Atkinson Lighthouse:** A network of paths through an unlogged forest leads to seaside viewpoints and the lighthouse. Surrounded with sparkling prisms, the 500-watt bulb is magnified to an illumination level of a quarter-million candlepower. If permission is obtained in advance, individuals are occasionally allowed inside the historic lighthouse.
Location: Marine Dr. and Beacon Lane, 8 km (5 mi.) west of the Lion's Gate Bridge.
Information: West Vancouver Municipal Hall, 922-1211, for a parks and recreation referral.

■ **Maplewood Farm and Petting Zoo:** Token admission. A variety of animals here provide city children with the chance to see farm animals close up. Soft furry bunnies live in the "rabbitat." Sheep-shearing day is held in early spring, and there are special events around Christmas.
Location: 405 Seymour River Place, North Vancouver.
Information: 929-5610.

■ **Mount Seymour Provincial Park Toboggan Runs:** On wintry days, an area is flagged off for family sleigh and toboggan runs and supervised by the Parks Board. In January, teams from as far away as Japan construct monolithic ice carvings in a spirited competition; phone ahead for details.
Location: On Mount Seymour Rd., North Vancouver.
Information: B.C. Parks, 929-1291.

■ **Park and Tilford Gardens:** There are several theme gardens here, including an herb garden, a native B.C. garden, and a Japanese garden. The sea of roses in June gives way to twinkling Christmas lights in November and December. The gardens won the 1991 Landscape Merit Award from the Canadian Society of Landscape Architects.
Location: #440 - 333 Brooksbank Ave., North Vancouver.
Information: 984-8200.

■ **Yew Lake Interpretive Trail:** Summer patches of wildflowers are identified by signs along this short, interpretive mountain-lake walk. A pamphlet, available at a kiosk, explains each stop of interest. Guided tours with a park naturalist are periodically available in summer; phone ahead. Other trails crisscross the mountainside and for a fee, a summer chairlift takes serious walkers to higher elevations. On the way up the mountain, stop at the Cypress Mountain lookout for a panorama of the whole of Greater Vancouver.
Location: Located in Cypress Provincial Park. Take the Upper Levels Highway to the Cypress Bowl turnoff, then 16 km (10 mi.) to the parking lot. Check the map at the on-site kiosk for walking directions.
Information: B.C. Parks, 929-1291.

■ **West Vancouver Centennial Seawall Promenade:** The sun setting over the ocean is especially notable when viewed from this 2-km (1.2-mi.) paved walkway with a parallel walk for dogs. From May through early September, between 5:00 p.m. and 7:00 p.m., cruise ships pass just offshore. Bring binoculars.
Location: Enter at the Dundarave Pier in the 2400 block Marine Dr., West Vancouver.
Information: Parks and Recreation, 922-1211.

■ **Ferry Building Art Gallery:** Before the Lions Gate Bridge was completed in 1939, this heritage building served passengers who crossed from Vancouver by water. Newly renovated, it is now a tiny art gallery featur-

ing a changing assortment of flower arrangements, sculptures, and paintings. Guided tours of the gallery may be available; phone ahead. While here, plan to stroll the Ambleside Shoreline Walk.
Location: 1414 Argyle Ave., West Vancouver.
Information: 925-3605.

■ **North Vancouver Museum and Presentation House:**
Small admission. Two adjacent galleries house Coast Salish artifacts, and a collection of 9000 heritage photographs; special revolving displays pay tribute to the logging and ship-building industries. Guided tours may be available and presentations are held at regular intervals; phone ahead.
Location: 333 Chesterfield, North Vancouver.
Information: Museum, 987-5618; Presentation House, 986-1351.

■ **Seymour Art Gallery:** A community art gallery showcases the works of local, well-known artists and their protegées in exhibitions of west-coast environmental subjects. Some education programs for children are held in the summer and visiting artists periodically give noontime lectures. Guided tours may be available; phone ahead.
Location: In the Deep Cove Cultural Centre, 4360 Gallant Ave., North Vancouver.
Information: 929-5744.

■ **Canadian Coast Guard Traffic Services Viewing Area:** The marine traffic in Vancouver's harbours is controlled 24 hours a day, like an airport; ships are assigned parking places and tugboats are summoned to emergencies. With advance notice, these federally operated services will sometimes allow a group to look through glass partitions at the control room. Trained personnel handle the complexities of marine traffic and an overhead recording explains marine operations. Groups only, by appointment; subject to the availability of staff.
Location: Kapilano 100 Building, West Vancouver. Ask for exact directions at the time of booking.
Information: 666-1003.

■ **Industrial Chemicals Plant Tour:** This facility produces chlorine, caustic soda, and muriatic acid for global distribution. The tour covers the chemical process with a good deal of emphasis on safety concerns, as the company is located in an urban setting. Groups with scientific interests only, by appointment.
Location: Canadian Occidental Industrial Chemicals, 100 Amherst, North Vancouver.
Information: 929-3441.

■ **Department of Fisheries and Oceans Tour:** Canadian research into the complexities of salmon production and the monitoring and preservation of water quality in the Pacific Ocean are the focus of this federal laboratory. Groups with scientific interests only, by appointment and subject to the availability of staff.
Location: West Vancouver Laboratory, 4160 Marine Dr., West Vancouver.
Information: Laboratory, 666-7928.

■ **Seymour Demonstration Forest Tour:** Why do foresters cut trees and leave them? Why does a young forest look delicious to deer? Can people really prune a forest? What is a "snag"? These questions and others are answered on a conducted forest tour. Guided tours for adults and older children are held on weekends most of the year; phone ahead. Allow 90 minutes to 2 hours. Alternately, visitors can cycle 11 km (7 mi.) to the fish hatchery, walk the interpretive forest trails, or explore the ruins of an old Chinese cedar shake operation.
Location: Drive along Lillooet Road, past Capilano College and the North Vancouver cemetery, up the gravel road to the forest entrance gate and parking lot. Obtain maps on-site before venturing on the trails.
Information: 432-6286 for times of scheduled tours; 520-1083 for recorded information; 985-1690 for fire hazard closings.

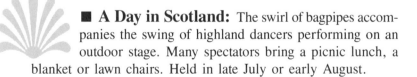

■ **A Day in Scotland:** The swirl of bagpipes accompanies the swing of highland dancers performing on an outdoor stage. Many spectators bring a picnic lunch, a blanket or lawn chairs. Held in late July or early August.

Location: Waterfront Park, next to Lonsdale Quay at the foot of Lonsdale Ave.
Information: Quay Market, 985-6261, keeps track of events at the park.

■ **Caribbean Day:** The calypso beat of the steel drums, and the music of island peoples are featured on an outdoor stage. Many spectators bring a picnic lunch, a blanket or lawn chairs. Held in late July.
Location: Waterfront Park, next to Lonsdale Quay at the foot of Lonsdale Ave.
Information: Quay Market, 985-6261, keeps track of events at the park.

■ **Concerts-By-The-Sea:** Musical concerts are held in the summer at two oceanside venues. Near the propeller fountain at Waterfront Park in Horseshoe Bay, calypso bands or classical quartets perform, children frolic in the water park and B.C. ferries slip in and out of the terminal. At Ambleside Beach in West Vancouver, performers enjoy the sandy setting surrounded by city highrises; concerts are held on Sundays and Wednesdays during the summer. Concerts are cancelled in inclement weather.
Location: For Waterfront Park, take the Upper Levels Highway. To avoid the ferry line-ups, stay left at the approach to Horseshoe Bay; the park is adjacent to the ferry terminal. Ambleside Beach is located at 13th and Marine Dr. in West Vancouver.
Information: Parks and Recreation, 922-1211, for a list of performances and locations.

■ **Harmony Arts Festival:** A week of performances and artistic encounters culminates with guided tours of artists' studios, free performances of rock, jazz, classical music, and "ArtBeat Tours of North Shore Artwork." Held in mid-August.
Location: Various venues in West Vancouver.
Information: 925-3605 for a list of festival activities.

■ **Lonsdale Quay Concerts:** Musical performances of folk, jazz, and classical music are featured on summer Sunday afternoons as trios, groups, and solo performers dance, sing, and harmonize on the outdoor plaza, beside the sea. During the

Christmas season, a number of carolers bring the Yuletide spirit to shoppers inside the market.
Location: At the foot of Lonsdale Ave., North Vancouver. Also accessible from the terminus of the SeaBus.
Information: Quay Market, 985-6261, for a list of performances.

■ **North Vancouver Folkfest Days:** Handicrafts from many lands are displayed; a guided Heritage Walk and several performances of folk dancing and cultural arts take place over the days of this festival. Held in June.
Location: Various venues, North Vancouver.
Information: 987-4488 or 987-7529 for a list of activities.

■ **Ambleside Beach Bonfire Evenings:** Watching the boats go by on a summer evening while roasting wieners and toasting marshmallows is a great experience. Bonfires are allowed on the beach here on specified summer evenings; firewood is not supplied and an adult must be in attendance.
Location: 13th and Marine Dr., in certain areas of the park, West Vancouver.
Information: Fire Marshall, 922-9311. Call in advance for instructions.

■ **Celebrations in North Vancouver:** Yearly events include Lynn Valley Days, Port Day in May; Lions Parade and North Van Folkfest, King Neptune Karnival in June; Edgemont Bavarian Festival (986-0961), Coho Festival in September; Christmas Carollers at Lonsdale Quay (985-6261) in December.
Location: Various venues in North Vancouver.
Information: InfoCentre, 987-4488, FAX: 987-8272.

■ **Celebrations in West Vancouver:** Yearly events include Community Day Parade on the first Saturday in June; Coho Festival in September; Christmas Carolers at Park Royal (922-3211), Christmas Carolers on the B.C. Ferries (669-1211) in December.
Location: Various venues in West Vancouver.
Information: InfoCentre, 926-6614, FAX: 926-6436.

Richmond

Information on the attractions and festivals of Richmond: InfoCentre, the George Massey Tunnel-Highway, #208 - 8171 Park Rd., Richmond, V6Y 1S9. Phone: 278-9333, FAX: 278-1265.

■ **Garry Point Park:** Considered at its best under the glow of the full moon, the light illuminating the waters, this park offers panoramic ocean views, trails, beaches, and a small Japanese garden. Guided walks such as the "Full Moon Dyke Walk" may be offered through the Richmond Nature Park. Other presentations are held periodically; phone ahead.
Location: End of Chatham and 7th Ave. From Highway 99, go west on Steveston Highway to the end, then turn south on 7th Ave.
Information: Richmond Nature Park, 273-7015.

■ **Iona Beach Regional Park Bird Watch and Nature Trail:** The extensive tidal flats at low and intermediate tides are home to thousands of birds which winter here; most notable are sandpipers, dunlins, and other shorebirds. Migratory geese periodically pass through the area. There is a 4-km (2.5-mi.) cycle and walking trail along the Iona Jetty. Best in the winter months.
Location: From McDonald Rd. turn left onto Ferguson Rd., then continue onto the Iona Island Causeway.
Information: Greater Vancouver Regional District Parks, 224-5739.

■ **Grocery Hall of Fame:** Purity Jam, Mrs. Pinkam's Blueing Agent, Rogers Golden Syrup cans used as lunch buckets in the 1930s—all are present on the shelves here. This collection of memorabilia includes about 30,000 items, mostly old packages, tins, and bottles from the turn of the century. Guided tours available Saturdays.

Location: 6620 No. 6 Rd.
Information: 278-0665.

■ **London Farm:** The pre-1900s farmhouse was once the home of two prominent Richmond families and is furnished to illustrate early rural life in Richmond. The farm is a fine example of early west-coast agricultural practises and is located on a reclaimed river inlet. Guided tours may be available in summer; phone ahead. Visitors can always walk the dyke trails here and experience the busy river environment.
Location: 6511 Dyke Rd. Turn left on London Rd., near south foot of No. 2 Rd.
Information: London Farm, 271-5220.

■ **Richmond Cultural Centre and Museum:** On display are works by juried artists who are just entering the arts world, or ongoing exhibitions featuring well-established artists. Once a year there is a formal celebration of Japanese flower arrangements. Heritage photographs, on permanent display in the museum (by donation), pay tribute to Richmond's agriculture and fishing industries. Presentations are held at regular intervals and guided tours may be available; phone ahead.
Location: #180 Minoru Park Plaza, 7700 Minoru Gate.
Information: 231-6440.

■ **Steveston Museum and Fishing Village:** Admission by donation. A re-created 1906 bank manager's office, three rooms of his frontier home, and historic farming implements make up the displays here. The museum is also close to the historic fishing village of Steveston. Fishermen offer their fresh catch direct to the public from the docks here.
Location: 3811 Moncton St.
Information: Museum, 271-6868.

■ **Canadian Coast Guard Hovercraft Dockside Visit:** The province of British Columbia owns 2 hovercraft for use in search-and-rescue operations, one stationed here and one on Vancouver Island. Both contain advanced elec-

tronics to navigate by satellite and are on emergency duty 24 hours a day. Allow for the possibility that arranged visits can be abruptly interrupted or cancelled at the last moment without notice. Groups only, by appointment.
Location: Just beyond the Seaplane Base, Sea Island, Richmond.
Information: 278-7717.

■ **Dyke Walk Guided Tours:** All of Richmond lies below sea level and the area is protected by dykes. Walkers and cyclists can take mini expeditions along the 7 km (4 mi.) of dykes that offer contrasting views of wetlands and the urban setting. Organized walks with naturalists from Richmond Nature Park are held periodically on weekends throughout the year; phone ahead.
Location: Various start points as arranged by the guide.
Information: Richmond Nature Park, 273-7015, for times of guided walks.

■ **Gulf of Georgia Cannery Visitor Centre:** This small interpretive centre features a small model of a cannery, photographs of pioneer fish nets, and a 10-minute audio-visual presentation with historical footage of canning lines. The visitor centre, operated by Gulf of Georgia Cannery Society, is a forerunner to a larger scheme to redevelop the pioneer cannery built in 1894, located behind the centre. The old cannery is designated as a National Historic Site and will be operated as a joint venture with Parks Canada. Guided tours may be available; phone ahead. Limited opening hours.
Location: 12138 4th Ave.
Information: Visitor Centre, 272-5045.

■ **Kuan Yin Buddhist Temple Visit:** Small admission. Palatial architecture, a bonsai garden, and exceptional embroideries intrigue the thousands of visitors who come each year to this temple, which is constructed in the same manner as those that guard the banks of the faraway Yangtze River. Scheduled visits are available; phone ahead. Be prepared to remove your shoes.
Location: 9160 Steveston Highway, between No. 3 and No. 4 Rd.
Information: 274-2622.

■ **Richmond Nature Park Programs:** Some programs are free, some for a fee. Peat bogs are nature's way of creating coal, but during the multimillion year process, a great variety of plants and animals thrive in the soggy environment. On the site of this natural peat bog, interpretive signs familiarize visitors with life in a wet environment. Guided tours are available; and a variety of nature presentations are held year-round at the on-site centre; phone ahead for a seasonal program. Operated by the Richmond Nature Park Society. **Location:** 11851 Westminster Highway, at the corner of No. 5 Rd. **Information:** 273-7015.

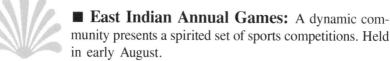

■ **East Indian Annual Games:** A dynamic community presents a spirited set of sports competitions. Held in early August.
Location: South Arm Community Centre and Park, 8880 Williams Rd.
Information: Community Centre, 277-1157.

■ **Obon Japanese Festival:** Origami, martial arts demonstrations, and a spirit of tradition are the basis for this Japanese festival, held in August. Richmond has a large Japanese community which dates from the early fishing industry.
Location: Steveston Buddhist Church, 4360 Garry St.
Information: Steveston Buddhist Church, 277-2323.

■ **Celebrations:** Yearly events include South Arm Days, Salmon Festival in June; Annual Workboat Parade in July; Multi-fest (273-3394) in August; Flatland Marathon in October.
Location: Various venues in Richmond.
Information: InfoCentre, 278-9333, FAX: 278-1265.

Burnaby

Events at the Pacific Coliseum: 253-2311.

Information on the attractions and festivals of Burnaby: InfoCentre, 6525 Sprott St., Burnaby, V5B 3B8. Phone: 293-1771, FAX: 299-0580.

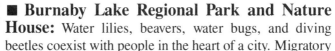

■ **Burnaby Lake Regional Park and Nature House:** Water lilies, beavers, water bugs, and diving beetles coexist with people in the heart of a city. Migratory birds are visible from a viewing tower that is found along an extensive 8-km (5-mi.) trail system around the lake. Young teams of scullers can often be seen practising their pulls on the rowing course. Trails around the lake are open year round. Burnaby Lake Discovery Day is held at the lakeside Burnaby Lake Sports Complex in early July. Presentations at the Burnaby Nature House are available in summer; phone ahead. The Nature House is closed in winter.

Location: Burnaby Lake Nature House, 4519 Piper St. Turn south off Winston St.

Information: Burnaby Lake Nature House, 420-3031; Greater Vancouver Regional District Parks, 224-5739; G.V.R.D., 432-6359.

■ **Burnaby Art Gallery:** Ceperly Mansion is a heritage home, today housing a collection of 20th-century art. While the remains of horse stables crumble nearby, the well-maintained formal gardens surrounding the mansion are a reminder of past elegance. Visitors sometimes combine their visit to the gallery with a Sunday afternoon picnic on the sloping lawns overlooking Deer Lake. Art presentations are held at regular intervals; phone ahead.

Location: 6344 Deer Lake Ave.

Information: 291-9441.

■ **Burnaby Village Museum:** Outstanding value at $5, especially during special celebration periods. This fully re-created pioneer town on a 4-ha (10-ac.) site is staffed by animators. A blacksmith, a teacher, and other late-19th-century characters work and play every day in a refurbished street setting recalling B.C.'s early days as a province. Visitors can see an old-fashioned ice cream parlour, peek into the one-room schoolhouse, or check up on the

news at the old-time printer's shop. Special heritage festivities are held on Canada Day, B.C. Day, and at Christmas. Allow 3 hours. Closed part of the year.
Location: 6501 Deer Lake Ave., entrance off Canada Way and Sperling.
Information: Recorded events line, 293-6500.

■ **Able Walker Museum and Factory Tour:** The history of transportation is outlined through life-sized artifacts: a stagecoach and wagon train with full-sized mules, a horse and rider, and a dog sled. Antique cars, including a Model S Ford (one of only 16 worldwide), are exhibited. The factory produces devices to assist those who have difficulty in walking. Guided tours are available; phone ahead.
Location: 2350 Beta Avenue, No. 16.
Information: 299-3444.

■ **Challenger Relief Map Tour:** This huge scale model configures the geographic contours of British Columbia by using over 948,000 hand-cut B.C. fir plywood pieces. Made by George Challenger and his sons, the relief map took seven years to assemble. Groups of 6 or more only, by appointment.
Location: At the B.C. Pavilion, PNE Exhibition grounds, Hastings and Renfrew.
Information: Pacific National Exhibition, 253-2311, local 429, to make arrangements.

■ **Compost Garden Demonstration Site:** The Greater Vancouver Regional District demonstrates various sizes and types of compost gardens to encourage the public to cut down on municipal waste. Presentation topics include handy tips on box construction, speeding the process of decomposition, and helpful hints for apartment dwellers. Free presentations are available on a regular basis; phone ahead.
Location: 4856 Still Creek Ave.
Information: 299-0659.

■ **Flower Growers' Auction:** Flowers are perishable and must be moved quickly from the producer, through the middle man, to the consumer. An early morning auction attended by flower wholesalers moves "lots," or trailer-loads, of flowers through the distribution system by means of a "countdown" bidding clock. Groups only can watch the process, subject to the availability of reserved seats; phone ahead.
Location: United Flower Growers' Auction, 4085 Marine Way.
Information: 430-2211.

■ **Simon Fraser University Tour:** This mountain-top campus features impressive architecture, houses a Museum of Anthropology and Ethnography, and boasts a "thousand" works of art. In the museum, a cutaway of the Namu trench reveals how archaeologists carve up a piece of land in order to date human settlements. The University Art Gallery features works from Pacific countries with an emphasis on Canada. Each facility can be visited separately. Scheduled campus tours are available in summer; phone ahead.
Location: Simon Fraser University, Burnaby Mountain Campus.
Information: Art Gallery, 291-4266; SFU Museum, 291-3325; campus tours, 291-3210; information, 291-3111.

■ **Taxidermy Demonstration:** The demonstration covers the process by which animals are preserved for museums or as tro-phies; the skin is tanned, placed over various forms, then artificial eyes and teeth are added. Participants must be emotionally prepared for the fact that the animals are dead. Groups only, by appointment.
Location: Steve Kulash Taxidermy, 3977 Kingsway.
Information: 437-4656.

■ **Ainu Poles and Totem Poles:** About 20 rough-hewn poles feature the mythological symbols of the Ainu people from the island of Hokkaido in northern Japan. They are now positioned in the park to draw attention to highlights in the Vancouver skyline. Also in the park is a collection of poles representing native totems. Two "touch poles," erected in 1992, are accessible to the smallest of children and are designed for the

carvings to be felt. The area is a popular spot for family picnics. Brochures with the story of the poles are available on-site or through the listed number.
Location: Burnaby Mountain Park. Follow Sperling to Curtis; turn east to the top of Burnaby Mountain.
Information: Burnaby Parks, 294-7450.

■ **Deer Lake Sunday Concerts:** What could be more relaxing than to laze beside the lake on a summer day listening to strains of Verdi while the sun shines warmly? Various performers from classical duos to soul music groups are presented on Sunday afternoons in the summer. Many spectators bring a blanket, lawn chairs, and a picnic lunch to the sloping lawns beside the lake.
Location: 6344 Deer Lake Ave.
Information: Burnaby Arts Centre, 291-6864, for a list of performances.

■ **Metrotown Summer Concerts in the Park:** Afternoon concerts, provided by a variety of performers, are part of the summer scene. Phone ahead for a program.
Location: Station Square, 4600 Kingsway, accessible from the Metrotown Station SkyTrain.
Information: Burnaby Arts Centre, 291-6864 for a list of performances.

■ **Celebrations:** Yearly events include Burnaby Days in May; Summer Theatre in July and August; Burnaby Lake Discovery Day, Annual Workboat Festival in July; Pacific National Exhibition Fair in August; Heritage Christmas at Burnaby Village Museum (294-1231) in December.
Location: Various venues, Burnaby.
Information: InfoCentre, 293-1771, FAX: 299-0580.

New Westminster

Information on the attractions and festivals of New Westminster: InfoCentre, 333 Brunette St., New Westminster, V3L 3E7. Phone: 521-7781, FAX: 521-0057.

■ **Japanese Friendship Gardens:** Cherry trees burst forth in whites and pinks throughout May in these gardens established as a tribute to New Westminster's sister city, Moriguchi, Japan; small pools and intricate plantings are carefully maintained. Opening hours are limited.
Location: 511 Royal Ave., near the City Hall.
Information: Parks and Recreation Department, 526-4811.

■ **Queen's Park:** As one of the Lower Mainland's principal parks, Queen's Park features a well-established rose garden of over 10,000 plants considered at its best in June. With a panoramic view of the North Shore, visitors can enjoy numerous picnic sites, sports venues, and a children's zoo. The on-site Arts Centre, sponsored by the Arts Council of New Westminster, mounts several yearly exhibitions. Phone for presentations and special events that take place throughout the park.
Location: 6th Ave. and 1st St.
Information: Arts Centre, 525-3244; City Parks, 526-4811.

■ **Canadian Lacrosse Hall of Fame:** Lacrosse is reputed to have been created by native peoples, and it is a little-known fact that lacrosse, not hockey, is Canada's official national sport. A small collection of historic field and box lacrosse exhibits can be seen here. Opening hours are limited; phone ahead.
Location: In the Community Centre Building at 6th Ave. and Cumberland St., near Queens Park.
Information: Community Centre, 526-2751.

■ **Irving House Museum:** Admission by donation. The 1864 restored home of a colourful riverboat Captain features 14 rooms of period furniture, plus memorabilia from the days when New Westminster was the capital city of British Columbia; adjacent is a collection of artifacts, such as an 1876 Dufferin horse coach. Guided tours may be available; phone ahead.
Location: 302 Royal Ave.
Information: 521-7656.

■ **Royal Westminster Regiment Museum:** Admission by donation. With little manpower and a great deal of gusto, the Military and the Royal Road Engineers kept order during B.C.'s frantic gold-rush days. This collection of photos and memorabilia, located in the old gun room of a 19th-century armoury, depicts the history of the oldest military unit in the Lower Mainland. Guided tours may be available; phone ahead.
Location: 530 Queens Ave.
Information: 666-4375.

■ *Samson V.* **Sternwheeler:** This old vessel was originally used to yank logs from the Fraser River; even in pioneer times, the waters were littered with snags and half-submerged logs. The last sternwheeler to operate on the Fraser is now permanently moored for visitors to explore. Guided tours may be available; phone ahead.
Location: 810 Front St., in front of the Westminster Quay Market.
Information: Museum, 521-7656, administrates the *Samson V.*

■ **Celebrations:** Yearly events include Jazz Festival, Antique Car Easter Parade in March or so; Hyack Nine-Day Festival in May; Portuguese Festival in June; Christmas Carol Cruise Ship Sail-Past, Sinter Klaas in December.
Location: Various venues in New Westminster.
Information: InfoCentre, 521-7781, FAX: 521-0057.

■ **Hyack Association Festivals:** From the exploding of the traditional anvil salute, a noisy substitute created for a Royal visit when no cannon was available, to an Easter Parade and Carol Ships, the Hyack Association is responsible for numerous yearly events. Ask about the headliners who will attend the annual Hyack Fraserfest and find out about free events surrounding the festivals. **Location:** Various venues throughout New Westminster. **Information:** Hyack Association, 522-6894.

Coquitlam, Port Coquitlam, and Port Moody

Information on the attractions and festivals of Coquitlam, Port Coquitlam, Port Moody: Seasonal InfoCentre, #3 - 1180 Pinetree Way, Coquitlam, V3B 7L2. Phone: 464-2716, FAX: 464-6796.

■ **Minnekhada Regional Park:** This forested park features a choice of walks from high knolls over the Pitt River to trails which connect with the Addington Marsh, a waterfowl and beaver habitat. Early October features the Annual Turkey Trek, a crowd-walk followed by a draw for a turkey. Every first and third Sunday of the month, from 12 noon to 4:00 p.m., a hunting estate, originally belonging to two lieutenant-governors, is open to the public; phone to confirm. Guided walks for the public are scheduled intermittently throughout the year; groups can book guided tours through the naturalist at Burnaby Lake Nature House which is open seasonally. Phone: 420-3031.
Location: From the Lougheed Highway turn north on Coast Meridian. Travel 2.5 km (1.5 mi.) to Apel Rd. Signs are present to Victoria Dr. Follow for 1 km (.6 mi.) to the crest of the hill and make a hard left turn. Travel northeast for 3.5 km (2 mi.) to the park entrance on Quarry Rd. To access the hunting estate, turn right on Quarry Rd., using the sign to Gilley's Trail. Travel .5 km (.3 mi.) south to Oliver Rd. Follow signs to the lodge.
Information: Greater Vancouver Regional District, 432-6200.

■ **PoCo Walking Trail:** The Fraser River is a working river with log booms, sawmills, and industrial operations, all visible from the vantage point of this specially blazed municipal trail. Self-guided tours anytime. Length: 28 km (17 mi.)

Location: Begin at the signs in downtown Port Coquitlam, or along Mary Hill Rd. and the ByPass, Port Coquitlam.
Information: Parks and Recreation, 944-5450.

■ **Place des Arts Gallery:** Paintings, quilts, stone carvings, and pottery are some of the exhibits featured in revolving exhibitions by local and visiting artists; focus is often on the emerging trend in wildlife and nature art. Presentations are held at regular intervals; phone ahead.
Location: 1120 Brunette Ave., Coquitlam.
Information: 526-2891.

■ **Port Moody Station Museum:** Admission by donation. Once pivotal in changing the railway builders advance away from the Fraser River and towards the potential commerce of the Pacific Ocean, the railroad station here represents an historic moment in the development of the trans-Canada railway. While here, take the opportunity to stroll a 2-km (1.2-mi.) walk, part of the Shoreline Park System between Rocky Point Park and Old Orchard Park. Guided tours may be available; phone ahead. Limited opening hours.
Location: Adjacent to Rocky Point Park on Moody Street, Port Moody.
Information: 939-1648.

■ **Andrés Wine-Tasting:** Small admission. This commercial winery is one of the oldest in British Columbia. As "old" is a good word to be associated with fine wines, the wine sampling here may be of interest. Opening hours for tastings vary seasonally; phone ahead.
Location: 2120 Vintner St., Port Moody.
Information: 937-3411. Not suitable for those under legal age.

■ **Dog Training Demonstration:** Dogs are trained for up to 4 months to assist a law officer or to guard without distraction; other dogs are trained in 2 languages or are prepared for work as

television extras. Demonstrations are available; phone ahead. Allow 1 hour.
Location: North American Guard Dog Training Academy, 1481 Pipeline Rd.
Information: 942-1940. Dress for outdoor weather conditions.

■ **Sawmill Tour:** A lumber and planer mill, part of British Columbia's largest industry, processes raw timber into dimensioned lumber used in building new homes. On this tour participants become familiar with some of the equipment and procedures used. Groups only, by appointment, in the summer. Allow 90 minutes.
Location: Fraser Mills, No. 2, King Edward Ave., Coquitlam.
Information: 520-8400. No children under the age of 12 years. For safety, no open-toed footwear or shorts are allowed, and participants should wear clothing which covers the arms.

■ **Celebrations:** Yearly events include the Festival Du Boise Francophone Celebration (Maillardville) in early March; Winter Carnival (Port Coquitlam) in March; May Day (Port Coquitlam, 941-5450), Dogwood Daze (Coquitlam, 526-3611) in May; All Saints' Festival (Coquitlam) in June; Kinsmen Sports Festival (Port Moody), Golden Spike Days (461-4411) in July; Children's Festival (942-0552) in September.
Location: Various venues.
Information: InfoCentre, 464-2716, FAX: 464-6796.

Surrey and White Rock

Information on the attractions and festivals of Surrey: InfoCentre, 15105A - 105th Ave., Surrey, V3R 7G9. Phone: 581-7130, FAX: 588-7549.
Information on the attractions and festivals of White Rock: InfoCentre, 1554 Foster St., White Rock, V4B 3X8. Phone: 536-6844, FAX: 536-4994.

■ **Serpentine Fen Wildlife Management
Area:** Ecosystem and wildlife habitats, under increasing
pressure from the encroachment of cities, are increasingly
in need of protection. This protected area, interlaced with walking trails, is rich in waterfowl, shorebirds, songbirds, birds of prey, and small mammals; observation towers are placed for maximum vantage with a minimum of disturbance to the wildlife. Allow 15 minutes to 3 hours, depending upon the trail. The White Rock and Surrey Naturalists' group will arrange guided tours for groups; phone ahead.
Location: 14343 - 44th Ave., Surrey, between King George Highway and Highway 99.
Information: Ducks Unlimited at Serpentine Fen, 591-1104; White Rock Naturalists, 535-2844. Secure car when parking.

■ **Tynehead Regional Park and Fish Hatchery:** Second-growth forests and salmon enhancement are two pertinent issues in British Columbia, and both are central themes in this park. The Serpentine Loop Trail of 4 km (2.5 mi.) winds along the Serpentine River; there are boardwalks which are wheelchair-accessible, and a viewing platform over the river. Allow a minimum of 1 hour to wander through second-growth forests, rolling meadowlands, and old orchards. Guided tours are held periodically in the summer; phone ahead. Groups can arrange guided walks year-round through the naturalist at Greater Vancouver Regional Parks. Nearby are privately operated salmon enhancement facilities at the Tynehead fish hatchery. The Serpentine Enhancement Society will arrange guided tours for groups; phone ahead.
Location: 16700 Tynehead Dr. off 96th Ave., between 160th and 176th St., Surrey.
Information: Greater Vancouver Regional District East, 530-4983; Serpentine Enhancement Society, 589-9127; G.V.R.D., 432-6359.

■ **Arnold Mikelson Mind and Matter Gallery:** This gallery sponsors periodic half-hour talks on the subject of B.C. artists, and mounts an annual Festival of the Arts in mid-July. Their sculpture gallery is situated along a 1-ha (3-ac.) garden. Pottery, paintings and sculpture are on display during opening hours year-round. Presentations are held at regular intervals; phone ahead.
Location: 13743 - 16th Ave., White Rock.
Information: 536-6460.

■ **Historic Stewart Farmhouse and Hooser Weaving Centre:** As the 1860 gold rush petered out, prospectors and settlers chose to make a new life in the lower mainland. This municipally designated heritage home, circa 1890, has been restored to evoke an active turn-of-the-century farmhouse; examples of weaving and spinning looms are tributes to the women whose "work was never done." Allow 1 hour to visit. Guided tours may be available and presentations are available at regular intervals; phone ahead. Limited opening hours.
Location: Elgin Heritage Park, 13723 Crescent Rd., South Surrey.
Information: 574-5744; Surrey Arts Centre, 596-7461, for information on presentations.

■ **Surrey Arts Centre:** Three spaces are used for art exhibitions: the main gallery features contemporary works by local, Canadian, and international artists; the Theatre Gallery space is used by community associations and emerging artists; the children's mini gallery features art for and about children. Guided tours may be available; phone ahead. Presentations are held at regular intervals.
Location: 13750 - 88th Ave., Surrey.
Information: 596-7461.

■ **Surrey Centennial Museum:** Admission by donation. B.C.'s third-largest museum features representative collections of native basketry, plains Indian leather, and bead work supplemented by full-size period room settings depicting pioneer settlement in

Surrey. Guided tours may be available; phone ahead.
Location: 6022 - 176th St.
Information: 574-5744.

■ **Educational Forest Tour:** What can be placed
in an envelope and 50 years later is too large to put on a
hectare of land? Answer: an arboretum. This guided tour covers
an old-growth forest, a mature second-growth forest, and an arboretum. The dawn redwood growing here was discovered on the
grounds of a remote Asian ashram. Guided tours are available from
spring to fall; phone ahead.
Location: B.C. Forestry Association, 9800A - 140th St., Surrey.
Information: Coast Region B.C. Forestry Association, 582-0100,
FAX: 582-0101. Free educational workshops and kits on forestry
are also available.

■ **Evergreen Seedlings Tour:** Canada's second-largest evergreen nursery, located on a 16-ha (40-ac.) site, grows well over
a million seedlings of fir, spruce, hemlock, Douglas fir, and pine
at any given time. The guided tour illustrates the process of "hardening to the elements" which is carried out before the seedlings are
replanted in southern B.C. Other operations include seed handling
and pest control. Operated by the Ministry of Forests. Groups only,
by appointment.
Location: Surrey Nursery, 3605 - 192 St.
Information: 576-9161, FAX: 574-4235.

■ **Hands Across the Border Celebration Day:**
Marching bands, waving flags, and an impromptu parade
honour the peaceful relationship between Canada and the
United States. The public is invited to bring a picnic lunch and
join in this yearly patriotic outburst, held in early June.
Location: Peace Arch Park, 138 Peace Park Dr., on the border
between Surrey, B.C., and Blaine, U.S.A.
Information: Peach Arch Park Supervisor, 531-3068; White Rock
InfoCentre, 536-6844.

■ **Celebrations:** Yearly events include Heritage Week (Surrey) in February; Cloverdale Rodeo (581-7130), Sea Festival and Sand Golf (White Rock 536-6844) in May; Festival of Arts (Surrey) in July; Surrey and Cloverdale Farm Fair (581-7130) in August, White Rock Sea Festival (536-6844), Crescent Beach Triathlon in August; Harness Racing (Surrey) from October through April.
Location: Various venues in Surrey and White Rock.
Information: InfoCentres, 581-7130, 536-6844.

■ **Barnston Island Ferry:** Although there are no designated parks here, some people like to pack a lunch and catch a little free ferry to an island in the Fraser River. Especially popular with bicyclists, there are fertile fields, dairy farms, some new housing developments, but no official picnic sites.
Location: Foot of 104 Ave., 179 St., is the start point.
Information: Western Pacific Marine, 589-2238.

■ **SkyBridge Crossing:** Token fee, about $2 one way. The SkyBridge is the longest cable-stayed rapid transit bridge in the world. Suspended 50 m (150 ft.) over the Fraser River, it is part of the $179 million rapid-transit link to Surrey. Visitors can cross it during a routine ride on the SkyTrain to or from Surrey.
Location: Board the SkyTrain at the Scott Street Station, Surrey.
Suggestion: travel to the end of the line, the Waterfront Station in Vancouver, then take the SeaBus, and visit Lonsdale Quay in North Vancouver.
Information: Transit Info, 261-5100, for fares and schedules.

Delta, Ladner, and Tsawwassen

Information on the attractions and festivals of Delta, Ladner, and Tsawwassen: 6201 - 60th Ave., Delta, V4K 4E2. Phone: 946-4232, FAX: 946-5285.

■ **George C. Reifel Waterfowl Refuge:** Small admission; free to the mentally handicapped, those in wheelchairs, and the blind. Waterfowl and migratory birds noisily occupy a 345-ha (850-ac.) sanctuary set aside to protect prime migratory routes along the Fraser River. Herons, ducks, and geese are abundant along the 3.2 km (2 mi.) of trails. Operated by the B.C. Waterfowl Society.
Location: 5191 Robertson Rd., Westham Island, located 10 km (6 mi.) west of Ladner.
Information: 946-6980. Pets are not allowed, and visitors are asked not to feed bread to the birds.

■ **Delta Museum:** Admission by donation. This 1912 restored heritage building features rooms furnished in Victorian style and a full-sized "streetscape" typical of turn-of-the-century Ladner. Permanent displays of native artifacts and a tribute to the fishing history of the area are also on display. Guided tours may be available; phone ahead.
Location: 4858 Delta Rd., Delta.
Information: 946-9322.

■ **Inverholme Schoolhouse, Burrvilla Victorian House, and Deas Island Regional Park:** A heritage one-room schoolhouse is now used as a Visitor's Centre. Nearby, a turn-of-the-century, Victorian-style Queen Anne residence is filled with antiques, many of which are for sale. Visitors can picnic on the dyke, savour the mountain panoramas, and watch the busy marine traffic on the Fraser River. Guided tours may be available; phone ahead. Opening hours are limited and the facility is closed in the winter. Campsites at Muskrat Meadows can be reserved for group activities. Phone: 432-6359.
Location: Travel south from the George Massey Tunnel, follow

the signs for Victoria Ferry - River Road, turn east on River Road, and follow the signs.
Information: Greater Vancouver Regional District, 432-6359.

■ **Celebrations:** Yearly events include Ladner Pioneer Days (946-5089) in May; North Delta Family Days (596-7960), Fraser River Festival in June; Annieville Days, Ladner Sports Festival in July; Tsawwassen Sun Festival (943-9186) in August.
Location: Various venues in Delta, Ladner, and Tsawwassen.
Information: InfoCentre, 946-4232.

Langley and Fort Langley

Information on the attractions and festivals of Langley: InfoCentre, Box 3422, 20420 Fraser Highway, Langley, V3A 4G2. Phone: 530-6656, FAX: 530-7066.

Information on the attractions and festivals of Fort Langley: InfoCentre, Box 75, 23325 Mavis St., Fort Langley, V0X 1J0. Phone: 888-1477, FAX: 888-2657.

Information kit on Fort Langley and its history: Fort Langley National Historic Park, Box 129, Fort Langley, V0X 1J0. Phone: 888-4424, FAX: 888-2557.

■ **Campbell Valley Regional Park:** The lush forest environment here changes into marsh, meadow, and river lands; sunny fields contrast with dark forests. The Little River Loop is a 3-km (2-mi.) walk along boardwalks; some trails have been upgraded to make them wheelchair accessible. The Annand-Rowlatt farmstead has remained virtually unchanged since the turn of the century. The Visitor's Centre, open in summer, features a display on how to attract wildlife into your own backyard. Guided tours may be available in the summer; phone ahead.

Organized groups can request the use of Coyote Camp, a group campsite.
Location: 8th Ave. and 200th St., located between 8th and 16th Ave., Langley.
Information: Greater Vancouver Regional District, 432-6350.

■ **B.C. Agricultural Museum:** Small admission. On display are old farm implements and devices, including hand scythes and an ingenious hollowed-out tree trunk used as a feeding trough. A re-creation of a blacksmith's forge and working scale-models of steam traction machines alternate with antique farm machinery in various stages of restoration. Guided tours may be available; phone ahead.
Location: 9131 King St., Fort Langley.
Information: 888-2273.

■ **Fort Langley National Historic Site:** Small admission. The fur-trading empire had scarcely stretched out to the west coast of North America when the demand for furs declined in Europe; nonetheless this west-coast fort continued to serve a commercial purpose for the few Europeans who lived in the region. Fort Langley National Historic Park is a restored 1850s fort, staffed by guides in costume who re-create the fur-trading era. During the early August celebration, voyageurs, accompanied by the swirl of pipes, arrive by cargo boat on the riverbank. Each November, members of the B.C. legislature arrive to simulate the first sitting of the provincial assembly. Guided tours are ongoing; phone ahead.
Location: 23433 Mavis St., Fort Langley.
Information: National Historic Park, 888-4424, for opening hours and presentations; tourist information, 888-1477, for walking tour maps.

■ **Langley Centennial Museum and National Exhibition Centre:** Admission by donation. On display here are the partial replica of a Coast Salish House, Indian artifacts, a full-sized re-creation of a homestead kitchen, a Victorian parlour and a general store. The National Exhibition Centre wing of the museum fea-

tures changing exhibits of art, science and history. Guided tours
may be available; phone ahead.
Location: 9135 King St., corner of Mavis and King St., Langley.
Information: 888-3922.

■ **Domaine de Chaberton Farm-Gate
Winery:** This is one of B.C.'s newest wineries and an example of B.C.'s farm-gate policy, in which wine sales are restricted
to the farm itself. The winemaker, Claude Violet, has constructed
a wine shop for tastings. Guided tours welcome year-round by
appointment; phone ahead. Opening hours for tastings vary
seasonally.
Location: 1064 - 216 St., South Langley.
Information: 530-1736.

■ **Celebrations:** Yearly events include Bradner Flower
Show in April; Langley Walk, May Day Celebrations
(Langley and Fort Langley) in May; Langley Country
Style Days, Little Britches Rodeo in June; Canada Day Celebra-
tions (Langley, 888-3678; Fort Langley) on July 1; J. R. Country
Jamboree (Fort Langley), Heritage Treasure Hunt (Fort Langley)
in July; Heritage Brigade Days and Fur Brigade Day (Fort Lan-
gley); Fort Festival of the Performing Arts (888-1477), Hot Air
Balloon Festival (Langley) in August; 49th to Fraser Relay Race
in September (530-1323); Celebration of Nature Regional Park
Canoe Race (432-6200) in October; Douglas Historic Re-creation
Day (Fort Langley) in November; Candlelight Carol Singing (Fort
Langley) in December.
Location: Various venues in Langley and Fort Langley.
Information: InfoCentres, 888-4424, 530-6656.

Maple Ridge and Pitt Meadows

**Information on the attractions and festivals of Maple
Ridge:** InfoCentre, 22238 Lougheed Highway, Maple Ridge,
V2X 2T2. Phone: 463-3366, FAX: 463-3201.

Information on the attractions and festivals of Pitt Meadows: Chamber of Commerce, 12492 Harris Rd., Pitt Meadows, V3Y 2J4. Phone: 465-7820.

Information and maps on Golden Ears Park: Ministry of Parks, Golden Ears Park, Box 7000, Maple Ridge, V2X 7G3. Phone: 463-3513, FAX: 463-6193.

■ **Kanaka Creek Park and Bell-Irving Fish Hatchery:** Meandering stream channels tumble over waterfalls and continue to carve out a small sandstone canyon at Kanaka Creek. The banks are overhung with alder and green ferns cling to the cliff walls; on warm summer afternoons, youngsters jump into the lagoon below the waterfall. Within the park, the Bell-Irving Fish Hatchery enhances stocks of chum and coho. Best viewing: from October to December at the hatchery's counting fence, located at the 240th St. Bridge. Groups only can phone ahead year-round for an appointment at the hatchery.
Location: Kanaka Creek Park is located on Dewdney Trunk Rd. Turn south on 253rd St. and park in the designated area; access to the creek is beyond the playing field. The fish hatchery is located 1 km (.6 mi.) south of Dewdney Trunk Rd. on 256th St.; watch for the sign at the entrance.
Information: Fish hatchery, 462-8643.

■ **Pitt Polder:** The 40 km (25 mi.) of trails here allow walkers and cyclists to observe a wildlife management area located in a natural marsh setting. Three observation towers are placed at strategic sites for viewing trumpeter swans, sandhill cranes, hawks and other bird life. Best viewing: from October to March. The northern boundary of Pitt Polder abuts Pitt Lake, the largest tidal freshwater lake in the world.
Location: Near the Pitt River, off DeKoster Rd., Renie Rd., or Koerner Rd.
Information: Dewdney-Allouette Parks Region, 462-8294.

■ **Haney House:** Admission by donation. Opening hours are limited. This 1878 pioneer farmhouse and garden is undergoing refurbishing; furniture, clothing, and household items are all originals representing three generations of possessions acquired from the family which lived here. There is no permanent phone on-site. Guided tours may be available; phone ahead. Groups only may order afternoon tea, in advance, for a small fee.
Location: 11612 - 224th, Maple Ridge.
Information: Museum curator's residence, 463-2594.

■ **Maple Ridge Museum:** Admission by donation. This was once the home of the manager of the Port Haney Brick Co. The 1907 house overlooks the Fraser River and the main CPR line. On display are pioneer and native artifacts from the local area, the story of the brickworks, and a working rail diorama of the Dewdney-Allouette Railway. Guided tours may be available; phone ahead. Open in summer.
Location: 22535 River Rd.
Information: 463-9563.

■ **Pitt Meadows Museum:** Admission by donation. Open only by arrangement. This heritage home contains paintings, historical photographs, and some artifacts of the local Coast Salish Indians. Guided tours may be available; phone ahead.
Location: 12479 Harris Rd., Pitt Meadows.
Information: 465-7820.

■ **Golden Ears Provincial Park Interpretive Program:** Mt. Blanshard frequently glows a golden colour at sunset, giving its twin peaks their name, Golden Ears. The heavily frequented park features several nature trails: the Spirea Nature Walk highlights a marsh zone and forest; the walk from the East Canyon Trail parking lot follows Gold Creek to the Lower Falls. Trail maps should be consulted before setting out, as the trails range

from easy to advanced. Interpretive programs with a park naturalist are available in summer; phone ahead.
Location: 15 minutes from Maple Ridge city centre, at Mount Blanshard.
Information: B.C. Parks Golden Ears, 463-3513, FAX: 463-6193.

■ **Heritage Self-Guided Walk:** Twenty-three historical sites, designated by the Maple Ridge Historical Society, have been placed on a special map obtained through Haney House or the InfoCentre. The map supplies commentary on each historical building.
Location: Haney House, 11612 - 224th St., Maple Ridge.
Information: Museum Curator of Haney House, 463-2594; InfoCentre, 463-3366.

■ **Pitt Meadows Airport Tour:** Aircraft takeoffs and landings are more thrilling when seen under the expert guidance of an air traffic controller. This conducted tour includes information on the workings of a local airport. Some aircraft may occasionally be available for inspection. Small groups only, by appointment.
Location: 2 km (1.2 mi.) south of Highway 7.
Information: Airport Tower, 465-6255. Children must be older than 12 and accompanied by an adult.

■ **Sawmill Tour:** This tour of a sawmill and planer operation covers the method by which raw timber is converted into finished lumber, mainly used by new home builders in Western Canada and the United States. Groups only, by appointment. Allow 2 hours.
Location: B.C. Forest Products, Hammond Division, 20580 Maple Crescent, Maple Ridge.
Information: 465-5401. Not suitable for persons under the age of 12. For safety, no open-toed footwear or shorts are allowed, and participants should wear clothing that covers the arms.

■ **UBC Demonstration Forest:** Managed by UBC's Faculty of Forestry, this area features two primary trails covered with bark mulch which total about 20 km (12 mi.). The trails pass through forests which demonstrate succession, pest management, and various eco-systems. Walking maps are available on-site. Allow from 1 to 2 hours for each of the two self-guided trail systems. Opening hours vary seasonally.

Location: Take Lougheed Highway to 232nd St. and turn north, then follow 232nd to Silver Valley Rd.
Information: 463-8148.

■ **Celebrations:** Yearly events include Mountain Festival and Homerama, Maple Ridge in May; Chamber Celebrity Golf Tourney, Pitt Meadows Days in June; Ridge Meadows Fair in July; Pitt Meadows Blueberry Festival in August; Santa Claus Parade Festivities in November.
Location: Various venues in Pitt Meadows and Maple Ridge.
Information: Maple Ridge InfoCentre, 463-3366.

■ **Albion Car-Passenger Ferry:** This free ferry ride across the Fraser River is used to bypass the Port Mann Bridge route to Surrey and can be used as a short-cut to Fort Langley; the ferry has a capacity of 24 vehicles and runs 24 hours a day, 7 days a week, from every 15 minutes to once an hour.
Location: At the foot of 240th St.
Information: Albion Ferry, 660-8770.

■ **Stave Lake Group Lodge and Campsite:** Not free, but of exceptional economy. Non-profit groups with a maximum of 24 members can seek permission to use an old B.C. Hydro work camp for holidays where comfort is not the main consideration. The heated lodge has running water and two dormitory-style sleeping areas. Beds, dishes and pots are not provided; inquire about cooking. The Warden will provide rules for use of the camp.
Location: 60 km (37 mi.) east of Vancouver, Dewdney Trunk Rd., right on Burma Rd. near Stave Falls Dam. Ask for exact directions when the application is accepted.
Information: Requests in writing only: B.C. Hydro Environmental Affairs, 970 Burrard St., Vancouver, V6Z 1Y3.

• • (2) • •

SHORT TRIPS FROM VANCOUVER

Vancouver is an exciting metropolis, but for most people there comes an urge to "get away from all." Fortunately for those in the Lower Mainland, a variety of environments await—just a few short hours from the city. This chapter covers the "quick" holiday in three directions: Vancouver to Whistler and beyond; the Sunshine Coast; the Fraser Valley, its canyon, and Harrison Hot Springs. Each offers a different environment and each promises friendly hospitality and a complete change of pace.

The "Sea to Sky" route takes a cliff-hugging highway that passes the deep-water port of Squamish to reach the mountains of

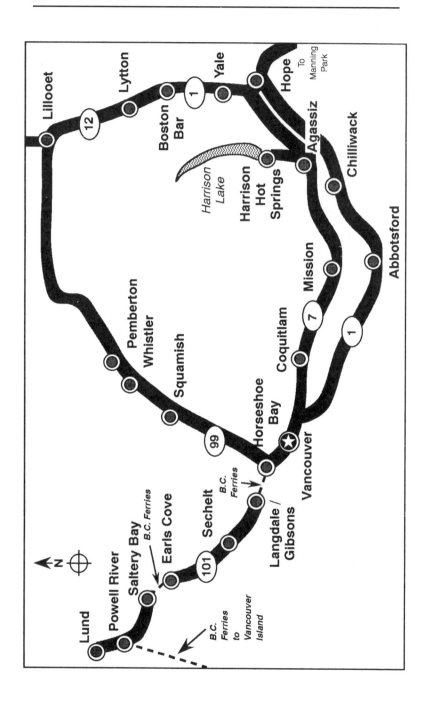

Whistler. This resort is famous for its winter skiing and summer alpine activities. Increasingly, travellers venture onward to Lillooet and area, a region rich in historical connections to the gold-rush days. Lillooet, situated in an arid region of hot sun and dry vegetation, is a novel change for deluge-soaked Lower Mainland residents.

The Sunshine Coast, accessible by a ferry ride or two, is a completely different experience featuring sea, surf, and a mild climate. The oceans around Powell River are known in diver's jargon as the "Emerald Sea," and numerous coves and harbours await discovery.

The Fraser Valley, also known as Rainbow Country, was the entryway for explorers and settlers on their way to the coast. Today, visitors can discover a restored mission, a fur-trading fort, and a country general store, each offering a vignette of life in simpler times. The pastoral countryside of the valley continues to provide the weekend traveller with a renewal of that connection to the land.

General Information

Information on daytrips or long weekends from Vancouver: Tourism Association of Southwestern B.C., #304 - 828 West 8th Ave., Vancouver, V5Z 1E2. Phone: 876-3088; from other Canadian provinces or the U.S.A., 1-800-667-3306; FAX: 876-8916.

Information and maps on B.C. parks in southwestern B.C.: Recreation Division, 1610 Mt. Seymour Rd., North Vancouver, V7G 1L3. Phone: 929-1291. Request descriptive brochures and maps of specific provincial parks by name, if possible.

■ Sea to Sky Country—Highway 99 ■

Highways Report for Highway 99 (taped message): 525-4997.

Squamish and Area

B.C. Rail Passenger Service to Squamish: 631-3500, FAX: 984-5005.

Information on the attractions and festivals of Squamish:
InfoCentre, 37950 Cleveland Ave., Box 1009, Squamish,
V0N 3G0. Phone: 892-9244.

Information and maps on Alice Lake: Ministry of Parks,
Alice Lake Park, Box 220, Brackendale, V0N 1H0. Phone:
898-3678, FAX: 898-4171.

■ **Climbing Areas:** In favourable weather, climbers
scale the sheer black walls of the Stawamus Chief rock face.
At 652 metres (2,140 ft.), the weeping rock, commonly
known as the "Chief," measures in as the second-largest granite
monolith in the British Commonwealth. Squamish natives consider
it bad luck to point at the rock—something interesting to keep in
mind as climbers labour upwards on summer weekends. Climbers
also scale the heights at the nearby Little Smoke Bluffs climbing
area.
Location: Stawamus Chief rock face can be seen from Highway
99 at the south end of Squamish; inquire at the InfoCentre for exact
directions to Little Smoke Bluffs climbing area.
Information: InfoCentre, 892-9244; Federation of Mountain Clubs,
737-3053.

■ **Eagle Walk and Tenderfoot Fish Hatchery:** The Fish
and Wildlife Service has determined that more than 2,500 bald
eagles live on the Squamish River system during the winter. The
public is invited to assist with the yearly predator count by joining
one of several weekend Bald Eagle Nature Walks held intermittently between November and January. Nearby is a hatchery, open
year-round, which enhances the chinook, coho, and steelhead populations. Best viewing: adult chinook from August to September;
coho, November to February; steelhead from March to May.
Location: Brackendale Gallery, headquarters for the walk: just north
of Squamish, on Government Rd.; seconds off Highway 99, at the
Depot Rd. turnoff, look for the unicorn. Tenderfoot Hatchery: turn
onto Cheekeye Rd., travel 5 km (3 mi.), cross bridge, turn right
on Paradise Rd., then right on Midway for 3 km (1.8 mi.).

Information: Brackendale Gallery, 898-3333; Tenderfoot Hatchery, 898-3657.

■ **Shannon Falls:** The Snohomish Indians say this cascading waterfall was created by a two-headed serpent as it crashed inland from the sea. A specially constructed platform at the base provides a good vantage point to view the falls. The water drops 335 m (1,100 ft.).
Location: Off Highway 99, 7 km (4 mi.) beyond Britannia Beach. Easy walk-in from the parking lot.
Information: B.C. Parks, 898-3678.

■ **Squamish Spit Windsurfers:** $5 to use the spit; free to watch. Squamish Spit is located at the end of a scenic river valley with mountains on either side and ocean waves crashing nearby. Cool air from Howe Sound is drawn north, past the spit, where it suddenly encounters hot air rising from the valley; the phenomenon is like air rushing through a wind tunnel. More than 9000 people a year come to this location—either to windsurf or to watch boarders in action.
Location: Start at McDonald's Restaurant near the sole traffic lights on the highway. Turn west at the intersection. Take the first right onto Buckley Ave. Cross the tracks onto Government Rd. Continue past the feed supply store and turn left onto the first gravel road. About 3 km (2 mi.) farther, turn left at the T-intersection, then go 2 km (1.2 mi.). Ask for exact instructions at the Infocentre before setting out.
Information: InfoCentre, 892-9244.

■ **Alice Lake Interpretive Trail:** The Parks and Outdoor Recreation and the Fish and Wildlife Branch have established a stream reclamation project at the outlet of this mountain lake. Interpretive signs explain the natural habitat of swamp lanterns, and several easy walking paths around tiny Alice, Fawn, and Stump lakes pass trout beds and offer views of the deep forest. In the summer, park interpreters present nature walks and give talks on wildlife and plants in the area; phone ahead.
Location: 13 km (8 mi.) north of Squamish, Highway 99.

Information: Alice Lake Park, 898-3678, FAX: 898-4171.

■ **Industrial Tours:** Located strategically on a deep-sea inlet, and having access to the timber harvests of the interior of British Columbia, Squamish is the base for 4 major industrial operations. Each of these facilities separately presents a guided tour to explain their operations. The Weldwood Logging Division illustrates the harvesting of timber and sorting of logs in a dryland operation. The Squamish Lumber Co. features equipment that rips through large trees to produce lumber for new-home construction. The Western Pulp Partnership Woodfibre Plant produces wood pulp that is ultimately made into high-quality paper such as that used for wedding invitations. Squamish Terminals handles ocean-going shipments through a double-berth deep-sea port and storage facility. Scheduled tours for each facility are held year-round; phone ahead. Allow a half-day for each industrial tour. Participants are asked to pack a lunch. Finally, the Sea to Sky Economic Development Commission offers varying yearly activities ranging from a public seminar to a tour of a demonstration forest; phone ahead.
Location: Ask for start point directions and times.
Information: Weldwood Logging Division, 892-5244; Squamish Lumber, 892-5236; Western Pulp Partnership Woodfibre Plant, 892-6600; Squamish Terminals, 892-3511; Sea to Sky Economic Development Commission, 892-5467. Not suitable for persons under the age of 12. For safety, no open-toed footwear or shorts are allowed, and participants should wear clothing which covers the arms.

■ **Celebrations:** Yearly events include Royal Hudson Train First Run Party and Trade Fair in May; Summer Festival on July first; Windsurfing Competitions from July through August; Logger Days, Squamish Folk Festival, Squamish Open Regatta Sailboat Championship (892-3333), Can Am Sailboard Championships in August.
Location: Various venues in and around Squamish.
Information: InfoCentre, 892-9244.

■ **First Run of the Royal Hudson Steam Train:** Each year, dignitaries and crowds assemble on the Victoria Day weekend in May for the first run of the Royal Hudson steam train. The bands play, children hold balloons, and Bunker C. Bear, the R.H. mascot, is in attendance; all are welcome to join in. The Squamish Chamber of Commerce usually sponsors a trade fair of local products during the same celebration.
Location: Squamish Train Station: turn left at the sole traffic light on the highway; turn right after passing the elementary school and before crossing the tracks; follow the tracks straight to the station.
Information: InfoCentre, 892-9244.

■ **Logger Days:** This annual celebration of forestry skills kicks off with a chainsaw contest followed by axe throwing and tree felling. Touted to be the largest "Logger Days" in British Columbia, find out about free events or demonstrations surrounding this festival. Held in early August.
Location: Various venues in Squamish.
Information: InfoCentre, 892-9244.

Whistler

Whistler Mountain Activities: 932-5528.

Blackcomb Mountain Activities: 932-3141.

Whistler Mountain Ski Conditions (taped message): 687-6761.

Blackcomb Mountain Ski Line (taped message): 687-7507.

Information on ski hills and winter vacations in B.C.: 387-1642. From Vancouver: 685-0032.

B.C. Rail Passenger Service to Whistler: 631-3500, FAX: 984-5005.

Information on the festivals and attractions of Whistler-Blackcomb Resort: Whistler Resort, 4010 Whistler Way, Whistler, V0N 1B4. Phone: 932-4222, FAX: 932-7231. Whistler Travel InfoCentre, 2097 Lake Placid Rd., Box 181, Whistler, V0N 1B0. Phone: 932-5528, FAX: 932-3755. Specific handouts to request: low-cost accommodations list, map of easy walking trails.

Map of Garibaldi Park: Garibaldi District, Ministry of Parks, Box 220, Brackendale, VON 1H0. Phone: 898-3678, FAX: 898-4171.

■ **Frozen Lakes for Skaters:** The small lakes in the Whistler area occasionally freeze solid enough to provide skaters with an old-fashioned Christmas-card setting. In order to use the lakes, ice surfaces must be inspected by the municipality and snow cleared away; skates can be rented at the KOA Campground.
Location: Inquire about locations in the valley.
Information: Municipal Hall, to verify safety, 932-5535; KOA Campground, 932-5181.

■ **Roadside Geology:** There is evidence of ancient volcanic activity from Squamish to Whistler and most can be seen from Highway 99 by amateur roadside geologists. Interesting formations include Garibaldi Mountain, a volcanic peak; Table Mountain; a lake of solidified lava at the 1333-m (4373-ft.) level; Opal Cone; a volcanic cone with evidence of a lava flow; Garibaldi Lake, glacier-fed and emerald blue; Black Tusk, the eroding core of a volcanic cone; the Barrier, a huge volcanically created boulder-dam holding in Garibaldi Lake; the Devil's rocks, eroding monolithic crystalline structures. The regular park map indicates the formations, and is available from B.C. Parks.
Location: Along Highway 99 between Squamish and Whistler.
Information: B.C. Parks, Garibaldi District, 898-3687, FAX: 898-4171. Write for Garibaldi Park map: Garibaldi District Ministry of Parks, Alice Lake Park, Box 220, Brackendale, VON 1H0.

■ **Toboggan Run:** The wintry slopes of Whistler and Black-comb mountains are monopolized by skiers and sledding is not allowed. However, a perfect spot for tobogganing has been set aside on the Old Rainbow Ski Hill.
Location: Old Rainbow Ski Hill, between Alpine Meadows and Emerald Estates, across from Green Lake.
Information: Whistler Activity and Information Centre, 932-2394.

■ **Chateau Whistler Lobby:** Engage in the tourist sport of "lobby walking." Constructed in the chateau style typical of grand hotels in Canada, this hotel features examples of Canadiana, such as hand-made woven carpets and hand-carved furniture, in its public areas. The recurring theme of the "leaf" is found entwined in the wall coverings, *trompe l'oeil*, specially commissioned carpets, fabric-covered walls, and even the chandeliers. One of the restaurants has a collection of bird houses, one of which is reputed to be haunted. **Location:** Blackcomb Base Area, Whistler Village. **Information:** 938-8000.

■ **Nancy Greene's Olympic Trophies and Awards:** At the 1968 Olympics in Grenoble, France, Nancy Greene was Canada's downhill skiing champion. Her Olympic gold medal is on display along with numerous trophies, plates, awards, and citations. **Location:** Two areas of the lobby of the Nancy Greene Lodge, along Village Stroll, between Village Square and Mountain Square. **Information:** 932-2221.

■ **Whistler Museum:** Admission by donation. Displays outline Whistler's appearance in the days before it became a world-class resort. Opening hours are limited. For a fee, groups can arrange a guided tour of the valley or a slide show featuring early photos. **Location:** Blackcomb Way in the Village. **Information:** 932-2019.

■ **Blackcomb Ski Area Orientation:** The variety of terrain and the numerous lifts which transport skiers up the mountain can be confusing for first-time visitors. Upon arrangement, the public relations department will provide a guided orientation tour of the mountain, any day in ski season. **Location:** Inquire about start points and times on Blackcomb Mountain.

Information: Guest Relations, Blackcomb Mountain, 932-3141; from Vancouver, 687-1032.

■ **Glacier Guided Walk:** Blackcomb Mountain has been open to year-round skiers ever since the Horstman glacier area was opened. Casual summer visitors can view that glacier in the company of a guide who explains the dynamics of glacier ice. Guided tours available about 4 times a day in summer; phone ahead. A corporate sponsor, such as General Motors, has in the past sponsored nature walks through alpine meadows at lower levels on the mountain; phone ahead. The walks are free, access is not free.
Location: Accessed by the Wizard chair at Blackcomb Mountain.
Information: Blackcomb Mountain, 932-3141; or from Vancouver, 687-1032.

■ **Log Homes Conducted Tour:** These customized log buildings are assembled on-site, numbered, taken apart, and then shipped. Guided tours are available in summer; phone ahead. Allow 45 minutes.
Location: Ultimate Log Homes, 1410 Alpha Lake Rd., Function Junction, Whistler.
Information: 932-6000. Not suitable for persons under the age of 12. For safety, no open-toed footwear or shorts are allowed, and participants should wear clothing which covers the arms.

■ **Whistler Mountain Guided Walks:** In the summer, there are 4 activities high on the side of this mountain. Guided nature-walks to Harmony Lake cover the geography of the mountain and the history of the Whistler town-site. The Paleface Loop is a 20-minute interpretive trail, sometimes available with a guide and sometimes self-guided. Here, visitors can spot a whistling marmot or two, pikas, soaring eagles, and the occasional black bear. The "lookouts" guided walk is held every hour on the hour; a guide takes visitors to several viewpoints on the mountainside and explains the sights. A display of snow-making and snow-grooming equipment with explanatory signs, is located beside the cafeteria. The walks are free, access is not free; phone ahead.
Location: Access at the top of the Whistler Express Gondola.

Information: Whistler Mountain, 932-3434; or from Vancouver, 685-1007.

■ **Whistler Ski Area Orientation:** Whistler Mountain is a winter world of intertwining ski lifts and varying levels of ski terrain. "Ski Ambassadors," who speak several languages, will show first-time visitors around at 11:00 a.m. and 1:00 p.m. every day in ski season.
Location: Meet at the Alpine Lightboard, near Pika's, the top of the Whistler Express Gondola.
Information: Guest Relations, Whistler Mountain, 932-3434; from Vancouver, 685-1007.

■ **Celebrations:** Yearly events include Ski Races on Whistler and Blackcomb Mountains, December to April; Snow, Earth, Water Race in May; Children's Art Festival in June; Canada Day on July 1, Country and Bluegrass Festival (932-3928) in July; Motor Sport Rally in August; Labour Day Extravaganza, Square Dance Jamboree in September; Fall Fair in October.
Location: Various venues at Whistler and Blackcomb.
Information: InfoCentre, 932-5528, FAX: 932-2027.

■ **Summer Magic, Ongoing Festivals:** An annual program of free street entertainment, occasional summer fireworks, and entertainment surprises takes place on the main streets of Whistler each summer. From jugglers to acrobats, from bluegrass to jazz, there are hundreds of free performances. To tap in to the activities, ask for the seasonal program.
Location: Main streets of Whistler.
Information: InfoCentre, 932-5528, FAX: 932-2027; Festival Coordinator, 932-3928. Write: Summer Entertainment Brochure, P.O. Box 1400, Whistler, V0N 1B0.

Pemberton and Area

Information on the attractions and festivals of Pemberton:
Arrange through Whistler Travel InfoCentre, Highway 99 and
Lake Placid Rd., Box 181, Whistler, V0N 1B0. Phone:
932-5528, FAX: 932-2027. Specify Pemberton.

■ **Meagre Creek Undeveloped Hot Springs:**
These naturally bubbling hot waters, emerging in their
natural state, can be reached by car along difficult gravel
roads; directions to the creek are hoarded and passed from generation to generation like a precious recipe. At the creek, a crude
dam has been constructed to create a small pool; people disrobe
along the banks. Note: in the cold of winter, garter snakes and reptiles congregate around the creek for its warmth. Best in summer;
bring a bathing suit and pack out all garbage.
Location: A typed page of detailed directions is available from
the sources below.
Information: Squamish InfoCentre, 892-9244; Whistler Travel
InfoCentre, 932-5528, FAX: 932-2027.

■ **Pemberton Historic Museum:** Admission
by donation. In the 1860s, Pemberton was part of the
supply route to the goldfields; before that natives lived
on the lands around Mt. Currie and D'Arcy for many generations.
The two cultures are represented through photographs and artifacts
displayed in this small museum. Opening hours are limited.
Location: 7424 Prospects St.
Information: Museum Curator, 894-6186.

■ **Tyax Mountain Lodge:** This building, said to be the largest log structure ever built on the west coast of North America,
encloses an area of 1,021 sq m (11,000 sq. ft.). It is somewhat isolated in a spectacular section of wilderness, and is in use as a
28-suite luxury resort. Casual visitors can browse the grounds and

walk the lobby. Bralorne, a modern-day ghost town is nearby and accessible for exploration. The town, constructed for a gold-mining operation, was recently abandoned when the claim ran out. **Location:** By all-season paved road between Pemberton and Lillooet. Ask for exact directions to the mountain lodge before setting out. **Information:** Tyax Resort, 238-2221, FAX: 238-2528.

Lillooet

B.C. Rail Passenger Service to Lillooet: 631-3500, FAX: 984-5005.

Information on the attractions and festivals of Lillooet: Travel InfoCentre, Box 441, Lillooet, V0K 1V0. Phone: summer, 256-4308; off-season, 256-4556, FAX: 256-4288.

■ **Recreational Gold Panning:** While meandering through hot, dry country, many people get the urge to strike a little "paydirt" on their own. Each year the swollen waters expose more of the precious metal, washing it downstream with ground runoff. Participants can bring a gold pan to a gold-bearing creek near town, where the provincial government has set aside a reserve for public use. This reserve is famous for gold "flour" so fine it floats. **Location:** Coming off Old Bridge, take trail to river just past the exit to Bralorne. Or, coming off New Bridge, turn left at Cayoosh Creek Park. Ask for the specifics at the InfoCentre. **Information:** InfoCentre, 256-4308 in summer or 256-4556 off-season; Public Information Unit of Energy and Mines, 356-2824.

■ **Rock-Hounding Safaris:** This area is known as a rock hound's paradise, where jade and many other semiprecious stones can be found; near here, the largest jade boulder ever found weighed in at 11 tonnes (12 tons). Set up a search for purple and yellow agate, hollow geodes, thunder eggs, jade, jasper, and serpentine. **Location:** Various locations around Lillooet. **Information:** Agate Country Lapidary and Gems, P.O. Box 196,

Lillooet, V0K 1V0; phone: 256-4860. InfoCentre, 256-4308 in summer or 256-4556 off-season. Public Information Unit of Energy
and Mines, 356-2824.

■ **Hanging Tree and Chinese Rock Debris:**
Judge Begbie, commonly known as the "Hanging
Judge," almost single-handedly kept order during the
gold rush of the 1860s. He exercised a combination of gusto, hand-
some looks, charismatic presence, British civility, a reasonable
knowledge of English law, and periodic hangings. It was said that
prospectors who arrived from the lawless scene of California's 49er
rush were warned, "If there's going to be a killing, there's going
to be a hanging." The Hanging Tree is a gruesome symbol of the
times, although the appropriate limb has rotted off. The Chinese
rock debris is a reminder of Chinese miners who washed and
rewashed tailings for specks of overlooked gold.
Location: Within walking distance of the train station; follow the
signs.
Information: InfoCentre, 256-4308 in summer or 256-4556 off-
season.

■ **Lillooet Museum and InfoCentre:** The museum, combined with the InfoCentre, is located in a disused church, site of
the former Anglican church, St. Mary the Virgin. The original,
brought in piece by piece on the backs of miners, was assembled
by number; interior furnishings were endowed by a wealthy English
gentlewoman and the doors of that first church were never locked
in 100 years. Itinerant miners slept in the pews and cooked food
on a stove designed for heating. Outside is a portable jail cell.
Location: Main St.
Information: 256-4308 in summer, or 256-4556 off-season.

■ **Golden Mile of History:** In its heyday in 1863,
Lillooet (then called Cayoosh Flats) had a population of
15,000, was the second-largest city north of San Francisco, and sup-

ported 13 saloons and 25 other liquor outlets. It served a population of miners, packers, gamblers, and ramblers. The exteriors and crumbling remains of some original buildings can still be seen. The Bridge of the 23 Camels was named after a caravan of dromedaries recruited to carry supplies. During the 1860s gold rush, shipping company employees grew tired of the twice-daily delays required to water mule trains. A few daredevils bought a group of camels from a U.S. army experimental unit in California, although the army neglected to mention the key features of the animals: easily injured feet, miserable dispositions, and offensive smell. In May of 1862, the desert animals arrived in Lillooet on a barge towed far, far behind a sternwheeler. First, horses refused to work around these beasts that kicked mules, oxen, horses, and men alike; their cloying odor especially upset the mules which proceeded to double their usual stubbornness when the camels were present. After valiant efforts to shoe the camels' tender feet with custom-made leather booties and the unsuccessful use of perfume sprays to disguise their exceptional smell, the owners gave up. Even camel steaks were met with disgust by the locals. In 1864, the remaining animals were scattered, and the last camel's offspring was said to have been sighted by a bewildered farmer in Alberta in the 1920s. Other points of interest on the map include the Miyazaki House with intricate gingerbread decorations, owned by an esteemed Japanese doctor; and the house of Ma Murray, flamboyant newspaper editor, whose lambasting of provincial politics won her acclaim.

Location: A walking tour map of the Golden Mile is obtained from the Lillooet Travel InfoCentre, Main St.

Information: InfoCentre, 256-4308 in summer or 256-4556 off-season. Write for historic information: Lillooet Historical Society, P.O. Box 441, Lillooet, V0K 1V0.

■ **Native Fish-Drying Racks:** In the desert-like climate here, the natives have long used hot river winds to preserve salmon. Traditional structures constructed of poles and boughs act as natural ovens using dry solar heat. The racks are in use in late July and August. Visitors are advised to

wear protective clothing, as the weather can exceed 42°C (107°F) in summer.
Location: On the river cliffs, near the Old Bridge at the confluence of the Bridge and Fraser rivers. Before setting out, ask for exact directions at the InfoCentre.
Information: InfoCentre, 256-4308 in summer or 256-4556 off-season; Lillooet Native Friendship Centre, 256-4146.

■ **Celebrations:** Yearly events include Mud Bog 4 X 4's in April; May Day Parade in May; Lillooet Days, Casino Night, Can-Can and Train Robbery, Forestry Days in June; District Fall Fair in September; Black Powder Shoot in October.
Location: Various venues in Lillooet.
Information: InfoCentre, 256-4308.

■ The Sunshine Coast ■

British Columbia Ferries Sunshine Coast Sailings: 669-1211; from Vancouver, 685-1021; from Victoria, 386-3431; from Seattle, (206) 441-6865; FAX for group reservations, 381-5452.

Langdale to Earl's Cove

Ferry Terminal, Langdale: 886-2242.

Information on the attractions and festivals of Gibsons: InfoCentre, 417 Marine Dr., or 668 Sunnycrest Rd., Box 1190, Gibsons, V0N 1V0. Phone: 886-2325.

Information on the attractions and festivals of Sechelt: InfoCentre, 5555 Highway 101, Box 360, Sechelt, V0N 3A0. Phone: 885-3100, FAX: 885-9538.

■ **Angus Creek Spawning Area and Porpoise Bay Park:** The Sechelt Indian Band is in charge of a facility that enhances chum, chinook, and coho salmon populations. Juvenile chinook can be seen from October through mid-June; juvenile coho February to mid-June; adults from September to November. The nearby Porpoise Bay recreational zone consists of a broad sandy beach giving way to a grassy open area followed by a dense second-growth Douglas fir and hemlock forest; there are several walking trails.
Location: From Sechelt, take Porpoise Bay road to signs, 4 km (2.5 mi.) east and north of Sechelt.
Information: Sechelt Indian Band, 885-5562.

■ **Exotic Tree Safari:** A number of unusual warm-weather tree species, including palm, eucalyptus, apricot, and fig, all grow in this area, evidence of the mild weather, light rainfall, and gentle winds which give the Sunshine Coast its name.
Location: Eucalyptus in a garden across from the Indian Cemetery at Sechelt; giant sequoia, monkey puzzle tree, and the windmill palm, a dozen unusual specimens on the grounds of the Rockwood Lodge on Cowrie Ave. in Sechelt; others located at Davis Bay, Wilson Creek, and Reception Point.
Information: InfoCentre, 885-3100.

■ **Sechelt Marsh Bird-Watching Area:** Kinglets and chickadees do insect patrol on spruce trees while brown creepers check the bark on fir trees. Many birds, including widgeons, grebes, coots, mergansers, jays, and several species of blackbirds, inhabit the marsh, depending upon the time of the year. The area was saved from destruction by concerned citizens and is in the early stages of development.
Location: Off Wharf Rd. near Porpoise Bay.
Information: InfoCentre, 885-3100.

■ **Skookumchuck Narrows Rapids:** *Skookumchuck* is a native expression for "turbulent, rapid torrent." On the incoming tide, ocean waters rush into the confines of Sechelt Inlet and then

build up again on the other side of the narrows on the outward flow. When the tide is running, boiling cauldrons, whirlpools, and swirling eddies create treacherous conditions for navigation. To catch conditions at their most turbulent (greatest tidal exchange) consult local tide tables. The highest tides are in the springtime and best viewing is during daylight hours. The local tour-boat operator listed below reports daily tide tables to the local newspaper. Allow 1 hour to walk each way from the parking lot.
Location: From the Egmont parking lot, take a 4-km (2.5-mi.) walking trail to Narrows Point and Roland Point.
Information: Local tour boat operator, 885-9802, for tides; InfoCentre, 885-3100.

■ **Elphinstone Pioneer Museum:** Admission by donation. The large Bedford seashell collection of about 25,000 shells features several rare specimens as well as the more familiar shoreside beauties. There are also pioneer exhibits, and native Coast Salish artifacts.
Location: Winn Rd., downtown Gibsons.
Information: 886-8232.

■ **Sunshine Coast Arts Centre:** Weavers, artisans, painters, and fashion designers choose to live in this region for its rural lifestyle and natural beauty. The arts centre presents exhibitions, arts events, and dramatic offerings by local and regional artists. The popular Sunshine Coast Craft Fair is held in August. Ask for a list of ongoing events.
Location: Junction of Trail and Medusa streets, Sechelt.
Information: 885-5412.

■ **Paper Mill Tour:** Now owned in partnership by Canadian Forest Products and Japan's Oji Paper, this company's tour familiarizes participants with the process of making newsprint. The original mill produced pulp products and was responsible for the establishment of an old-time community called

Port Mellon. During this tour there are many stairs to climb. Phone ahead for scheduled tour times; alternate tour times may also be arranged. Allow 2 hours for the tour.
Location: Howe Sound Paper Mill, in Port Mellon on the lower Sunshine Coast. Inquire about start point.
Information: 884-5223, local 575. Not suitable for persons under the age of 12. For safety, no open-toed footwear or shorts are allowed.

■ **Sechelt Nation Cultural Complex:** The House of Hewhiwus, meaning "house of chiefs" is a multipurpose facility for the use of band members, but part of the facility is open to the public. The Tem Swiya Museum features artifacts of the "Salmon People," a store offering local native handicrafts, and a permanent totem-pole collection.
Location: Centre of Sechelt.
Information: Band Office, Sechelt, 885-2274; Band Office, Vancouver, 688-3017.

■ **Celebrations:** Yearly events include Polar Bear Swim in January; Pender Harbour Days (886-2561), April Fools' Race in May; Sunshine Coast Fishing Derby in June; Sechelt Celebration Days, Halfmoon Bay Country Fair (885-3230), Gibsons Sea Cavalcade and Tugboat Races, Drama Festival in July; Writers' Festival, Festival of the Written Arts, Annual Sunshine Coast Craft Fair "Eaire" in August; Gambier Island Craft Fair, Gibsons Fall Fair in September.
Location: Various venues in and around Sechelt, Gibsons, and Pender Harbour.
Information: InfoCentre, 885-3100.

Powell River to Lund

B.C. Ferries, Saltery Bay terminal (Sunshine Coast connections): 485-9333.

B.C. Ferries, Westview Harbour (Vancouver Island connections): 485-2943.

Information on the attractions and festivals of Powell River: InfoCentre, 6807 Wharf St., Powell River, V8A 1T9. Phone: 485-4701, FAX: 485-4272.

■ **Cranberry Lake Wildlife Sanctuary:** Admission by donation. The circuit trail around this 4-ha (10-ac.) sanctuary is designed to allow wildlife viewing in a protected habitat. Muskrat and beaver, geese, trumpeter or tundra swans, waterfowl, and birds of prey can be observed in season. Opening hours vary from season to season. No dogs, except seeing eye dogs, are allowed. Visitors are requested not to touch or feed the birds.
Location: 5570 Park Ave.
Information: 483-2122.

■ **Lang Creek Hatchery:** More than a million chum and coho fry are released annually from this hatchery. The facility is at peak capacity for pinks late August to October in odd years, and for chum from October to early December each year. An interpretive trail leads visitors around the forested setting. Guided tours may be available; phone ahead.
Location: Take the road to Haslam Lake and continue on Duck Lake Rd. Turn right after the Duck Lake outlet bridge and follow the signs. Check instructions at the InfoCentre.
Information: Hatchery, 485-7612; InfoCentre, 485-4701, will arrange guided tours.

■ **Mountain Ash Farm Petting Zoo:** Small admission. Youngsters can visit a "pot-bellied" pig, pygmy goats, rabbits, ducks, geese, and ponies.
Location: South of Powell River, take Highway 101; turn northeast on Silinsky Rd., then north on Nassichuk Rd. Follow the signs.
Information: 487-9340.

■ **Powell Lake Trapped Seawater:** Powell Lake is a geological anomaly. Although it appears to be a large freshwater lake, pockets of ocean brine have been trapped within its depths for nearly 10,000 years. The salt layer begins at a depth of 110 m (360 ft.), supports no marine life, and contains methane; fish thrive in the upper layers. The souvenir store sells vials of brine that have been brought up from the depths, and date back to the last Ice Age. **Location:** Just northeast of Powell River townsite. Ask at the InfoCentre. **Information:** InfoCentre, 485-4701.

■ **Powell River to Lund Mini-Adventure:** The hundreds of eagles that gather around the salmon-spawning creeks from October to December are the subject of numerous photographs and film documentaries. The Sliammon Indian Band operates a remote chum enhancement facility. Guided tours may be available; phone ahead. Okeover offers a look at commercial oyster cultivation and marine shore life. Highway 101 terminates at Lund, a picturesque fishing village. Stop by the historic Lund Hotel or browse the Huber Ink Studio and Gallery, open May to September. **Location:** Consult a detailed map. Sliammon Hatchery is downstream from the second bridge on the road to Sliammon Village. Okeover oyster-cultivating area is 3 km (2 mi.) south of Lund; turn east onto Malaspina Road, travel 5 km (3 mi.) east. For Huber Ink Studio and Gallery, take the third right on Finn Bay Rd. at Lund. Ask for exact instructions at the Powell River InfoCentre before setting out. **Information:** InfoCentre, 485-4701; Sliammon Band Administration, 483-4111, for guided tours.

■ **Recreational Site for the Physically Challenged:** This unique area is a model recreational experience featuring a fully accessible trail. The viewpoints have been arranged to accommodate wheelchairs, and theme areas, such as a scent garden for the blind, allow maximum advantage for specific senses. Recommended between April and November. **Location:** Inland Lake, in Powell River. Ask for start point. **Information:** InfoCentre, 485-4701; Recreation Resource Officer, 485-9831; Chamber of Commerce, 485-6291. Write for a list of wheelchair-accessible cabins, restaurants, and accommodation: Powell River Chamber of Commerce, 6910 Duncan St., Powell River, V8A 1V4.

 ■ **Mill Lookout:** Just offshore lies an imposing structure constructed from the intact hulls of abandoned ships. Old war ships were filled with concrete and are now anchored in place to serve as a breakwater for logs in the MacMillan Bloedel mill pond. Though the assembly dominates the view, there are few published photographs of it; the looming structure is aptly nicknamed the "incredible hulks." Interpretive signs describe the history of the area, its totem poles, and the story of the mill.
Location: Pull-off on Marine Ave., near the golf course.
Information: InfoCentre, 485-4701.

■ **Powell River Historical Museum and Nature Walks:**
Token admission. This museum features a collection of native carvings, baskets, masks, pioneer furniture, and the third-largest photograph archives in B.C. The cabin of a notorious local character named "Billy Goat Smith" has been restored. Guided tours may be available; phone ahead. Nearby are two interpretive nature walks: the 1.6-km (1-mi.) Willingdon Creek Nature Trail starts beside the museum, and Beach Trail begins across the street at Willingdon Beach.
Location: Willingdon Park, in the centre of Powell River. Obtain maps of the walks at the museum or the InfoCentre.
Information: 485-2222.

■ **Pulp Mill Tour:** This complex was once one of the world's largest single unit mills, encompassing a power generator, pulp mill, paper-producing system, and sawmill. The guided tour takes visitors into the operational parts of the mill, including a look at the "Bellingham Barker" which uses powerful, ripping, water jets to strip huge trees. The complex covers a large area and the tour requires a great deal of walking. Guided tours are available in summer; phone ahead. Allow 2 hours. **Location:** MacMillan Bloedel, along Highway 101. **Information:** Regional office, 483-3722, for booking tours; InfoCentre, 485-4701, will also book mill tours.

■ **Lime Quarry Tour:** Lime is used in the manufacture of fertilizers, cement, glass, and chemicals. This tour covers the removal of the raw stone from one of four open pit quarries and allows a look at the barges transporting crushed rock to the mainland. Groups of 6 or more may prearrange guided tours. On another note, rock hounds can hunt for "flower" rocks that are unique to this island. Sometimes used for jewellery, the rock appears to have a white flower embedded within its structure; try looking at Shelter Point overlooking Georgia Strait. Watch for deer: there are reputed to be 5 times as many deer as people on the island. **Location:** On Texada Island, served by B.C. Ferries from Powell River to Blubber Bay. No public transportation is available on the island. **Information:** Ideal Cement, 486-7627; Powell River InfoCentre, 485-4701, for a referral to book the tour.

■ **Celebrations:** Annual festivals include Music Festival in March; Tour de Lund Bike Race, Algerine Passage Sailing Event in May; Wildlife Sanctuary Week in June; Texada Sand Contest, Seafair and Loggers' Sports (485-4051), Choral Festival featuring thousands of singers in July; Lund Days in August; Sunshine Folkfest, Soccer Tournament in September; Sailing Club Race in October; Old-timers Hockey Tournament in November. **Location:** Various venues in Powell River, Texada Island, and Lund. **Information:** InfoCentre, 485-4701.

■ Heritage and Rainbow Country ■ The Fraser Valley and Canyon

Information on the attractions and festivals of the Fraser Valley and the Fraser Canyon: Tourism Association of Southwestern B.C., #304 - 828 West 8th Ave., Vancouver, V5Z 1E2. Phone: 876-3088.

Information and maps on B.C. Parks in the Fraser Valley: Ministry of Parks, Fraser Valley Parks District, P.O. Box 10, 2950 Columbia Valley Highway, Cultus Lake, V0X 1H0. Phone: 858-7161, FAX: 858-4905.

Abbotsford and Matsqui

Information on the attractions and festivals of Abbotsford and Matsqui: InfoCentre, 2462 McCallum Rd., Abbotsford, V2S 3P9. Phone: 859-9651, FAX: 850-6880.

■ **Matsqui Trail Regional Park:** An 11-km (7-mi.) riverside dyke located beside pastoral fields is the setting for one of 16 Lower Mainland parks operated by the Greater Vancouver Regional District. The dyke here provides a level gravel surface ideal for walking, cycling, or horseback riding. Guided tours may be available; phone ahead.
Location: 70 km (43 mi.) east of Vancouver. From Lougheed Highway, turn south at the junction of Highway 11 and cross over the Mission Bridge. Turn right at Harris Road, then right at Riverside St.
Information: Greater Vancouver Regional District, 432-6350.

■ **Trethewey House, and Heritage Gallery:** Admission by donation. Trethewey House is a designated heritage house restored to the 1925 era. The main floor is open to the public, but an attendant must accompany visitors through the upstairs rooms. The restored yard features trellis and lattice work, benches, period fencing, and an outdoor gazebo; the original garage is now converted into an exhibit gallery and presentation area. Groups only can arrange for demonstrations, lectures on native lore, weaving, and dying fabric. The public is invited to join in scheduled activities, such as making raspberry vinegar, old-time theatre, or a Hallowe'en stomp. Ask for a seasonal program of events. Guided tours may be available; phone ahead. **Location:** 2313 Ware St., Abbotsford. **Information:** 853-0313.

■ **Brick Manufacturing Tour:** This tour familiarizes groups with the making, firing, and shipping of bricks at an established refractory and face-brick manufacturer. After the 1-hour tour, visit the nearby village of Clayburn to see historical buildings built from Clayburn bricks. Groups only, by appointment. **Location:** Clayburn Industries, 33765 Pine St., Abbotsford; to get to Clayburn, take Mission Highway heading north, then go right on Clayburn Rd. **Information:** 859-5288. No children under the age of 13 years.

■ **Irrigation Pump-Station Tour:** The original pump station, started in 1920, has served the area well, draining approximately 6,500 ha (16,000 ac.) of rich agricultural farmland and 2,000 ha (4,900 ac.) of steep wooded hillside. Once drained, the land was protected from flooding by a system of dykes. A new pumping station with a total project value of $25 million was opened in 1985. This guided tour reviews the modern and historic installations, built to protect prime B.C. farmland. Best viewed in May, June and July. Guided tours are available by appointment. **Location:** Barrowtown Pump Station, 16 km (10 mi.) east of Abbotsford on Highway 1. **Information:** Pump Station, 823-4678; or Abbotsford Municipal Hall, 853-1155.

■ **Moccasin Factory Demonstration:** Fine-quality deerskin moccasins, mooseskin muk-luks and soft leather shoes are

produced at this small facility. Natives create Indian-style footwear using a combination of modern equipment and traditional methods. Small groups only, by appointment.
Location: Sto:Lo Bigfoot Moccasin Factory, #6 - 2009 Abbotsford Way.
Information: 854-8380.

■ **Trout Hatchery Tour:** B.C.'s largest trout hatchery features 9 large glass aquariums with push-button displays that provide information on the life cycle of the trout. Glassed-in walkways overlook the fry-rearing area and there are hourly slide shows. Guided tours are available; phone ahead.
Location: Fraser Valley Trout Hatchery, 34345 Vye Rd., Abbotsford.
Information: 852-5388.

■ **Fraser Valley International Arts Festival:** This international festival features entertainment, ethnic food, a craft market, artists at work, children's entertainment, and displays from many nations. Held in mid-May.
Location: Central Fraser Valley Exhibition Park. Inquire for exact location.
Information: 852-9358 for a list of activities.

■ **Celebrations:** Yearly events include Bradner Flower Show, Abbotsford-Matsqui International Band Festival in April; Sheep and Wool Fair in May; Canada Day Celebration, Abbotsford Berry Festival in July; Agrifair, Abbotsford International Air Show (852-8511) in August.
Location: Various venues in and around Abbotsford and Matsqui.
Information: InfoCentre, 859-9651.

■ **Abbotsford Berry Festival:** Admission is free. Take part in a celebration of the goodness of local strawberries, raspberries, and blueberries, continuous stage entertainment, hourly bingos, a children's costume contest, arts and crafts tables, fresh berries

and good food. Held annually in July.
Location: Montrose Ave. and Essendene.
Information: InfoCentre, 859-9651.

■ **Sheep and Wool Fair:** Admission is free. Of special interest
to weavers and knitters, a contest called "From Sheep to Shawl"
features teams producing garments from the fleece of a live animal.
Sheep-shearing contests are demonstrations of strength and speed
and 4H Club members fluff up little lambs or deck them out in
bow ties. There is a traditional lamb barbecue with "lamburgers."
Held annually in May.
Location: Central Fraser Valley Exhibition Park; inquire for exact
location.
Information: InfoCentre, 859-9651.

Mission

Information on the attractions and festivals of Mission:
InfoCentre, St. Mary's Park, 34033 Lougheed Highway, Box
3340, Mission, V2V 4J5. Phone: 826-6914, FAX: 826-5916.

■ **Inch Creek Hatchery:** One of the many locations
in B.C. where the public is invited to see chum, coho and
chinook raised to enhance fish stocks. Best viewing: adult
chum, chinook and coho, November to December; juvenile chum,
March to April; juvenile chinook, December through April. Guided
tours may be available; phone ahead. After a visit to the hatchery,
plan to stop at nearby scenic Cascade Falls Regional Park.
Location: 38620 Bell Rd. in Dewdney, east of Mission.
Information: 826-0244.

■ **Hatzic Rock Archaeological Site:** This
archaeological site is now being excavated by the Sto:lo
Tribal Council with assistance from the University of
British Columbia. The site represents what may be the oldest dwell-

ing ever unearthed in B.C.; only the hardened floor, blackened fire pit, and crude post holes remain of a dwelling which may be more than 5,000 years old. Simple pebble tools and flakes of sharp rock are now being sifted from the soil. Single boulders frequently mark places of special significance to prehistoric peoples and according to native legend, the lone glacial rock that guards the area imprisons the frozen spirit of a disobedient ancestor. Guided tours are occasionally available through the Tribal Council; phone ahead. **Location:** Take the Lougheed Highway east of Mission to Hatzic. It is just east of the Esso Station and Dewdney Trunk Road Intersection. The rock is on private property and may be viewed from the highway. **Information:** Sto:lo Tribal Council, 885-3366; UBC Department of Anthropology and Archaeology, 822-2567.

■ **Mission Museum:** Admission by donation. An eclectic collection of artifacts includes farm equipment, minerals, army memorabilia, a homestead kitchen, and a Chinese display. All are housed in a stately white heritage building formerly used as a Bank of Commerce; the 1907 two-storey building is an early example of a prefabricated structure. **Location:** 33201 2nd Ave., downtown Mission. **Information:** 826-1011.

■ **Electricity Generating Tour:** Tours of the Stave Falls hydroelectric site and the Ruskin Generating Station can be arranged. The tour leader explains how electricity is generated by moving water and turbines, and the group can sometimes see water released through the penstocks. Groups only, by appointment. **Location:** Stave Falls Dam, start point as arranged. **Information:** B.C. Hydro, 462-7145.

■ **Dam Driving Tour:** Mission's hydroelectric dams have been used as backdrops for film productions, including *We're No Angels,* starring Sean Penn, and the television series "MacGyver." Ruskin Dam was used in a "MacGyver" episode that focused on the destruction of rhinoceros in Africa; Hayward Dam and Stave Falls

Dam were the backdrop for a $2.6 million movie set depicting a dilapidated frontier town. The set was dismantled after it was used for two movies. Take a self-guided driving tour of the three dams. **Location:** Start at the Mission InfoCentre, 1.5 km (1 mi.) east of Mission on Sasquatch Dr., Highway 7. Ask for exact directions to explore the three sites. **Information:** InfoCentre, 826-6914.

■ **Fraser River Heritage Park Tour:** Early in the history of British Columbia, Christian missionaries assumed responsibility for the education of native people. Today, visitors can see the Oblate cemetery, the ruins of St. Mary's Oblate Mission and the old Indian Residential School—the original mission that gave the municipality its name. Take in broad vistas from this hilltop overlooking the Fraser River; the Blackberry Kitchen offers afternoon tea. Open from May to Labour Day; Canada Day celebrations and the Mission Folk Festival are held here in July. Scheduled walking tours for visitors are held in summer; phone ahead. Groups can prearrange guided tours. Unscheduled entertainment takes place at the park during the summer; phone for details. **Location:** Log Reception and Interpretation Centre, 3 km (2 mi.) east of downtown Mission just off the Lougheed Highway. **Information:** InfoCentre, 826-6914; Mission Heritage Association, 826-0277.

■ **Westminster Abbey Visit:** Admission by donation. Thousands of people visit this serene church high above the Fraser Valley. Designed by Asbjorn Gathe, the building features 64 stained-glass windows and the dome of coloured glass over the altar allows shafts of light into the heart of the church. Ten bells peal at 9:45 a.m. and 4:15 p.m. on Sunday. Mass is sung at 10:00 a.m. Sundays and 6:30 a.m. weekdays. Public visits are encouraged each Sunday from 2:00 p.m. to 4:00 p.m. and weekdays from 1:30 p.m. to 4:30 p.m. At the Benedictine monastery, monks carve out a self-sufficient lifestyle, tending crops and raising livestock in a continuation of monastic practises from the Middle Ages. Modest dress is requested. **Location:** East of downtown Mission. **Information:** 826-8975.

■ **Celebrations:** Yearly celebrations include Mission Raceway, March to October; Folkfest, Mission Indian Pow Wow and Native Dancing (826-1281), Agricultural Parade Fair & Arts and Crafts, Pioneer Days in July; Raft Race, Drag Boat Races in August; Christmas Craft Fair in November; Candle-light Parade in December.
Location: Various venues in and around Mission.
Information: 826-6914.

Chilliwack

Information on the attractions and festivals of Chilliwack: InfoCentre, 44150 Luckachuck Way, Sardis, V2R 1A9. Phone: 858-8121, FAX: 858-0157.

■ **Chilliwack River Hatchery:** This facility raises more than 7 million chum, chinook, coho and steelhead fry in a year. Best viewing times: adult chum from November to December; coho from October to December; chinook from August to November; and steelhead from March to April. Guided tours may be available; phone ahead.
Location: Take the Sardis exit south from Highway 1, drive to the Chilliwack River crossing and turn east. The hatchery is located at the junction of Slesse Creek and the Chilliwack River.
Information: 858-7227.

■ **Canadian Military Engineers Museum:** The first military engineers were an intrepid lot who were responsible for the construction of the first eastern forts as early as 1610. During the First and Second World Wars, Canadian Engineering Units cleared mine fields, demolished bridges, and constructed airfields. Items of interest on display here

include military uniforms, weapons, and medals. Old military pieces used in engineering operations are stored on the grounds along with a log cabin circa 1860. Guided tours may be available; phone ahead. **Location:** Take Highway 1 to the Canadian Forces Base exit and continue south on Vedder Rd. for 5 km (3 mi.). The museum is the first building on the right after the traffic lights at Keith Wilson Rd.
Information: 858-3311, local 462, for general information; 858-3311, local 261, for guided tours.

■ **Chilliwack "Powerland":** Free, except for threshing bees. Officially called the Atchelitz Thresherman Association Museum, this collection of old farm equipment is more commonly known as Powerland. Among the collection of threshing and farm equipment dating from the last 100 years, some pieces are in working order, others are restored to their original condition. Periodically, a blacksmith gives live demonstrations. *Atchelitz* is a native Indian word meaning "friendly meeting place" and the thousands who trickle through each year have come to appreciate the sentiment. Guided tours may be available; phone ahead.
Location: Southeast corner of Lickman Rd. overpass, just off Highway 1.
Information: 858-2119.

■ **Chilliwack Museum:** Admission by donation. This imposing white building with Grecian pillars was designed by English-born Thomas Hopper. Formerly used as the city hall, it was built in the neoclassical style to fit the theme of justice. Artifacts are arranged in time capsules from 1858 to 1950; items range from Sto:lo native tools and pioneer Isaac Kipp's organ, to a baby's high chair, bibles, quilts, china pieces, walking canes, kitchen utensils, and an old-fashioned sewing machine. Guided tours may be available; phone ahead.
Location: 45820 Spadina Ave.
Information: 795-5210.

■ **Apple Farm Tour:** Token admission. The owners here sell 17 varieties of apples and pears, mostly grown on

special trees less than 2 m (7 ft.) high; the resulting varieties are sold in health-food stores and specialty outlets. This tour reviews the "slender spindle" method of trimming. Allow about 90 minutes for a tour and plan to buy some apples; phone ahead. Best from September through November.
Location: 4490 Boundary Road, Yarrow.
Information: 823-4311, FAX: 832-4669.

■ **Forests-In-Action Tours:** Chilliwack's Chamber of Commerce and the B.C. Ministry of Forests have prepared several self-guided tours to familiarize visitors with various aspects of the forest. Following the routes indicated in a forestry brochure, participants pass through old forests, new forests, a tree nursery, and a fish hatchery. The route is easily driven at moderate speeds in a family vehicle; allow 2 hours.
Location: Chilliwack "Forests-in-Action" brochures available by writing or in person: Chilliwack InfoCentre, 44150 Luckachuck Way, Sardis, V2R 1A9.
Information: InfoCentre, 858-8121.

■ **Cultus Lake Interpretive Program:** The name *Cultus* is derived from an Indian word meaning "worthless"; in native lore, the lake was reputed to contain a bad bear spirit responsible for whipping up dangerous storms. Today, it is a popular lake with several campgrounds. A self-guided interpretive trail up Teapot Hill demonstrates the power of natural electricity: where lightning struck a huge fir tree, the trail has been rerouted and an interpretive sign added to view the damage. Scheduled naturalist programs that focus on wildlife, flowers, or edible wild plants are held at the campground and change regularly throughout the summer; phone ahead. Every long weekend in summer, park interpreters present special events such as slug races, pioneer lore, or old-fashioned games for the children.
Location: South of Chilliwack on Vedder Rd., 13 km (8 mi.).
Information: B.C. Parks, Fraser Valley District, 858-7161, FAX: 858-4905, for details on programs.

■ **Nut Farm Visit:** In the past, the preferred method of harvesting nuts was to hire a team of people with hard hats and have

them shake each tree, but times have changed. Now the owner of this nut farm hires a helicopter to fly low and blow the nuts off. While it is not possible to time a visit to coincide with the arrival of the helicopter, visitors can see the farm when it is ready for harvest. Guided tours available only around the first week in October; phone ahead.
Location: 50621 Yale Rd. E., Rosedale. Ask for exact directions.
Information: 794-7139.

■ **Volksmarch Walking Route:** Small admission fee. Pick up a "start card" and take part in a volksmarch, derived from a German word meaning "people-walk." Participants navigate a specified walking route and their card is checked off at control points. Walks are sponsored by a European club and are open to all; the purpose is to see new sights and stay in shape. Routes are changed twice each year; each walk is 10 km (6 mi.) or more in length.
Location: Various venues near Chilliwack.
Information: InfoCentre, 858-8121, for referral to the appropriate person. Mailing address is Rainbow Country Volksport Club, MPO 612, CFB Chilliwack, V0X 2E0.

■ **Cultus Lake Indian Festival:** Outstanding value; individual events may be charged for separately. Established in 1920, the Cultus Lake Indian Festival today features a field of more than 25 11-paddle canoes, B.C.'s largest annual gathering of Indian war canoes. There is native entertainment and a competition for Sto:lo Indian Princess. Held in late May or early June.
Location: Cultus Lake, various venues.
Information: Sto:lo Band Office, 794-7924.

■ **Celebrations:** Yearly events include Old-Fashioned Antique Threshing Bee in April; Chilliwack Horses and Country Living Festival (828-8121), Chilliwack International Jazz Festival (795-3600) in May; Square-Dance Demo and

Jamboree, Yarrow Days, Drama Festival in June; Canada Day
Celebrations, Cultus Lake Yacht and Krafty Raft Race (858-3334),
Triathlon Tin Man in July; Chilliwack Exhibition and Fall Fair,
Rod Show for Fishing Enthusiasts, Loggers' Sports Days, Bluegrass
Festival (792-2069) in August.
Location: Various venues in and around Chilliwack.
Information: InfoCentre, 858-8121.

■ **Krafty Raft Race:** Groups of 8 people create home-made
rafts which must not use conventional techniques and cannot be
motor-powered; results are hilarious. Held in July.
Location: Various venues, Cultus Lake.
Information: 858-1204; entries before June 15 to Rotary International, P.O. Box 330, Chilliwack, V2P 6J4.

Agassiz and Harrison Hot Springs

**Information on the attractions and festivals of Agassiz and
Harrison Hot Springs:** InfoCentre, Highway 9, 499 Hot
Springs Rd., Box 255, Harrison Hot Springs, V0M 1K0.
Phone: 796-3425, FAX: 796-3188.

■ **Hot Springs Source:** Harrison Lake is the largest
lake in southwestern B.C., yet, surprisingly, 40 percent of
first-time visitors do not even know it exists. Native Indians
used the waters as a trade route, and explorer Simon Fraser named
it. A clumsy, or perhaps tipsy, prospector fell into the supposedly
frigid water of Harrison Lake and was shocked to discover it was
warm. Two hot springs emerge from the base of the mountain, each
a different temperature and chemical composition; the hot waters
are now captured for use in a public swimming pool and resort
hotel. Anyone may explore the source of the warm waters, a short
stroll away from the front door of the hotel. A tap is provided to
drink the mineral water—called "taking a cure" in other parts of
the world.
Location: Village Esplanade Walk, past Harrison Hot Springs
Hotel, along the waterfront walkway to the cement structure. If

lost, ask the doorman at the hotel to point the way.
Information: Harrison Hot Springs Resort Hotel, 796-9339.

■ **Industrial Ruby Hunt:** Rock hounds can sometimes find industrial-grade (not of gemstone quality) rubies and garnets. Best time for the hunt is late winter before the annual spring runoff. Significant finds, such as pebble choppers and arrowheads, common in the area, should be donated to the Chilliwack Museum.
Location: Ruby Creek as it flows under Highway 7, 18 km (11 mi.) beyond Agassiz, at the Fraser River where the red-and-white natural gas pipeline crosses the road. For exact directions and other sites, ask at the InfoCentre before setting out.
Information: InfoCentre, 796-3425; Public Information Unit of Energy and Mines, 356-2824.

■ **Rock Hound Country:** Rock hounds all over North America quietly emerge as the spring runoff subsides along the Fraser River. More than 600 interesting varieties, including rhodonite, orbicular jasper, and B.C. jade, can be found in this area. With effort, amateur explorers can find fossils from the early Cretaceous and Jurassic periods. Do not disturb ammonite fossils; they are to be left intact and in place.
Location: Rock specimens: along the Harrison East Forestry Rd. to the headwaters of the Big Silver River. Cretaceous fossils: along Harrison West Forestry Rd. to Lookout Trail for about 30 km (18 mi.). Jurassic fossils: farther along Harrison West Forestry Rd. to Mystery Creek. Ask for complete instructions at the InfoCentre before setting out.
Information: InfoCentre, 796-3425; Public Information Unit of Energy and Mines, 356-2824.

■ **Weaver Creek Spawning Channel:** Sockeye salmon do not thrive in hatcheries; they require a long, winding spawning channel and clean oxygenated water. At this shallow man-made extension to the original creek, the full-sized salmon returning from the ocean actually protrude out of the shallow water. Observe the care taken to ensure the water supply is adequate and the winding channel clean. Fish productivity has increased 200 times since construction. Best viewing is during the second, third and fourth weeks

of October; the greatest numbers of fish arrive about October 15, with peak activity for the following 10 days. Guided tours, for groups only, may be available.
Location: From the Lougheed Highway, turn north on Morris Valley Rd. at the Sasquatch Inn. Take the right fork in the road about 300 m (1000 ft.) from the highway. Follow the signs to the spawning channel past the Chehalis Hatchery. The distance is about 13 km (8 mi.) from the main highway.
Information: 796-9444.

■ **Kilby General Store Museum:** Small admission. In pioneer times, the country store served as post office, grocery store, clothing store, shoe store, hardware, and legal office; this general store, circa 1910-1930, also features an upstairs rooming house for weary travellers. The store, rooming house, creamery, and gardens have now been restored to their former condition, with supplies on the shelves and letters in the postal boxes; animator-guides in costume may strike up a conversation on the price of milk. Guided tours may be available as well as occasional free open houses and story-telling events; phone ahead. From November through April, bald eagles are frequently sighted in the area; bring binoculars. Operated by the Ministry of Recreation and Culture.
Location: Kilby Provincial Historic Park; turn off Route 7 (the Lougheed Highway) at the east end of the Harrison River Bridge and travel 1.6 km (1 mi.) south on School House Road. The Museum is 16 km (10 mi.) west of Agassiz.
Information: 796-9576, FAX: 796-9592.

■ **Agricultural Research Station and Railway Station Museum Tour:** Established well over 100 years ago by the federal government, this 144-ha (355-ac.) experimental farm has been engaged in various types of agrarian experimentation ever since. With renewed interest in the quality of foodstuffs, livestock, and grasses, historical knowledge is back in fashion. The

guided tour covers the old Clydesdale horse barn, the mature arbore-tum planted in 1892, and the stone barn; a historic weather station on-site is approaching its 100th birthday. Guided summer tours for the public start from the Railway Station museum; phone ahead. Group tours available year-round by appointment.
Location: Just past the intersections of Highway 7 and Highway 9 in Agassiz. Watch for signs.
Information: 796-2221.

■ **Forests-in-Action Tour:** This self-guided tour follows a route through B.C.'s coastal forest. Participants pass by the old Har-rison Ranger Station, Raake Marine Services, an old logging camp, the old logging railway grade, examples of forest management, wood lots, old growth, and recently planted forest. The whole route is easily driven at moderate speeds in the family vehicle. Allow 2 hours.
Location: Harrison "Forests in Action" brochure available by writ-ing B.C. Ministry of Forests, District Office, 9850 McGrath Rd., Rosedale, V0X 1X0. Pamphlet also available at the InfoCentre in Harrison.
Information: B.C. Ministry of Forests, District Office, 794-3361.

■ **Sasquatch Park Interpretive Programs:** Park Rangers give short lectures on wildlife, flowers, or outdoor lore and sto-ries. These informative programs are usually held in an outdoor amphitheatre in the evening in summer, but occasionally take the form of a guided walk. Designed for amateurs, subjects change from week to week and focus on the environment; phone ahead.
Location: Various campgrounds, north of Harrison Hot Springs.
Information: B.C. Parks, Fraser Valley District, 858-7161, FAX: 858-4905.

■ **Harrison Festival of the Arts:** Outstanding value; occasional free demonstration events. This colourful event is held for 9 days in early July and features hundreds of international, national, or local performers providing musical, artistic, and dramatic presentations; attendance hovers around 5,000.
Location: Various venues. Potential participants are asked to

contact H. H. S. Arts Festival, Box 399, Harrison Hot Springs, V0M 1K0, or phone for the program list. **Information:** 796-3664, FAX: 796-3694.

■ **Seabird Island Indian Band Festival:** A native festival featuring First People's games, food, and war canoe races is held over a 2-day period in late May. Charges may be made but there are free events surrounding the festival. **Location:** Various venues, 7 km (4 mi.) east of Agassiz, Highway 7. **Information:** Band Office, 796-2177.

■ **Celebrations:** Yearly events include Kids' Easter Egg Hunt during Easter season; Daffodil Tea in April; Canada Day in July; World Championship Sand Sculpture Competition in August or September; Haney Harrison Road Relay (987-1924) in November. **Location:** Various venues in and around Harrison Hot Springs. **Information:** InfoCentre, 796-3425.

■ **Hang Gliders' Informal Fly Meets:** Hang gliders can often be seen on pleasant weekend afternoons from April through October, gliding up and away, then landing again in the favourable air currents around a modest-sized hill. Pull well to the side of the road and watch for oncoming traffic; meets are cancelled in inclement weather. Bring binoculars. **Location:** Mount Woodside: the landing area is alongside Highway 7. Ask for the exact location at the InfoCentre. **Information:** InfoCentre, 796-2585.

■ **Sand-Castle Building:** Join in Harrisons' most engaging activity: sand-castle building. In August or September, crowds watch as teams of experts build sand sculptures, later judged on engineering skills such as height, arches, and towers. Entrants to the World Championship Sand Sculpture Competition are allowed 10 hours to build their creations, as opposed to seaside contests that are limited by nature to about 4 hours between tides.

Location: By the lake, Harrison Hot Springs.
Information: InfoCentre, 796-3435. Register a kite at 796-2824.

Hope and Area

Information on the attractions and festivals of Hope: InfoCentre, 919 Water Ave., Box 370, Hope, V0X 1L0. Phone: 869-2021, FAX: 369-2160.

Maps of the Skagit Valley or Manning Park: Fraser Valley District Provincial Parks, P.O. Box 10, 2950 Columbia Valley Highway, Cultus Lake, V0X 1H0. Phone: 858-7161, FAX: 858-4905.

■ **Bridal Falls and Mineral Museum:** Like a tiered veil, this high cascade plummets in stages towards the valley floor. The waterfall is best viewed on a 20-minute return walk from the parking area. Afterwards, browse among the gift shops housed in old-time false-fronted buildings or stop by the Sandstone Mineral Museum, featuring a collection of B.C. rock samples (admission charged).
Location: Turnoff on Highway 1, junction of Highway 1 and 9.
Information: 794-3003.

■ **Fraser River Rock Hounding:** Besides gold, the immense drainage system of the Fraser River churns up colourful rocks of interest to collectors. Experts have discovered more than 600 varieties around the Fraser River, some semiprecious. Stones include green and black nephrite, rhodonite, orbicular jasper, dumortierite of a rare violet colour, obsidian, fossils, garnet, serpentine, jade, olivine, and jasper.
Location: Specimens are found at the Coquihalla River, Emory Creek, and Ruby Creek. Ask for exact locations at the InfoCentre.
Information: InfoCentre, 869-2021; Public Information Unit of Energy and Mines, 356-2824.

■ **Hope Slide:** Early on the morning of January 9, 1965, a small earthquake triggered an enormous slide. Suddenly, without warn-

ing, the mountain slumped, sending tonnes of rock, mud, and trees onto the main highway. Four people were buried; two victims are still entombed. The adjoining valley and a valley floor creek were filled to a depth of 61 m (200 ft.), totally displacing Outram Lake and causing a devastating secondary mud slide. The slide can be seen from a roadside viewpoint and parking area.
Location: On Highway 3, 15 minutes east of Hope.
Information: InfoCentre, 869-2021.

■ **Recreational Gold-Panning Reserve:** Open to the public. Fresh placer gold washes down from the cliffs every winter and is found after the swollen waters of spring begin to subside. Bring a gold pan and try panning out a few specks of dust. Finding flakes larger than the lower case letters on this page is a lucky event. Best in early spring, and August through November.
Location: To get there, before the Fraser Bridge, take a left turn and continue along Landstrom Rd. until a road leads straight to the gravel beds beside the river. Ask for exact instructions at the InfoCentre before setting out.
Information: B.C. Parks, Fraser Valley District, 858-7161; Public Information Unit of Energy and Mines, 356-2824.

■ **Sucker Creek Salmon-Spawning Channel:** A specially constructed boardwalk allows visitors to wander along a stream where the salmon return each October. This is not a hatchery: one school of thought counsels that hatchery-bred stock may eventually weaken wild stocks, and certain areas have been set aside to permit wild stocks to propagate naturally. These channels are continuously inspected for free-running water with adequate volume and oxygen levels, clean gravel, and overhanging shade trees; even here in the wild, the fish are pampered.
Location: On the outskirts of Hope. Cross the bridge over the Coquihalla River on Kawkawa Lake Rd.; turn left.
Information: InfoCentre, 869-2012.

■ **Hope Museum, Travel InfoCentre, and Ball Mill:** Admission by donation. Outside the museum is a huge gold concentrator or "ball mill" used in the 1920s by mining companies. Its function was to pulverize enormous rocks into bite-sized pieces in order to extract flakes of gold and minerals. Inside, there are informal displays depicting the fur trade, the gold-rush era, and early logging history. There are also a few photographs of the nearby Japanese internment camp which housed displaced persons during World War II.
Location: 919 Water St.
Information: Museum in summer, 869-7322; museum in winter, 869-2021; InfoCentre, 899-2021.

■ **Othello Tunnels:** Pioneer engineer-surveyor Andrew McCulloch surveyed this canyon from a wicker basket hanging over the gorge and then decided to build 5 separately designed tunnels. The Kettle Valley Railway utilized the tunnels from 1916 to 1961, when its hard-won route was no longer necessary. Carved from solid rock, the tunnels recently served as the dramatic setting for Sylvester Stallone in his movie *First Blood*. Three other movies were subsequently filmed along this dramatic gorge where river waters churn between 100-m-high (300-ft.) cliffs. All five tunnels are now open to the public. Be forewarned: the tunnels drip. Closed in winter.
Location: Kawkawa Lake Turnoff, Highway 5. Ask for exact directions at the Hope InfoCentre.
Information: InfoCentre, 869-2021.

■ **Rainbow Junction Art Centre:** Designed and built by the Great Northern Railway in 1916 at the outlandishly high cost of $7,200, this building served its original purpose for many years. The former CN railroad station was relocated intact, and is now rechristened and operated as a restaurant and art gallery, where you can browse among the works of local craftspeople and artists.
Location: Junction of Highway 1 and old Hope-Princeton Way, in Hope.
Information: 869-9495.

■ **Anglican Christ Church Tour:** Admission by donation. Christ Church is the oldest active house of worship in British Columbia. Designed by Royal Engineer Captain John Grant and consecrated in 1861, the original furnishings were brought by sailing vessel from England around Cape Horn. The founding vicar's prime concern was to offer an alternative to the many saloons providing services to pioneer gold miners. Guided tours may be available by appointment; phone ahead.
Location: 681 Fraser Ave.
Information: InfoCentre, 869-2021, for a referral.

■ **Forestry or Mill Tour:** Local forestry companies sometimes sponsor bus tours in the summer months. Choose between a woods tour that is 4 hours in duration and sometimes includes a look at the active felling of trees, or a sawmill tour that is 2 hours in duration and features the cutting and finishing of lumber. Advance booking is mandatory; dress casually as the bus ride is dusty.
Location: Start point: Hope Travel InfoCentre, 919 Water Ave.
Information: InfoCentre, 899-2021. Not suitable for persons under the age of 12. For safety, no open-toed footwear or shorts are allowed, and participants should wear clothing which covers the arms.

■ **Movie Stars' Footsteps:** Walk in the steps of movie stars Sylvester Stallone, Brian Dennehy, and Richard Crenna—stars in the movie *First Blood* filmed in and around Hope. The town hall became the "sheriff's office" and an exact replica of the town's gas station was built to explode.
Location: Pick up a self-guided "Rambo Tour Map" at the InfoCentre in Hope.
Information: InfoCentre, 869-2021.

■ **Celebrations:** Yearly events include Brigade Days in September; Lights of Hope Festival in December.
Location: Various venues in and around Hope.
Information: InfoCentre, 869-2021.

Manning Park

Maps and information on Manning Park: B.C. Parks, Manning Park, V0X 1R0. Phone: 840-8836, FAX: 840-8700.

■ **Subalpine Floral Meadows/Rare Rhododendrons:** This beautiful meadow is said to be one of the only true car-accessible subalpine meadows in the world. Located at an altitude of 2,000 m (6,500 ft.), fragile mountain wildflowers bloom in late July: avalanche lilies, lupines, and phlox nod against the panorama of the Cascade mountains. Park interpreters lead occasional public tours to the meadows; phone ahead. At another location, the annual flowering of the rare red California rhododendron (*Rhododendron macrophyllum*) is cause for celebration; it is one of only three flowers protected by special B.C. legislation. In June, its deep pink blooms contrast with its evergreen leaves.
Location: Subalpine meadows, up Blackwall Mountain; rhododendrons located at Rhododendron Flats. Exact locations are available from the Park naturalist at the Visitor Centre, Manning Park Resort.
Information: B.C. Parks, 840-8836; Manning Park Resort, 840-8822.

■ **Meet the Naturalist Program:** Park experts give informative nature talks, lead morning and evening walks, or present slide shows at an outdoor amphitheatre. These public programs on environmental subjects change from week to week. Participants may explore a beaver dam, investigate the secret lives of animals, peer into a pond, or hike trails through a sea of subalpine flowers; phone ahead.
Location: Visitor Centre Information Bulletin Board, Manning Park Resort, midway between Hope and Princeton on Highway 3; Amphitheatre on Gibson Pass Rd.
Information: B.C. Parks, 840-8836; Manning Park Resort, 840-8822.

■ **Celebrations:** Yearly events include Bird Blitz Bird-watching Tips in June; Rhododendron Rhapsody Guided Walks in June; Canada's Parks Day, Elderhostel in July; Old-Fashioned Picnic, Family Frolic in August.
Location: Various venues in Manning Park.
Information: Manning Park Lodge, 840-8822.

■ **The Last Resort:** Outstanding value. This largely unserviced rustic lodge with kitchen is available to groups of up to 37 intrepid friends at a nominal fee. It is fun for those big group gatherings, where comfort is not the main consideration; ask about rates, accessibility, and the services available at the old lodge.
Location: Manning Park Resort, 45 minutes east of Hope on Highway 3, about 3 hours from Vancouver. The exact location of the old lodge is not far from the new resort.
Information: Manning Park Resort, 840-8822.

The Fraser Canyon

Information on the attractions and festivals of the Fraser Canyon: Lytton Travel InfoCentre, 400 Fraser St., Box 450, Lytton, V0K 1Z0. Phone: 455-2523, FAX: 455-6669.

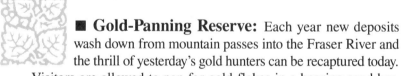

■ **Gold-Panning Reserve:** Each year new deposits wash down from mountain passes into the Fraser River and the thrill of yesterday's gold hunters can be recaptured today. Visitors are allowed to pan for gold flakes in a bearing sand bar. Hand-panning only; no commercial or motorized operations are allowed. Bring gold pans.
Location: Along the Fraser River, in a public reserve set aside by the government, near Lytton. A map is available at the Lytton or Yale InfoCentre.
Information: Lytton InfoCentre, 455-2523, FAX: 455-6669. Public Information Unit of Energy and Mines, 356-2824.

■ **Lytton Jellyroll:** Roadside geologists can watch for a rock formation that is evidence that a layer of silt along an ancient lake bottom suddenly rolled into a jelly-roll shape and was enclosed in a larger bed of coarser sand. The unusual event was probably the result of a single geologic episode, rather than the pressures of millions of years. A pamphlet, obtained from the Lytton InfoCentre, details the phenomenon. A fibreglass replica is mounted in the Lytton Village Square, near the InfoCentre.
Location: The structure, or what is left of it, is visible in the wall of a small sand pit just south of Lytton; located on the east side of the Fraser River, it can be clearly seen from Highway 1 when travelling north.
Information: Lytton InfoCentre, 455-2523, FAX: 455-6669. Hope InfoCentre, 869-2012.

■ **Alexandra Bridge:** Constructed in 1926, this cable suspension bridge was built on the site of the old 1863 Cariboo Wagon Road bridge that washed away in the flood of 1894. The bridge has openwork iron decking that allows a see-through into the raging river below. From here the two railway lines can be seen, and, in season, natives fishing the river, or river rafting in progress.
Location: 1 km (.6 mi.) north of Spuzzum on Highway 1. Walk to the bridge along remnants of the old highway.
Information: B.C. Parks, 858-7161.

■ **Gold-Rush Monuments:** Yale rightfully claims to be the "birthplace of British Columbia" and was the beginning of the treacherous Cariboo supply road to the Barkerville goldfields. Beginning in 1858, over 30,000 prospectors passed here on their way to the interior. Arriving by river steamer, goods, animals, and supplies had to be unloaded; treacherous Lady Franklin Rock was a barrier to further navigation upriver. The Royal (Road) Engineers constructed a crude road from this point through the Fraser Canyon and onward to the Cariboo. The circa 1860 Pioneer Cemetery, Lady Franklin Rock, the Cariboo Wagon Road National Monument, and the Barnard Express

Commemorative Plaque are reminders of Yale's colourful past.
Location: Various locations around Yale; obtain a locator map at
the Yale Travel InfoCentre, Highway 1.
Information: Yale Seasonal InfoCentre, 863-2324.

■ **Yale Museum and InfoCentre:** Admission by donation.
On display are artifacts from the days of the gold rush and the later
building of the Canadian Pacific Railway. The museum itself is
a heritage home built in 1868; in front stands a monument to the
Chinese workers who, in the 1880s, were pivotal in constructing
the first rail lines. Guided tours may be available; phone ahead.
Location: 31179 Douglas St.
Information: Yale and District Historical Society, 863-2324; Yale
Seasonal InfoCentre, 863-2324.

■ **Church of St. John the Divine:** Admission by donation.
Claiming to be the oldest Anglican church in B.C., this mellow
wooden building was constructed by Royal Engineers who took time
out from the laborious task of road building to bring some godli-
ness to the prospectors. Built in 1863, the church was set among
a city of tents, crude dwellings, and liquor and gambling establishments. The church was designed by a leading architect of the
day, B. Wright; the interior is fully furnished with original pews
and altar.
Location: Next door to 31179 Douglas St.
Information: Yale and District Historical Society, 863-2324,
administrates the site. Heritage properties branch of the B.C.
Government, 356-1040.

■ **Forestry Tours for Groups Only:** Several
facilities either offer tours of sawmill operations that produce
finished lumber, or bush tours that illustrate active cutting and sorting in the woods. Pre-book conducted tours through each facility
separately. Groups only, by appointment; ask about dates, times,
and restrictions.
Location: Various start points as arranged.
Information: Lytton Lumber, 455-2246; Ainsworth Lumber,
867-8885. Not suitable for persons under the age of 12. For safety,

no open-toed footwear or shorts are allowed, and participants should wear clothing which covers the arms.

■ **Celebrations:** Yearly events include Boston Bar May Days (869-2021), May Day Celebrations and May Day Crowning (Lytton) in May; The Strawberry Social (Yale) in July.
Location: Various venues in the Fraser Canyon.
Information: InfoCentre, 869-2021.

■ **Fraser River Barrel Race:** With much pomp and ceremony, barrels are dropped into the Fraser River at Hell's Gate and a competition is held to judge the arrival time of the barrels downstream in Yale. The journey may last from 3 to 11 hours. Cash prizes are won for guessing the exact time. Held late in August; proceeds to the Yale Enhancement Society.
Location: Central Yale.
Information: Yale InfoCentre, 863-2324.

■ **Reaction Ferry:** This fine example of energy efficiency was established in 1894, before the advent of modern energy forms. The two-car ferry crossing the Fraser River is tethered to an overhead cable, powered by the river current and has been crossing the river on demand (or when the attendant is there) for almost a century. The ferry crosses near the *cumchin,* or "friendly meeting place of Salish natives." Lytton is the point where the jade-coloured water of the swift-flowing Thompson River merges with the silt-laden water of the Fraser; explorer Simon Fraser first noted this spectacular confluence in 1808.
Location: On Highway 12, 1.5 km (1 mi.) northwest of Lytton. Ask for exact directions at the InfoCentre in Lytton, 108 km (67 mi.) north of Hope on Highway 1.
Information: Lytton InfoCentre, 455-2523, FAX: 455-6669.

• • ③ • •

VICTORIA AND AREA

Victoria is considered by many to be British Columbia's most romantic city; quaint shops offer English tweeds, Scottish tartans, and china plates for tea. Horse-drawn carriages take tourists through the downtown area and double-decker buses mimic those of London. A profusion of flowers, plantings, and English gardens thrive in the temperate climate. While the Spanish and Russians may have predated the English on this coast, the British were often the first to document their explorations and officially lay claim to the land. Buffalo were still roaming the empty prairies in 1799, while the British were prac-

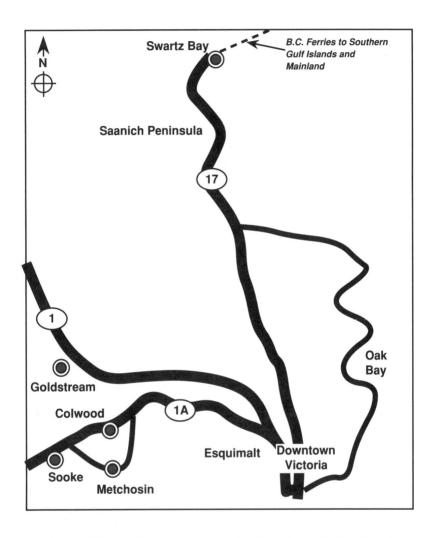

tising civility in the emerging naval colony here. Today, the city still reflects the old-world charm of England, half a world away.

To the north of Victoria is the Saanich Peninsula, notable for its ferry terminals, flowers, and peaceful farming communities which preserve a rural way of life. Gardening secrets are shared by the students of the Horticulture Pacific Landscape Gardeners Institute on the Saanich Peninsula, which keeps a showcase garden-complex of its own, and is listed in this chapter.

Beyond the city of Victoria on its western edge, Highway 14 leads to Sooke and the windward side of Vancouver Island, where the coast—exposed to wild weather systems sweeping in from the open Pacific—is carved into rugged contours. Many beautiful parks and gardens, as well as excellent camping spots, line this route, which is most noted for its beaches, rich with intertidal marine life.

General Information

Ferries from Vancouver: B.C. Ferries: recorded information from Victoria, 656-0757; recorded information from Vancouver, 669-1211; inquiries from Victoria, 386-3431; inquiries from Vancouver, 685-1021; inquiries from Nanaimo, 753-6626; inquiries from Seattle (206) 441-6865; FAX for group reservations, 381-5452. Royal SeaLink Jetfoil for passengers: inquiries, 687-1464.

Ferries from Port Angeles: MV *Coho:* inquiries from Victoria, 386-2202; inquiries from Port Angeles: (206) 457-4491; inquiries from Bellevue, (206) 622-2222.

Ferries from Seattle: Victoria Clippers: inquiries from Victoria, 382-8100; inquiries from Seattle: (206) 448-5000.

Ferries from Anacortes and Sidney: Washington Ferries: inquiries from Victoria, 381-1551; inquiries from Seattle, (206) 464-6400.

Information and maps on B.C. parks in the Victoria-Sooke area: B.C. Parks, Malahat Zones, 2930 Trans-Canada Highway, Victoria, V8B 5T9. Phone: 387-4363. FAX: 478-9211. Specify Goldstream, Bamberton, or Ruckle parks.

Greater Victoria

Bus Transit Service Greater Victoria: 382-6161.

Information on the attractions and festivals of Victoria and area: Tourism Victoria InfoCentre, 812 Wharf St., Victoria, V8W 1T3. Phone: 1-800-663-3883, 382-2127, FAX: 382-6539.

Information on the heritage attractions of Victoria: B.C. Heritage Attractions, Southern Region, Ministry of Municipal Affairs, Recreation, and Culture, 5th Floor, 800 Johnson St., Victoria, V8V 1X4. Phone: 387-1619, FAX: 387-5129.

■ **Beacon Hill Park:** Set against a panoramic view of the Olympic Mountains, this expansive park features legendary Garry oak trees up to 350 years old, what is reputed to be the world's second-tallest totem pole, and forested lakes. More than 30,000 flowers per annum are planted here; daffodils create a riot of colour in early springtime. For "tree safari" hunters, there are ginkos, a single california nutmeg, and a very rare dawn redwood, a species originally cultivated in a Chinese monastery. Art buffs will encounter several outdoor displays. **Location:** Douglas St. leads into Beacon Hill Park. **Information:** InfoCentre, 382-2127; Victoria City Hall, 385-5711 for a referral to the parks department.

■ **Government House Gardens:** This is the residence of the lieutenant-governor, who represents the Queen for the province of British Columbia. The residence is off-limits, but the grounds are open to the public except when the Queen or other members of the royal family are visiting. The gardens feature flowering shrubs, manicured lawns, flower beds, a lily pond, and a waterfall. **Location:** 1401 Rockland Ave.; look for pillared gates. Ample parking inside and outside the grounds. **Information:** Government House, 387-2080.

■ **Antique Row:** As old-country English estates slowly disappear, their contents are auctioned off, bought up, and some of the valuable pieces shipped here for sale. A street of Tudor-style antique and collectibles shops features furnishings and knick-knacks reminiscent of those offered on London's Kensington Church St. An antique, by definition, must be 100 years or older; a collectible is less than a century old. Both are found here. **Location:** Fort St. from Blanshard to Cook. **Information:** 384-2817.

■ **Art Gallery of Greater Victoria:** Admission by donation on Thursdays from 5:00 to 9:00 p.m., and small admission at other times. Housed in the gracious 1889 Spencer Mansion, this gallery features a collection of Japanese art and a range of contemporary works. The structure itself includes a dramatic staircase, Jacobean ceiling, and a fireplace faced with tiles depicting the Arthurian legend. A Shinto shrine has been added to the courtyard. Special services include an art reference library, wheelchair accessibility, and tactile tours for the visually challenged.
Location: 1040 Moss St., off Fort St.
Information: 384-4101.

■ **Carr House:** Small admission. Built in the 1860s, this house was the birthplace of Emily Carr (b. 1871), one of British Columbia's foremost artists. Much of her life was spent in remote coastal communities among natives whose environment and mythology inspired her writings and paintings. Today her family home is open seasonally and staffed by animator-guides in costume. Guided tours may be available; phone ahead.
Location: 207 Government St.
Information: Carr House, 387-4697.

■ **Craigdarroch Castle:** Small admission. At the height of his fortune in 1887, coal baron Robert Dunsmuir built a stone mansion located in the exclusive Rockland area. His wife, Joan, plus a few of their 10 offspring, moved in. Today, many of the original furnishings have been returned and are on display. Take in the city view from the fifth-floor tower, up 86 (or is it 87?) stairs. Guided tours may be available; phone ahead.
Location: 1050 Joan Crescent.
Information: Historic Society, 592-5323; FAX: 592-1099.

■ **Craigflower Farmhouse and Schoolhouse:** Small admission charged to each facility. These farm buildings were completed in 1856 and the main door of the farmhouse is made of heavy oak reinforced with iron to protect against possibly hostile natives. The circa-17th-century furnishings include bedwarmers, pots, and linens, and were imported from Scotland. Residents and Esquimalt navy officers found the manor to be the centre of social life

in the area. The schoolhouse, built in 1854, served children from nearby districts and housed the teacher and boarders in the upstairs rooms. It is said to be the oldest surviving schoolhouse in Canada. Reduced hours in winter. Special events held periodically, with a notable celebration at Thanksgiving. Guided tours may be available; phone ahead.
Location: 110 Island Highway. At Admirals and Craigflower Rd., Highway 1A.
Information: Craigflower Farmhouse, 387-3067.

■ **Emily Carr Gallery:** Small admission. British Columbia's eminent pioneer artist was little recognized in her lifetime. Although many of her original works are in the Vancouver Art Gallery, 25 representations of her style can be seen here. A documentary film on her life is shown daily, along with historic vintage films from the archives of the British Columbia Historical Recording Service.
Location: 1107 Wharf St.
Information: 384-3130.

■ **Empress Hotel Lobby and Victoria Conference Centre:** Indulge in the tourist sport of "lobby walking." The refurbished Empress Hotel, poised at the water's edge, is one of the world's grand hotels. The Empress Dining Room, the Garden Café, the plush, club-like Bengal Room and the Library Bar are typically English. Tea drinkers can enjoy a brief sojourn in the conservatory, complete with aviary. The attached conference centre features an artful blend of modern design and historical form with an indoor waterfall and garden; parts of the centre are open to the public.
Location: 721 Government St.
Information: Hotel, 384-8111; Conference Centre, 361-1000.

■ **Helmcken House:** Small admission. Dr. Helmcken's medicine chest is on display along with other articles he brought over from England during the colony's early days. He practised both medicine and politics, and married Cecelia, daughter of Governor Douglas. The house was built in 1852, when Victoria was still a fur depot for the Hudson's Bay Company. Reduced hours in winter. Special events are held periodically and are especially notable at

Christmas. Guided tours may be available; phone ahead.
Location: 675 Belleville. On its original site near the Royal B.C. Museum.
Information: InfoCentre, 382-2127.

■ **Centennial Fountain and Market Square:** Fringed with a formal miniature Elizabethan knot garden, the Centennial fountain was a gift from surrounding municipalities on the occasion of Victoria's 100th birthday. Today, Market Square is made up of some 40 gift shops and craft stores converted from yesteryear's saloons and bawdyhouses.
Location: Fountain: on the corner of Fisgard and Douglas streets, across from City Hall; Market Square: between Yates, Wharf, and Johnson streets.
Information: InfoCentre, 382-2127.

■ **Christ Church Cathedral:** Donations appreciated. The first Anglican cathedral was destroyed by fire, the second became too constricted, the third and present building was first consecrated in 1929. In the manner of Gothic-style medieval cathedrals, some of which required 200 years to complete, this building is still under construction. The choir screen and massive organ originate from London's Westminster Abbey. The pulpit, carved from a 500-year-old oak, stands amid sparkling stained-glass windows. Open daily to the public. Christ Church holds free recitals on Sundays in July and August, as well as a one-day open house in July; phone ahead.
Location: 912 Vancouver St.
Information: 383-2714.

■ **Ogden Point Breakwater:** With a navigational light at one end, this huge breakwater stretches 750 m (2,500 ft.) into the sea. Built of 18-tonne (20-ton) granite blocks, it was completed in 1917 at a staggering cost of $1.8 million. It required nearly twice the budget of the B.C. Legislative Buildings built around the same period.
Location: East side of the entrance to Victoria Harbour.
Information: InfoCentre, 382-2127.

■ **Point Ellice House:** Small admission. This 1861 Victorian heritage home is furnished with restored antiques cluttered in every

nook, accumulated by three generations of the O'Reilly family. The lush nineteenth-century garden has been replanted to reflect its former sumptuous glory. Closed in winter. Guided tours may be available; phone ahead.
Location: 2616 Pleasant St., close to downtown.
Information: 387-4697.

■ **Royal British Columbia Museum:** Free on Mondays from October 1 to April 30. The largest museum in B.C. features the story of human settlement in British Columbia juxtaposed against dioramas of natural history. A giant woolly mammoth greets visitors, who can then wander through a coastal forest, seaside environment, and river delta. Native cultures are represented in a full-sized longhouse and through a collection of important artifacts. Scale models of early industry and a reconstruction of Captain Vancouver's ship offer a glimpse at the more recent past. Outside the main exhibit building the tracks of a dinosaur mark the entrance to the native plant gardens. Other features are the totem poles in Thunderbird Park and St. Ann's Academy Schoolhouse—Victoria's first schoolhouse for proper young ladies. Theatre programs, gallery demonstrations, speaker's tours, and travelling exhibitions are all available through the museum.
Location: 675 Belleville St., Inner Harbour area.
Information: 387-3014 for recorded information; 387-3701 for general information; 387-5822 for theatre programs.

■ **Whale Wall:** An outdoor mural depicts killer whales and views of life below the surface as seen by these giants of the deep. The side wall was painted by muralist A. Wyland.
Location: Chandler Building, corner of Wharf and Yates St.
Information: InfoCentre, 382-2127.

■ **Canadian Forces Base Tour:** Visitors can occasionally take a guided tour that includes walking, as well as transportation by water taxi, around snug Esquimalt Harbour. The tour covers the dockyards, destroyers in port, and the headquarters of the Marine Forces Pacific Naval Fleet. Without official signatures, visitors will not be allowed access to the base.

Location: End of Esquimalt Rd., via the Johnson Street Bridge. Start point for tours: Main Gate, or as arranged. **Information:** 363-5795. Write for formal permission for a tour: C.F.B. Esquimalt, Base Information Office, F.M.O. Victoria, V0S 1B0.

■ **Goldstream Park Interpretive Program and Hatchery:** Salmon spawn in the hatchery: adult chinook in late October and early November; chum in November; coho in November and December; steelhead in early February. Nearby are a salt-marsh estuary and virgin forests of Douglas fir and 600-year-old western red cedar, as well as ferns, mushrooms, and wildflowers. On-site is a Visitor's Centre. Miners struck gold here in the late 1800s; a few modern-day hobby prospectors still try their hand. Guided naturalist programs for the public are held in the summer; phone ahead. **Location:** 2930 Trans-Canada Highway. Drive north of the city centre for 20 km (12 mi.) on Highway 1. **Information:** B.C. Parks, Malahat Zones, 387-4363.

■ **Legislative Buildings Tour:** Tour leaders point out interior details: sea-green Italian marble, the dizzy heights of the dome, the once-misplaced Diamond Jubilee Window, the Legislative Chambers, and the Provincial Library. The seat of government in British Columbia receives visits from over a quarter-million people a year. Drop-in tours are offered weekdays except when parliament is in session. Group visits year-round, by appointment; tours in foreign languages are available by prior arrangement. To arrange tickets to the opening session pageantry, call a provincial MLA; to reserve seats to a regular sitting, see below. **Location:** 501 Belleville St. Tour start place: main doors. **Information:** Tours, 387-3046; Sergeant-at-Arms, 387-0952, to reserve seats for regular parliamentary sessions.

■ **Old Cemeteries Guided Tour:** Admission by donation from September through June; in summer, a fee is charged. Every Sunday at 2:00 p.m. this society respectfully conducts tours of the gravesites of the famous and not-so-famous at the Ross Bay Cemetery or at the Greater Victoria Cemetery. Devotées of Emily

Carr can visit her grave in the Ross Bay Cemetery, 1495 Fairfield Rd., during daylight hours or in the company of these tour leaders. **Location:** Start point: as arranged. **Information:** 384-0045, for recorded information. Write: Old Cemeteries Society of Victoria, P.O. Box 40115, No. 27, 910 Government St., Victoria, V8W 3N3.

■ **Swan Lake Sanctuary Guided Walks:** When annual water levels rise, birds flock to these flooded fields and provide a noisy show. Features include a floating boardwalk, trails, ponds, and permanent bird blinds. The Nature House has a "senses" display of natural materials for feeling and smelling, and live reptiles from the local area, in cages; special displays are created each season. Best bird watching is November through March. Ongoing "bird walks" led by volunteer naturalists are held 2 or 3 times a week; phone ahead. **Location:** 3873 Swan Lake Rd. **Information:** 479-0211.

■ **Victoria City Hall Tour:** The recent renovation of the 1897 City Hall was a major impetus to the revitalization of several other heritage buildings in Victoria. Groups only may occasionally arrange guided tours of the interior, by appointment. **Location:** 1 Centennial Square. **Information:** Municipal Hall, 385-5711.

■ **Victoria Scenic Drive and Inner Victoria Walking Tour:** The driving tour covers the classic sights of Greater Victoria, including the Oak Bay Hotel and marina, the shopping centre known as "behind the tweed curtain," and the gardens, farms, and ferries in the direction of the Saanich Peninsula. The drive continues to Esquimalt and past its naval base, and then travels back to the tussle of the Inner Harbour. The walking tour covers the Inner Harbour and its historic sights, such as Bastion Square and Trounce Alley. Once the main site of Fort Victoria, established 1843, many of Victoria's original buildings have been renovated into shops and restaurants. The restored House of Assembly and Law Courts remain of interest to those with architectural leanings, and the new contents of many of the historic buildings will please shoppers.

Location: Driving map or walking tour map available from the InfoCentre, 812 Wharf St.

Information: InfoCentre, 382-2127, FAX: 361-9733. Maps are available by mail through Tourism Victoria, 6th Floor, 612 View St., Victoria, V8W 1J5.

■ **University of Victoria Campus Tour:** The playing fields at this campus remain the only place in Canada where English skylarks thrive in their adopted home. The guided campus tour covers the rhododendron gardens, lecture rooms, recital halls, the School of Music, the library, and the Maltwood Art Gallery sculpture collection. Check newspapers for information on special activities. Guided tours are available in summer; phone ahead.

Location: Finnerty Rd.; follow University Circle.

Information: Campus directory, 721-7211; drop-in summer tours, 721-7645. For on-campus accommodation, available at budget cost in the summer, write: University Housing, P.O. Box 1700, Victoria, V8W 2Y2. Phone: 721-8395.

■ **Chinatown:** Victoria's Chinese heritage is evident in a neighbourhood which dates back to 1858. It grew in size with the Chinese labourers who helped to build the railroad. Fan Tan Alley, once notorious for opium dens and gambling houses, is now a place of modern-day commercial pursuits. The ornate red entrance to Chinatown, called the Gate of Harmonious Interest, features two hand-carved lions—a gift from the city of Suchow, China.

Location: Fisgard Street at Government St.

Information: InfoCentre, 382-2127, FAX: 361-9733.

■ **Terri-Vic Dixieland Jazz Party:** Jazz Bands rap, jive, jam, and oomph their way through a lively week featuring some free sample performances. Terri-Vic Jazz is the highlight of Victoria's annual Dixieland extravaganza held in late April. Over 500 volunteers are recruited to help with the festivities and some receive free tickets.

Location: Various venues in Victoria.

Information: 381-5277, FAX: 381-3010. To volunteer, write: Dixieland Jazz Party, #207 - 633 Courtenay St., Victoria, V8W 1B9.

■ **Celebrations:** Yearly events include Annual Journey for Sight—Institute for the Blind (382-0900), Teacup Races (598-4647), Decorated Boat Parade, Inner Harbour Sail Past (598-4647), Swiftsure Sailing Classic, Victoria Day Parade, (478-6035), Annual B.C. Festival of the Arts (383-4241), Buccaneer Days—Esquimalt (385-8666), Annual Swiftsure Walk past Heritage Homes (727-9569) in May; Gorge Canoe Regatta (361-3534), Annual 8-km Run (477-1826), Folkfest (388-5322) in June; Canada Day Fireworks, Sunday Recital Series at Christ Church Cathedral (383-2714), Victoria International Classical Music Festival (386-6121) in July; International Festival of Dance, Classic Boat Festival—Inner Harbour (385-7766) in August; Fringe Festival in September.
Location: Various venues in and around Victoria.
Information: InfoCentre, 382-2127, FAX: 361-9733.

■ **British Fortnight Celebration:** Shops in Victoria put on an absolutely spiffy "light up" for jolly old Father Christmas. Join in a celebration of British heritage with early seasonal events and entertainment, including street presentations of carollers and singing. Held mid-October through November.
Location: Various venues.
Information: InfoCentre, 382-2127, FAX: 361-9733.

■ **Dr. Helmcken's Christmas Celebration:** Small admission. Be part of an old-fashioned Victorian Christmas or join a Yuletide singing celebration. Period-costumed actors take guests of one of British Columbia's oldest homes back to a time when Christmas traditions were strongly British. Held mid-December through the Christmas season with the exception of December 25 and 26; phone ahead.
Location: Helmcken House, 675 Belleville.
Information: 387-3067.

■ **Remembrance Day Ceremony:** Particularly elaborate ceremonies are held in inner Victoria, with the participation of students from military colleges and members of the legislature; services are held, and silence observed in remembrance of those who lost their lives in war. Held November 11 at the eleventh hour.
Location: War Memorial to the Unknown Soldier, Legislative Buildings, Inner Harbour.
Information: InfoCentre, 382-2127.

Saanich Peninsula

Information on the attractions and festivals of Sidney: InfoCentre, 10382 Patricia Bay Highway, Sidney, V8L 3S3. Phone: 656-0525.

■ **Horticulture Pacific Garden Centre:** Token admission. Enjoy an excellent, almost free experience at a large garden centre: a 44-ha (109-ac.) parcel tended by agriculture students. Flowers bloom every month of every year: Doris Page Winter Garden, November through March; rhododendrons, April; the Lily Circle, June and July; dahlia beds, August; and mums in September and October. Also featured are an edible garden, fragrant rose gardens, a conifer collection, a pond, and a creek. The gardens are staffed by students in Horticulture Pacific Centre's landscape gardeners' program, who are pleased to give advice and offer pamphlets on garden care.
Location: On Beaver Lake Rd., west of West Saanich Rd., Highway 17A.
Information: 479-6162.

■ **Stargazing:** Three telescopes, including a large reflecting telescope, are housed in an observatory atop a small mountain here. The panoramic views of the city in the daytime are matched by the outstanding views of the universe through the 1.8-m (72-in.) telescope at night. Presentations are held at regular intervals; inquire in advance. Groups should phone ahead for an appointment. Maintained by the National Research Council of Canada.

Location: Dominion Astrophysical Observatory, 5071 Saanich Mountain Rd. On the east side of Highway 17A, 5.5 km (3 mi.) south of the Keating Crossroad.
Information: 363-0001.

■ **B.C. Aviation Museum:** Small admission. An eclectic collection of flying machines features everything from completely restored artifacts in mint condition to restoration projects in process. On display are a 1944 Avro Anson, 1941 Cessna Crane, and a 1930s Pietenpol, as well as many other machines. Visitors sometimes have the opportunity to talk to volunteers involved in ongoing restorations; phone for times. Guided tours may be available; phone ahead.
Location: #3 - 3539 Norseman Rd., Patricia Bay Airport, Sidney, V8L 4R1.
Information: 655-3300, FAX: 656-3936.

■ **Ocean Sciences Tour:** This tour covers the work of two research departments: Fisheries and Oceans collects samples of plankton to analyze the richness of the ocean and the content of sea "bubbles"; Energy, Mines, and Resources records earthquakes and develops techniques to predict large quakes. Since the oceans act as one of the earth's lungs (the other is the rainforest) it is important to analyze the ocean's ability to absorb carbon dioxide. Paleomagnetics studies shifts in the earth's magnetic field, and researchers monitor Vancouver Island as it drifts slowly northward a few millimetres per year. Groups only, by appointment.
Location: Institute of Ocean Sciences; 9860 West Saanich Rd., Sidney.
Information: 363-6518. Not suitable for persons under the age of 12.

■ **Sidney Museum:** Admission by donation. The remarkable evolution of the whale is traced through interpretive displays featuring an ancient whale fossil and two blue whale jawbones; also on display are pioneer and native artifacts. Guided tours may be available; phone ahead.

Location: 2586 Beacon Ave.
Information: 656-1322.

■ **Working Artifact Demonstration:** Admission
by donation. Featured here on a 12-ha (30-ac.) site are displays of pioneer farming equipment, a model railroad, an old-time
sawmill, steam-run equipment, and a planer mill. If visitors make
arrangements, volunteers from the Vancouver Island Model
Engineers, Model Shipbuilder's Society, or the Historic Artifacts
Society will demonstrate the operation of historic equipment. These
societies cooperate to collect, restore, and display items of interest.
Most of the machinery is in working order. Presentations are held
at periodic intervals; inquire in advance. Groups or individuals can
drop in during opening hours or check when demonstrations are
being held.
Location: 7321 Lochside Rd., Saanich Peninsula. East off Highway 17 on Island View Rd.
Information: Saanich Historic Artifacts Society, 652-5522.

■ **Arts and Crafts Show:** Flowers are the specialty
of the peninsula and the creative people who arrange them
are featured here, along with other arts and crafts ven-
dors. Held annually in early May.
Location: Sanscha Hall, 2243 Beacon Ave. in Sidney.
Information: 656-5824.

■ **North and South Saanich Agricultural Society Fair:**
This old-fashioned country fair features livestock competitions,
flowers, vegetables and home baking. Held on Labour Day
Weekend.
Location: 7910 East Saanich Rd.
Information: 652-1540.

West of Victoria

Information on the attractions and festivals of Colwood and Langford: Juan de Fuca InfoCentre, 697 Goldstream Ave., Victoria, V9B 2X2. Phone: 478-1130, FAX: 478-1584.

Information on the attractions and festivals of Sooke: Sooke Travel InfoCentre, 2070 Phillips Rd., Box 774, Sooke, V0S 1N0. Phone: 642-6112, FAX: 642-7089.

■ **Royal Roads Military College Gardens:** This academy was originally called Hatley Castle and was commissioned by James Dunsmuir, with the proviso that no expense was to be spared. James was the son of Robert, who built Victoria's Craigdarroch Castle from a fortune founded on coal. Completed in 1908, Hatley Castle was complemented by 263 ha (650 ac.) of groomed gardens. During W.W.II the Royal Canadian Navy purchased the property for use as a military training facility. The public can make arrangements to attend academy-graduation ceremonies, including a march-past and the firing of cannons in May; phone ahead. The gardens of this military academy are open to the public every day.
Location: Hatley Park, 2050 Sooke Rd.
Information: Military College, 363-4660; 388-1885 for an invitation to march-pasts.

■ **Fort Rodd Hill National Historic Park and Fisgard Lighthouse National Historic Site:** The ruins of this 19th-century coastal fortification contain the guns and cannons deemed necessary for the defense of Victoria (and Canada). The original magazine emplacements, barracks, searchlight facilities, and other buildings are now open to the public. Still active, adjacent Fisgard Lighthouse was built in 1869. From mid-May to Labour Day, there are on-site interpreters.

Location: 604 Belmont Rd., outskirts of Victoria.
Information: Historical and visitor information: National Historic Site, 501 Belmont Rd., Victoria, V9C 1B5, 363-4662. Phone: 363-4662.

■ **Metchosin Schoolhouse:** Admission by donation. Opened in 1872 and operated continuously until 1949, this was the first school established in the province after British Columbia joined Confederation in 1871. Open Sunday afternoons from April to October.
Location: Corner of Metchosin and Happy Valley Rd., along Highway 14.
Information: InfoCentre, 642-6112.

■ **Sooke Regional Museum:** Admission by donation. Logging and fishing artifacts, Coast Salish objects and a scale reconstruction of the Sheringham Point Lighthouse are featured here. Sooke Museum holds an annual open house and barbecue in late June. Guided tours may be available; phone ahead.
Location: Sooke-Jordan River, west side of the Sooke River Bridge, Highway 14, 35 km (22 mi.) west of Victoria.
Information: Sooke Museum, 642-6351, FAX: 624-7089.

■ **Pearson College of the Pacific Tour:** As one of seven United World Colleges, this institute promotes world peace and understanding through a special program for high-school students. The nondenominational college is open to students from all over the world. The grounds are open to self-guided tours at all times. Guided tours of the campus may be available; phone ahead.
Location: Pearson College Dr. Take William Head Rd. from the end of Metchosin Rd., located on the shores of Pedder Bay on the outskirts of Victoria.
Information: 478-5591.

■ **Witty's Lagoon Interpretive Program:** Seals are often seen along the long sandy beach here. The area is interspersed with creeks and waterfalls and a lagoon supports abundant waterfowl

and bird life. An on-site nature house features permanent displays on intertidal marine life and the flora and fauna of the area. Naturalists lead conducted walks and interpretive programs in summer; phone ahead.
Location: 6 km (4 mi.) from the Metchosin Rd. turnoff at Highway 14.
Information: Regional Parks Recorded Information, 474-7275; Nature House, 474-2454.

■ **Celebrations:** Yearly celebrations include Arts and Crafts Fair (Sooke) in March; Luxton Rodeo (Colwood) in May; Gilangcolme Fun Days (Colwood), Sooke Museum Open House and Salmon Barbecue in June; Canada Day Celebrations at Colwood, Fort Rodd Hill Day, Sooke Annual Festival of History, All Sooke Day in July; Sooke Fine Arts Festival in August; Luxton Fair in Colwood, Sooke Fall Fair in September; Arts and Crafts Fair (Sooke) in November.
Location: Colwood and Sooke.
Information: InfoCentre, 642-6112.

■ **All Sooke Day:** Logger's sports day features the competitive skills of loggers along with local celebrations. Find out about free events surrounding this festival. Held in mid-July.
Location: Various venues, 35 km (22 mi.) from Victoria along Highway 14.
Information: InfoCentre, 642-6112.

VANCOUVER ISLAND

Vancouver Island is as long as Great Britain, minus Scotland. Yet, on a map, snuggled in the far west against the enormous width of Canada, it seems like an afterthought. Visitors are advised to keep in mind that exploring British Columbia's "big" island is similar to covering an area the size of England with one major difference: there are relatively few roads. The main route along the eastern side of Vancouver Island, Highway 1-19, extends from the city of Victoria in the south to Port Hardy in the north. Highway 4 cuts across the centre of the Island to the west coast and centrally located Nanaimo is a major arrival point

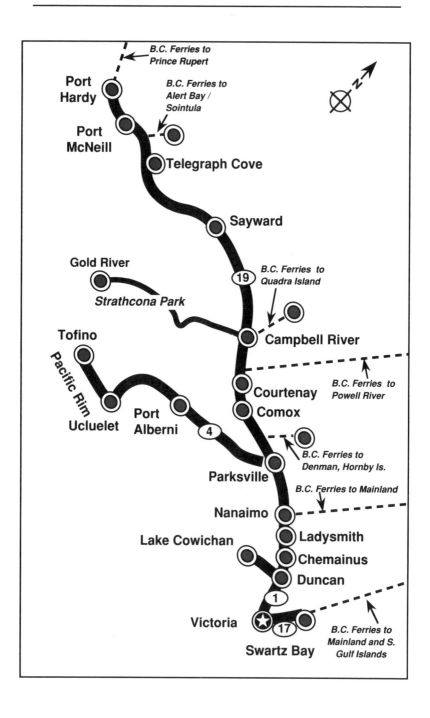

from the mainland by ferry. The island is noted for the snow-capped spine of the Insular Mountain range, lakes, rivers and ocean inlets, and rolling pastoral farmlands.

In the gap between the mainland and Vancouver Island are scattered more than 300 small islands. Above the 49th parallel, they are called the Gulf Islands and belong to Canada; below the same parallel, they are the San Juan Islands and belong to the United States. The most prominent among them have become favourite tourist destinations, noted for their unspoiled beauty and natural attractions. Because the Gulf Islands can all be accessed from Vancouver Island, they have been included in this section. Only those islands that offer specific free attractions are listed here, but many travellers will find that the experience of exploring these beautiful islands is enough of a free experience in itself, and justifies the cost of the ferry. Travellers to the islands should phone in advance, as ferry lineups are frequent and accommodation is limited.

Pacific Rim National Park, on the west side of Vancouver Island, faces the wind-swept expanses of the open Pacific, resulting in miles of rolling surf, and a landscape carved by ceaseless wind and waves. Here are found excellent naturalist programs, including whale watching from shore and storm watching from high points on the coast.

This chapter is organized into three sections. South Vancouver Island covers the area from Swartz Bay along Highway 1 to the outskirts of Nanaimo. Central Vancouver Island explores the features of Nanaimo through to Campbell River, with a side trip to the west coast. North Vancouver Island starts with a side trip to Strathcona Park and Gold River, then continues along Highway 19 to Port Hardy. Those Gulf Islands with specific free attractions are listed in geographic sequence according to the Vancouver Island ferry terminal that services them.

General Information

Information on the attractions and festivals on Vancouver Island and the Gulf Islands: Tourism Association of Vancouver Island, #302 - 45 Bastion Square, Victoria, V8W 1J1. Phone: 382-3551, FAX: 382-3523.

Information on B.C. Ferries: 1112 Fort St., Victoria, V8V 4V2. Phone: 669-1211. For phone numbers on ferry service to Victoria see chapter 3.

Information and maps on B.C. parks on Vancouver Island: B.C. Parks, 2nd Floor, 800 Johnson St. Phone: 387-4609.

■ South Vancouver Island ■

Salt Spring Island

Ferries from Vancouver Island and Tsawwassen: There are three landing docks for B.C. ferries on Salt Spring Island: Fulford Harbor, accessed from Swartz Bay (crossing time: 35 min.); Vesuvius, accessed from Crofton (crossing time: 20 min.); and Long Harbour, accessed from Pender Island. There is another route to the islands from Tsawwassen. Phone: B.C. Ferries to Salt Spring Island, 537-9921.

Information on the attractions and festivals of Salt Spring Island: InfoCentre, 121 Lower Ganges Rd., Box 111, Ganges, V0S 1E0. Phone: 537-5252, FAX: 537-4276.

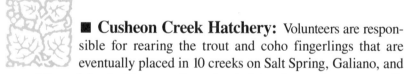

■ Cusheon Creek Hatchery: Volunteers are responsible for rearing the trout and coho fingerlings that are eventually placed in 10 creeks on Salt Spring, Galiano, and Mayne islands. There are 2 rearing tanks and a nearby nature walk through a swampy area. In the stream that runs beside the hatchery, fish congregate and respond actively to being fed. Open 3 times a week to the public; phone ahead.
Location: Corner of Stuart Rd. and Cusheon Lake Rd.
Information: 537-2232.

■ Petroglyph: Weighing in at several tonnes and measuring about 2 m (7 ft.) in diameter, this sandstone carving is thought to be of a seal—although the meaning of all

petroglyphs is open to interpretation. One legend says it may be a woman changed into a rock. It was originally found in the harbour and later moved to its present location.
Location: Located in Drummond Park on Musgrave Rd.
Information: InfoCentre, 537-5252.

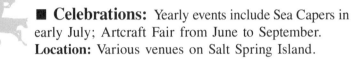

■ **Celebrations:** Yearly events include Sea Capers in early July; Artcraft Fair from June to September.
Location: Various venues on Salt Spring Island.
Information: InfoCentre, 537-5252.

■ **Ganges Farmer's Market:** Vibrant and successful, this mixed market sells fresh seafoods and organic produce, along with high-quality crafts, such as pottery and weaving. Open from early morning to about 2:00 p.m. on Saturdays, year-round.
Location: In Centennial Park during the summer months. In the Farmer's Institute in the winter.
Information: Parks and Recreation Commission, 537-4448.

Other Southern Gulf Islands

Ferries from Vancouver Island and Tsawwassen: B.C. Ferries travel various routes to Salt Spring, Pender, Saturna, Galiano and Mayne islands; there are some inter-island connections. The landing dock on Pender Island is at Otter Bay; on Mayne Island at Village Bay; and on Galiano Island at Sturdies Bay. B.C. Ferries to Gulf Islands, 629-3215.

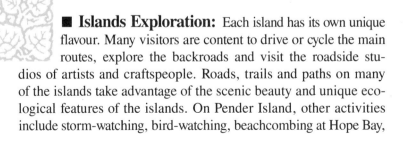

■ **Islands Exploration:** Each island has its own unique flavour. Many visitors are content to drive or cycle the main routes, explore the backroads and visit the roadside studios of artists and craftspeople. Roads, trails and paths on many of the islands take advantage of the scenic beauty and unique ecological features of the islands. On Pender Island, other activities include storm-watching, bird-watching, beachcombing at Hope Bay,

or spotting seals and sea lions. The sandstone formations of Galiano
are particularly noteworthy and the southern Gulf Islands have huge
concentrations of eagles. The annual July 1 lamb-bake on Saturna
is a longstanding tradition.

Duncan and Area

Information on the attractions and festivals of Duncan:
InfoCentre, 381 Trans-Canada Highway, Duncan, V9L 3R5.
Phone: 746-4636, FAX: 746-8222.

■ **Cowichan Hatchery:** In addition to the hatchery
here, visitors can see the Skutz Falls fishway and Rotary
Park side channel for spawners; best from November
through January. Best hatchery viewing: juvenile chinook April
and May; juvenile coho February through June. Contact the band
office for permission to visit this salmon facility and to walk the
trail along the Cowichan River.
Location: After the first bridge south of Duncan, turn east on Boys
Rd. Then follow Mission Rd. to the end and keep right on the gravel
road. Contact the Band office before proceeding.
Information: Band office, 746-5741.

■ **Cowichan Valley Museum:** Admission by
donation. A parlour, bedroom, and kitchen are wall-
papered and furnished to 1912 standards; a general store
is overflowing with wares dating from the 1890s to the 1940s;
historic medical equipment, the town's first gas pump and an old
mail cart are on display. A photo collection is filed away in the
archives. Guided tours of the museum may be available; phone
ahead. Groups only may periodically book a guided walking tour
of the downtown, which originates here.
Location: 120 Canada Ave., in the old Via Rail Station.

Information: 746-6612. Write: Cowichan Historical Society, Box 1014, Duncan, V9L 3Y2.

■ **Totem Poles:** Duncan, which calls itself the "City of Totems," has some 40 totem poles on display in public areas. Eleven Indian carvings can be seen along the main highway; 2 are displayed outside city hall; 8 poles were unveiled in 1987 near the train station. Overlooking the fountain next to the city hall, "The King of the Cedar Forest" pole was carved by a New Zealand Maori native. Five poles are found near the Court House complex on Government St.; one was erected in the downtown core in honour of Rick Hansen's "Man in Motion" world tour. Totem poles were originally symbolic figures representing native family histories, but some of these poles are modern interpretations of tradition.
Location: Various locations; see above.
Information: InfoCentre, 746-4636; City Hall, 746-6126, for information on the poles.

■ **Whippletree Junction:** This centre, which includes several restored buildings assembled from Duncan's Chinatown and elsewhere, now features an old-fashioned boardwalk along which visitors can browse for antiques, crafts, food, and gifts in more than a dozen boutiques, an ice-cream parlour, and a log-cabin restaurant.
Location: 6 km (3.5 mi.) south of Duncan on Highway 1.
Information: Whippletree General Store, 748-1100.

■ **Outdoor Eco-Museum Self-Guided Tour:** The Eco-museum, a brand-new concept and one of a kind in Canada, is a 1000-sq-km (386-sq.-mi.) museum without walls. Using a tour map and a vehicle, visitors can explore the lakes, forests, and attractions in the Cowichan and Chemainus valleys. The society which created the concept believes this is the best way to introduce outsiders to the heritage, beauty, wildlife, and value of the region. Guided tours may also be available; phone ahead.
Location: Map available at local InfoCentres in the area or from the address below.

Information: 746-1611, FAX: 746-1622. Write: Eco-Museum Society, 160 Jubilee St., Box 491, Duncan, V9L 3X8.

■ **Celebrations:** Yearly events include the Cowichan Indian Days in June; Duncan-Cowichan Summer Festival in mid-July; Cowichan Exhibition in September; Christmas Chaos in November; Santa Claus Parade in December.
Location: Various venues in and around Duncan.
Information: InfoCentre, 746-4421.

Side Trip to Lake Cowichan

Information on the attractions and festivals of Lake Cowichan: Seasonal InfoCentre, Box 824, Cowichan Lake Rd., Lake Cowichan, V0R 2G0. Phone: 749-4141, FAX: 749-3900.

■ **Wildflower Reserve:** In British Columbia, an Order-in-Council can quickly set aside small reserves of special ecological significance. One such place is Vancouver Island's largest known concentration of pink fawn lilies. Other wildflowers are also abundant here: bleeding hearts, wood violets, white trillium, and wild ginger. Removal of vegetation is strictly prohibited.
Location: Honeymoon Bay; on the south shore of Lake Cowichan, 1 km (.6 mi.) past Gordon Bay Park. Ask at the InfoCentre before setting out.
Information: InfoCentre, 749-4141.

■ **Kaatza Station Pioneer Museum:** Logging and local history displays, as well as small dioramas, are housed in a former railway station; children can ride on a real railway pumping car. Outside, a short nature walk

to a pond passes near a beaver habitat. Guided tours may be available; phone ahead.
Location: 125 Southshore Rd.
Information: 749-6142.

■ **Forest or Sawmill Tour:** The timber tour covers an active logging site, a walk through a second-growth forest, and a dryland log sort at Honeymoon Bay, with a rest stop at Heather Lake campsite on Lake Cowichan. Allow 4 hours and bring a lunch. A guided tour of a sawmill is also scheduled at regular intervals in the summer; allow 1 hour. Phone to determine times.
Location: Fletcher Challenge Canada. Inquire about start points.
Information: 749-3244. Sawmill portion of tour is not suitable for persons under the age of 12. For safety, no open-toed footwear or shorts are allowed, and participants should wear clothing which covers the arms. Sturdy footwear is required.

■ **Lake Cowichan Demonstration Forest:** The forests on Vancouver Island are in transition. A self-guided driving tour with notes elaborates on the contrast between newly forested areas and the remaining wilderness. The tour is designed to illustrate forest management practises. Suggestions for optional walking tours along the way are included.
Location: A circle tour map is available at local InfoCentres. The demonstration forest is found along Highway 18, around the shore of the lake.
Information: InfoCentre, 749-4141. Map available from Tourism Development Officer, Lake Cowichan, Box 278, Duncan, V9L 3X4.

■ **Celebrations:** Yearly events include Heritage Days in May; Lake Cowichan Celebration Days in June; Honeymoon Bay Summer Festival in July; Water-skiing Tournament, Drag-Boat Races, Youbou Regatta in August; Model Float Plane Day in September.

Location: Various venues in and around Lake Cowichan.
Information: InfoCentre, 749-4141.

Chemainus

Information on the attractions and festivals of Chemainus:
Seasonal InfoCentre, 9758 Chemainus Rd., Box 575,
Chemainus, V0R 1K0. Phone: 246-3944, FAX: 246-3251.

■ **Chemainus Murals:** When it faced economic extinction due to the rerouting of the main highway, Chemainus, "the little town that did," set out to survive. As part of an ambitious revitalization scheme, artists were hired to paint large murals on the downtown buildings depicting the area's history and folklore. Today, thousands of tourists follow footsteps painted on the sidewalks for a self-guided tour of Waterwheel Park, Heritage Square and the murals. For a token admission, guided tours depart from the red caboose in the town centre, several times a day in summer. Street performances are held throughout the summer.
Location: Downtown Chemainus.
Information: Chemainus Festival of Murals Society, 246-4701.

■ **Celebrations:** Yearly events include Crofton Salmon Barbecue and Fair, Scottish Ceilidh in July; Festival of Murals from July through August.
Location: Various venues in and around Chemainus.
Information: InfoCentre, 246-3944.

Ladysmith

Information on the attractions and festivals of Ladysmith:
Seasonal InfoCentre, 12 Gatacre St., Box 598, Ladysmith,
V0R 2E0. Phone: 245-2112, FAX: 245-8545.

■ **Black Nugget Museum:** Small admission. The name of this museum is derived from the nick-name for coal. Located in a restored 1881 hotel, it retains its saloon with the original ornate bar, polished brass foot rail, and mirror trimmed in 24-carat gold leaf. On display are native artifacts, historic clothing items, furniture, and household goods. Guided tours may be available; phone ahead.
Location: 12 Gatacre St., half block from Highway 1.
Information: 245-4846.

■ **Heritage Buildings Self-Guided Tour:** Lady-smith is rather circuitously named after the wife of "battling" Harry Smith, a gallant English fighter of the early 1800s. During a battle in Spain, he rescued a 13-year-old convent girl from the clutches of his own soldiers and soon married young Juanita Maria de Los Delores de Leon, shortened to a more convenient Lady Smith at the time of her husband's knighting. In 1899, during the Boer War, a town in South Africa (which bore her name) was liber-ated after a rather nasty battle. The founder of Ladysmith heard the joyful news on the eve of naming the new centre—and several streets also came to bear the names of Boer War generals. Lady-smith's buildings are somewhat reminiscent of the early days of San Francisco, and the revitalization of its downtown was successful enough to earn it one of four national "Main Street Canada" awards in 1988. A numbered map, available at the seasonal InfoCentre, or through the Chamber of Commerce, explains the history of ownership behind each of the buildings.
Location: Map available at InfoCentre or Chamber of Commerce.
Information: Chamber of Commerce or InfoCentre, 245-2112.

■ **Celebrations:** Yearly events include the Miss Lady-smith Pageant in May; Dogwood Days in August; Ladysmith Fall Fair in September; Festival of Lights in late November and December; Santa Claus Parade in December.
Location: Various venues in Ladysmith.
Information: InfoCentre, 245-2112.

■ **Festival of Lights:** Some 50,000 twinkling lights are found in displays of toy soldiers, teddy bears, snowmen and starbursts. Turn-on ceremony is the last Thursday in November. Stage entertainment and fireworks are held throughout December. Call for program.
Location: Throughout town and in Bob Stuart Park at the north entrance to the town.
Information: InfoCentre, 245-2112.

■ Central Vancouver Island ■

Information and maps on B.C. parks in Central Vancouver Island: Ministry of Parks, Arrowsmith Zone, Rathtrevor Beach Park, Box 1479, Highway 19, Parksville, V0R 2S0. Phone: 248-3931, FAX: 337-5695.

Nanaimo

Ferries from Vancouver: B.C. Ferries: recorded information from Nanaimo, 753-6626; inquiries, 753-1261.

Information on the attractions and festivals of Nanaimo: InfoCentre, 266 Bryden St., Nanaimo, V9S 1A8. Phone: 754-8474 or 1-800-663-7337, FAX: 754-6468.

■ **Morrell Wildlife Sanctuary:** Some 12 km (7 mi.) of interpretive trails lead through a representative stand of Pacific coast forest and around a beaver pond. Wildlife

frequently seen includes birds, raccoons, deer, and other small woodland creatures. Visitors who phone ahead can pick up an interpretive brochure from a nearby office. Tours for groups only are available for a small fee; phone ahead.
Location: Corner of Nanaimo Lake and Dogwood Rd., 1050 Nanaimo Lakes Rd.
Information: 753-5811.

■ **Nanaimo Community Hatchery:** This hatchery was established to enhance the salmon populations along the Nanaimo River. The self-guided tour is best in the autumn, but open all year round. There is a nature walk and a picnic area. Guided tours may be available; phone ahead.
Location: Take Beck Rd. beside the Cassidy Inn, past the bridge for 5 km (3 mi.). Follow the signs. The hatchery is a total of 10 km (6 mi.) south of Nanaimo.
Information: 245-7780.

■ **Newcastle Island:** Newcastle Island is accessible by passenger-only ferry for a small charge. The little island features tree-lined pathways, gravel beaches, sandstone cliffs, caves, old rock quarries, and Indian middens. Coal was once mined here and the Japanese operated a saltery for fish. A 1931 pavilion, built by the Union Steamship Co. for weekend excursions, has been restored and houses displays of natural history. Excellent for bicycles. In the summer, interpretive nature and history programs are available; phone for details.
Location: Passenger-only ferry leaves several times a day during the summer from Swy-a-lana Lagoon (Maffeo-Sutton Park), behind the Civic Arena. Restricted service March-April; no service Thanksgiving to mid-March.
Information: InfoCentre, 754-8474.

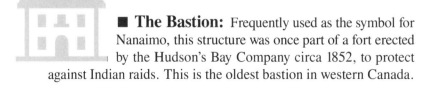 ■ **The Bastion:** Frequently used as the symbol for Nanaimo, this structure was once part of a fort erected by the Hudson's Bay Company circa 1852, to protect against Indian raids. This is the oldest bastion in western Canada.

In summer, guards in 19th-century uniforms fire a cannon precisely at noon.
Location: Corner of Bastion and Front St.
Information: 754-8474.

■ **The Lions "Great" Bridge:** Vancouver has the Lions Gate Bridge; Nanaimo boasts the Lions Great Bridge. A footbridge, built by the Lions Club, connects two non-continuous parts of a foreshore footpath. An interesting addition is an 18-tonne (20-ton), 19-m (62-ft.) bridge that rotates, allowing vessels to enter the river.
Location: Between Departure Bay and Cameron Island in Swy-a-lana Lagoon.
Information: InfoCentre, 754-8474.

■ **Malaspina College and Nanaimo Art Gallery-Exhibition Centre:** A self-guided walking tour around the campus covers the college forest, exhibits at the Nanaimo Art Gallery-Exhibition Centre, and koi-fish at Tamagawa Japanese Gardens. The campus is surrounded by sweeping harbour views. Presentations at the art gallery are held at regular intervals; phone ahead. More insistent visitors can prearrange to see a beaver display at the Museum of Natural History or visit an active bee-yard tended by apiary students; phone ahead. Groups with scientific interests only can book an appointment to tour the Pacific Institute of Aquaculture and Fisheries, presently carrying out research on fish farms and the health of local species.
Location: 900 Fifth St., on the lower slopes of Mount Benson; map available at the InfoCentre.
Information: Nanaimo Art Gallery-Exhibition Centre, 755-8790; Malaspina College, 753-3245, for referrals to access the bee-yard, to open the Museum of Natural History, or to book a group tour of the Aquaculture Institute.

■ **Nanaimo District Museum:** Token admission. The gallery features an old working printing press and Chinatown artifacts, a diorama of Coast Salish activities that depicts life prior to the arrival of whites, and artifacts which illustrate the story of coal. In nearby Piper's Park, there is a reconstruction of a miner's cottage, a coal

mine, and a pioneer town. Guided tours may be available; phone ahead.
Location: Adjacent to Harbour Park at Front St.
Information: 753-1821.

■ **Heritage Walk or Harbourside Walk:** The city of Nanaimo has two designated self-guided walking tours. The heritage walk passes the Bastion, old hotels, the original stone Post Office, St. Paul's Anglican Church, and the Great National Land Building; it is designated by the Heritage Advisory Committee and sponsored by British Columbia Heritage Trust. The harbourside walk takes in the boat basin, the Bastion, the Mark Bate heritage tree, Swy-a-lana Lagoon (a man-made tidal pool), the ferry terminal to Newcastle Island, evidence of native cultures, the Nanaimo Yacht Club, and the Chinese Memorial Gardens; the walk is designed by the Nanaimo Harbour Commission. The harbourside walk continues onward to link with the Queen Elizabeth Promenade.
Location: Consult walking maps for tour routes. Maps available from the Nanaimo InfoCentre, 266 Bryden St., just past the Pearson Bridge at the corner of Highway 19 and Bryden St.
Information: InfoCentre, 754-8474; Harbour Commission, 753-4146, FAX: 753-4899.

■ **Pulp Mill Tour:** The tour takes visitors through the complex chemical operation of breaking down chipped wood into a sort of "cardboard," called pulp. Scheduled tours are offered from May through August; phone ahead for reservations.
Location: Harmac Division of MacMillan Bloedel. Ask for start point when booking.
Information: 722-3211, local 4315. Not suitable for persons under the age of 12. For safety, no open-toed footwear or shorts are allowed, and participants should wear clothing which covers the arms.

■ **Petroglyph Park:** Some of the carvings represent birds, wolves, lizards, mythical beasts, sea monsters and occasionally humans. Easy trails through the park lead to the petroglyphs. The Nanaimo Museum (100 Cameron St.) has castings of other petroglyphs.
Location: Off Highway 1, south of Nanaimo, about 2 km (1.2 mi.) north of Cedar Rd.
Information: 754-8474.

■ **Celebrations:** Yearly events include the Polar Bear Swim on January 1, Eagle-Watching Tours from January to April; Empire Day Celebrations in May; Heritage Days in June; Canada Day Fireworks, Marine Festival and Bathtub Race, Pacific Rim Quarter-Horse Circuit in July; Theatrical Festival from May through July; Salmon Festival, Vancouver Island Exhibition, Agricultural Fair in August; Dixieland Jazz Affair in September.
Location: Various venues in and around Nanaimo.
Information: InfoCentre, 754-8474 or 1-800-663-7337, FAX: 754-6468.

■ **Bathtub Race:** Perhaps the zaniest spectacle in Nanaimo is the annual Nanaimo-Vancouver bathtub race held in mid-July. Hundreds of local daredevils and international competitors take to the waters of Georgia Strait in modified "bathtubs." Prizes are large, so the competition is heated, just as a good bath should be.
Location: Newcastle Channel or viewpoint along Front St.
Information: InfoCentre, 754-8474.

■ **Nanaimo Bar Sweets:** No journey to Nanaimo would be complete without sampling the chocolate delight called the "Nanaimo Bar." Sometimes dubbed the "ultimate sweet," it was reputedly named during a magazine recipe contest in the 1930s; other stories link the bar to rum-running in the 1920s, when bottles of "Nanaimo bar flavouring" were said to conceal alcoholic substances. Whatever the real story, the bar is now immortalized in the world of cuisine. Visitors can obtain authentic (nonalcoholic) Nanaimo Bar recipes straight from the source, or gourmands can sample recipe variations throughout the city.

Location: Authentic Nanaimo bar recipes are available by writing Nanaimo Tourist Bureau, 266 Bryden St., Nanaimo, V9S 1A8.

Information: InfoCentre, 754-8474, 1-800-663-7337, FAX: 754-6468.

Parksville and Area

Information on the attractions and festivals of Parksville: InfoCentre, 1275 East Island Highway, Box 99, Parksville, V9P 2G3. Phone: 248-3613, FAX: 248-5210.

Information and maps on B.C. Parks on Central Vancouver Island: B.C. Parks, Strathcona District, Rathtrevor Beach Park, Box 1479, Highway 19, Parksville, V9P 2H4. Phone: 755-2483.

■ **Cathedral Grove:** This aging forest was donated to the province in 1944 by Harvey Reginald MacMillan, first provincial forester for B.C. and later head of MacMillan Bloedel. The tract is about 12 ha (30 ac.) in size, part of a larger bequest of over 122 ha (300 ac.). Lush undergrowth and verdant vegetation bring the hush of a cathedral to this special stand of ancient giants; the oldest tree is probably around 800 years old and the largest is about 3 m (10 ft.) in diameter, over 9 m (30 ft.) around and 75 m (246 ft.) high. During the summer months, pamphlets can be obtained at the on-site information kiosk. Allow 30 minutes to walk the easy trail.

Location: Alongside Highway 4, 31 km (19 mi.) west of Parksville.

Information: InfoCentre, 248-3613.

■ **Wild Rhododendron Reserve:** On Vancouver Island there stand a few tattered remnants of flowers that time forgot: a species of rhododendron that has survived the last Ice Age, retained its ability to bloom, and survived the wall of ice which drastically altered all other living things on the island. Scientists have studied

the unique strain of small, wild rhododendron protected on an ecological reserve beside Rhododendron Lake. Best in May and early June. Access to the lake is by private forestry road; open on weekends and summer evenings only. Removal of vegetation is strictly prohibited.
Location: 7 km (5 mi.) south of Parksville on Highway 4, and then 14 km (9 mi.) along a forestry road. Ask for exact instructions at the InfoCentre before setting out.
Information: InfoCentre, 248-3613.

■ **Coombs Country Market and Emporium:** At the turn of the century, the Salvation Army was responsible for bringing more than a quarter of a million disadvantaged English and Welsh citizens to this area. Today, Coombs is an eclectic mix of small-town shopping and the simple living of former times. Goats sometimes graze on the sod roof of a cleverly designed building at Coombs. The rebuilt Country Market, General Store, and Bakery seem trapped in time—but what era? Old west? Early sixties? Late seventies? Check the dates for the Coombs Country Rodeo and perhaps visit Butterfly World (admission charged). The complex is closed during the winter.
Location: 9 km (6 mi.) west of Parksville.
Information: 248-2812.

■ **Craig Heritage Museum and Park:** Admission by donation. This museum displays local artifacts from the pioneering era and has photographs and newspaper archives. At the adjacent park, several heritage buildings may be viewed: Knox United Heritage Church built in 1912, the French Creek Post Office, a 1942 fire hall with a 1946 fire truck, a log house first used by MacMillan (the pioneer behind MacMillan Bloedel), the Craig Crossing post office, and the Mount Rose school—first used as a surveyor's cabin. Guided tours may be available; phone ahead.
Location: 1110 East Island Highway.
Information: 248-6966; InfoCentre, 248-3613.

■ **Water Bombers at Sproat Lake:** The world's largest water bombers, Martin Flying Tanks, are about the height of a two-storey building from the ground to the top of the tail. The wingspan measures 61 m (200 ft.) and they carry 27.5 tonnes (30 tons) of water for each dump. Informal drop-in visits are occasionally available. The lake itself is famous for its mirror reflections. Bring paint brushes or load film into a camera for a classic mountain reflection picture. The reflection in the lake is usually there but the bombers may be away on forest fire duty.
Location: On Highway 4, 10 km (6 mi.) beyond the turnoff to Stamp Falls.
Information: West Coast Rangers, 723-2952.

■ **Canadian Coast Guard Hovercraft Dockside Visit:** This rescue craft, which serves Vancouver Island, is one of two in B.C.; the other is stationed in Vancouver. Hovercraft vehicles navigate by satellite and are on call for emergencies, including medical evacuations or rescues after boating accidents. Allow for the possibility that arranged visits can be abruptly interrupted or cancelled at the last moment without notice. Groups only, by appointment.
Location: From Highway 19, turn off at Corfield Rd., then onto Beachside Dr.
Information: 248-2724.

■ **Englishman River Falls Interpretive Programs:** This nature stop in a beautiful forest setting features guided nature walks led by a park naturalist in the summer; phone ahead. Bring a snorkel and air mattress for a unique swimming experience in crystal-clear pools, or plan to walk among scenic waterfalls. The river gushes over cataracts into deep chasms and the easy trails offer breathtaking vistas.
Location: Take Highway 4 about 5 km (3 mi.) west of Parksville and continue 9 km (5 mi.) to the park.
Information: B.C. Parks, Strathcona District, 755-2483; FAX: 248-8584.

■ **Rathtrevor Park Interpretive Programs:** High tide

at this beach is said to offer the warmest ocean swimming in British Columbia. More than 150 species of birds have been recorded in the area and there are more than 2 km (1.2 mi.) of sandy shoreline waiting to be explored. There are also 4 km (2.5 mi.) of walking trails and a nature house. Summer naturalist programs focus on knowledge of the sea, sand, and shore life; phone ahead.

Location: On the southern outskirts of Parksville.

Information: B.C. Parks, 755-2483; Rathtrevor Park, 248-3931.

■ **Petroglyphs:** A persistent explorer will be able to find the exact location of two ancient native petroglyphs. One is of two whales and the other is a bear; both are of uncertain meaning and uncertain age. The location of petroglyphs and pictographs throughout B.C. is protected due to vandalism; for exact directions, inquire at the local InfoCentre or ask knowledgeable locals.

Location: Between Nanaimo and Parksville along the Englishman River. Take the Port Alberni cutoff road, then take the first left at the overpass. Turn down Allsbrook Rd., travel .75 km (.5 mi.). The trail to the river is about .75 km (.5 mi.). Ask for a diagram of the route at the InfoCentre before setting out.

Information: InfoCentre, 248-3613.

■ **Celebrations:** Yearly events include Coombs Rodeo, Coombs Country Music Festival, Open Sandcastle Competition, Pageant Days in July; Coombs Country Bluegrass Festival, Croquet Tournament, Great Nanoose Days, Rocking Horse Rodeo in August.

Location: Various venues in and around Parksville.

Information: 248-3613.

■ **Little Mountain Dropoff:** Those who like lump-in-the-throat surprises can drive along this relatively gradual hill with ho-hum views of the Englishman River. At the top the view of Georgia Strait and the mid-Island mountain ranges is matched by the

sharp cliff drop-off at your feet. Trailers are prohibited, as it is impossible to turn around at the summit; parking is limited.
Location: West on Highway 4, turn left on Bellevue Rd. and left again on Little Mountain Rd. Ask for exact directions at the InfoCentre before setting out.
Information: InfoCentre, 248-3613.

■ **Sand-castle Competition:** As the tide goes out, the feverish activity begins, because when the tide turns, the game will be over. This frenzied sand-castle competition draws thousands of spectators who watch competitors create complex constructions. Expert teams work against mother nature's clock, often to a selected theme. Cash prizes are large and so are the sand creations. Competitions continue for a week during July.
Location: Various venues on the beach at Parksville.
Information: InfoCentre, 248-3613.

Port Alberni

Information on the attractions and festivals of Port Alberni: InfoCentre, Highway 4, R.R. 2, Site 215, Comp. 10, Port Alberni, V9Y 7L6. Phone: 724-6535, FAX: 724-6560.

■ **MV** *Lady Rose* **or MV** *Frances Barkley*: Outstanding value with rates in the range of $30 to $45 return; reservations are mandatory. Here is the opportunity to take a budget mini-cruise aboard a passenger and cargo boat serving remote communities and passing through a scenic fiord where waterfalls cascade down the sides of mountains, eagles soar, and porpoises sometimes play in the wake of the boat. During W.W.II, the *Lady Rose* carried supplies to 7,000 servicemen stationed on the coast. Now she and a companion ship take people and cargo along Vancouver Island's longest inlet, passing through the Broken Group Islands in Barkley Sound and stopping at Bamfield or Ucluelet. Depending on the itinerary, allow 9 or 10 hours round trip.
Location: Dock in Port Alberni at the Argyle St. pier.
Information: 723-8313. Contact: Box 188, Port Alberni, V9Y 7M7, for a brochure, itinerary, or schedule information.

■ **Robertson Hatchery and Stamp Falls Fishway:** Built in 1959 to enhance pink salmon runs, this facility was expanded in 1980 and is now producing millions of sockeye, coho and chinook smolts for the Stamp-Somass river systems. Best salmon viewing is from September to November, and again in February when the steelhead spawn. At a second location, a fish channel was constructed to avoid a waterfall. Best viewing: adult sockeye in mid-July, coho in August and September, chinook in September and October. Picnic facilities are located nearby.
Location: Robertson Hatchery: drive through Port Alberni on Highway 4, turn right on Great Central Lake Rd. and follow the signs to the hatchery. Stamp Falls Fishway: drive west on Highway 4 out of Port Alberni and turn right on Beaver Creek Rd., proceed for 12 km and turn left into Stamp Falls Provincial Park.
Information: Robertson Hatchery, 724-6521; B.C. Parks, 755-2483.

■ **Alberni Harbour Quay:** Built in 1984 for about $2.1 million, the quay is home port for the *Lady Rose,* a passenger and cargo ship which serves the remote communities of Barkley Sound. An old steam donkey and 2-spot, a Shay steam locomotive, are on display at the restored 1912 E & N railway station. Browse the stores, restaurants, InfoCentre, and craft outlets. A climb up the clock tower is rewarded with a panoramic view of the harbour and a peek at the oversized berths for deep-sea vessels. During the annual NHL Celebrity Derby, visitors may catch a glimpse of famous hockey players; phone for dates.
Location: Foot of Argyle St., south Port Alberni.
Information: 724-6535.

■ **Alberni Valley Museum and Art Gallery:** Admission by donation. On display here are an innovative water wheel that generates electricity, and several model steam engines that illustrate the principles of steam. The collection of artifacts, both pioneer and native, include two canoes carved from red cedar. The art facility houses a display of West Coast native art, three art galleries, two permanent historical displays, and a centre for visiting displays. Adults can have access to the archives of the Alberni Historical Society. Guided tours may be available; phone ahead. **Location:** 4255 Wallace St. **Information:** 723-2181.

■ **MacMillan Bloedel Visitor's Centre:** Hands-on displays provide children with a look at modern forestry practises. Youngsters can play forestry computer games or climb through and over the stump of a tree. Logging tours of the forest originate here; phone ahead. **Location:** 5440 Argyle St. **Information:** 724-7890.

■ **Sawmill, Pulp and Paper, or Forestry Tours:** Port Alberni is the centre of an enormous wood-processing facility. Four tours familiarize visitors with the industry. Two separate sawmill tours cover the equipment used to make finished lumber. Allow 90 minutes; tours are limited in size to 12 participants each. The pulp and paper mill tour follows trees from chipped wood to the final product. Allow 90 minutes; tour is limited to 20 participants. Another tour takes visitors into the woods for a look at logging operations. Allow 2 hours; tour is limited to 14 participants. Guided tours are available in summer; phone ahead. **Location:** Various start points. **Information:** Tourism Information, 724-6535; pulp and paper tour, 723-2161 extension 4696; Alberni Pacific sawmill tour, 724-7438; Somas sawmill tour, 734-7474; MacMillan Bloedel logging operation tour, 724-7888. Not suitable for persons under the age of 12. For safety, no open-toed footwear or shorts are allowed, and participants should wear clothing which covers the arms.

■ **Marine Biology Station Visit:** This marine biology study centre monitors the abundant sea life on the surf-battered side of Vancouver Island. Visits are available during the summer— Saturdays and Sundays at 1:30 p.m. to coincide with the stopover of the *Lady Rose;* phone ahead. Allow 30 minutes. **Location:** Western Canadian Universities Marine Biology Station in Bamfield; access from Port Alberni by the *Lady Rose.* Bamfield is also accessible by secondary road from Port Alberni. **Information:** 728-3301.

Ucluelet

Information on the attractions and festivals of Ucluelet: Seasonal InfoCentre, 1620 Peninsula Rd., Box 428, Ucluelet, V0R 3A0. Phone: 726-4641, FAX: 726-7289.

■ **Thornton Hatchery:** An enhancement society improves chum, some chinook and coho runs. Best viewing: adult chum, mid-October to November. Guided tours may be available: phone ahead.
Location: From Highway 4 at Ucluelet, turn towards Port Albion; turn right at the end of the pavement and proceed another 2 km (1.2 mi.). The hatchery is on the right-hand side.
Information: Thornton Enhancement Society, 726-7566.

■ **Amphitrite Lighthouse Viewpoint and VTS Facility:** This lighthouse, established in 1905, affords commanding views out to the open Pacific and Barkley Sound. A $5-million traffic services complex monitors shipping activity in coastal waters, including sea traffic, ship-to-shore communications, search and rescue operations, and weather information. Stroll the paved pathways, especially at dusk; sunsets are sensational.
Location: On the southern tip of the Ucluth Peninsula, at the foot of Ucluelet's main street.
Information: InfoCentre, 726-4641.

■ *Canadian Princess* **Hotel:** In downtown Ucluelet, the *Canadian Princess* is permanently moored as a floating hotel. Formerly a historic west-coast steamship built in 1932 and named the *William J. Stewart,* the vessel provided hydrographic services in her 43 years of service along the coast. In wartime she was armed and carried out top-secret assignments for the Canadian Navy. On June 11, 1944, she was yet another casualty of Ripple Rock (see Campbell River entries). It took a month to refloat her. Visitors can admire the restoration work and polished brass fittings of the ship's interior.

Location: Downtown Ucluelet, on the water.

Information: 726-7771.

Pacific Rim National Park

Information on Pacific Rim National Park: Canadian Parks Services, Information Services, Western Regional Office, Room 520, 220 - 4th Ave. S.E., Box 2989, Station M, Calgary, Alberta T2P 3H8. Phone: (403) 292-4440.

Brochures on wildlife, walking, and hiking trails: National Park, P.O. Box 280, Ucluelet, V0R 3A0.

Information and maps on Pacific Rim: Pacific Rim Park InfoCentre, Box 428, Ucluelet, V0R 2Z0. Phone: 726-4212, visitor information services.

■ **Long Beach Exploration and Storm Watching:** The raw glory of nature is the prime reason for visiting this once-remote area. The deafening pounding of the waves never ceases among rocky outcroppings and tidal pools; a permanent colony of sea lions basks in front of Combers Beach. Stand atop Radar Hill on a clear day and gaze seaward for 22 km (14 mi.) by Coast Guard reckoning. Walk for hours along the beach or the headland trails. Storm watching comes naturally. Stand on a promontory, high above the crashing waves, feel the wind quicken and appreciate the drama as the sky darkens and looming clouds roll and swirl in dramatic formations. Nature gives full vent to her most dramatic manifestations here. Bring a portable cassette player and music by Wagner. Occasionally, storm-walks are offered from the Wickaninnish Interpretive Centre.

Location: A map of 20 easy trail walks is available at the InfoCentre.

Recommended high points: Amphitrite Point, Wya Point, Quistis Point, Portland Point, Radar Hill, or Cox Point.
Information: InfoCentre, 725-3414. Write for a one-page sheet describing the location of remote beaches and walking trails: Pacific Rim Resort, Box 570, Tofino, V0R 2Z0.

■ **Wickaninnish Visitor Centre:** This structure incorporates the timbers, rafters, and stone hearth of the historic lodge named *wickaninnish* which means "roaring waters." Observation decks are equipped with telescopes. Inside, the story of great whales is told in a mural, animated exhibits, and a film or video. Workshops and interpretive tours are held from early spring through the summer; during March and April, whale-spotting walks may originate from the parking lot. Phone ahead for all activities. Note that evening fires are allowed on the beach here; gather firewood in the daylight as it is completely dark most nights. The centre is closed in winter.
Location: At the end of Long Beach Rd., picturesquely located on the point.
Information: Wickaninnish Interpretive Centre, 726-7333; Wickaninnish workshops, 726-4254. Write for a list of interpretive programs: Wickaninnish Centre, Box 280, Pacific Rim National Park, Ucluelet, V0R 3A0.

■ **Interpretive Programs:** Three separate interpretive programs are offered for visitors throughout the early spring and summer months. At Green Point Theatre in the Green Point Campground, park staff give daily evening lectures on the park's history and ecological concepts, or they arrange occasional nature walks. Park-naturalist-led outdoor hikes and whale-watching walks are posted at the Tofino and Ucluelet Co-op Bulletin Boards, published weekly in the Ucluelet newspaper, *Westerly News,* posted on a sandwich board located near the entrance to Green Point, and listed at both Ucluelet and Tofino Travel InfoCentres; the Wickaninnish Centre (see previous entry) features displays, video, films, and is the start point for guided tours. All interpretive programs are free.

Location: Various locations in Tofino, Ucluelet, and Pacific Rim National Park.

Information: InfoCentre, 725-3414.

■ **Whale-Watching From Shore:** Vapour spouts are the telltale signs of the 20,000 or so gray whales that migrate past this coast. From late February through March and April, virtually the entire world population of Pacific gray whales passes the west coast of Vancouver Island on their northward migration. The whales feed on small organisms, such as plankton and small crustaceans. Best sightings are from one of the rocky headlands along Long Beach, but whale sightings are not guaranteed. Guided walks to view whales may be offered seasonally from the Wickaninnish Centre in March and April; phone to inquire.

Location: Wickaninnish Centre, located at the end of Long Beach Rd., is the place to source free guided walks. Recommended high points: Amphitrite Point, Wya Point, Quistis Point, Portland Point, or Cox Point.

Information: InfoCentre, 725-3414; Wickaninnish Centre, 726-7333; Wickaninnish workshops, 726-4254.

■ **Pacific Rim Whale Festival:** Have fun at a "whale of a festival" in celebration of the annual return of the gray whales. Coastal communities and surrounding native villages host an annual festival to coincide with the peak migration season. Competitions such as the Geoduck (pronounced gooey-duck) Competition, Crab Races, art exhibits, concerts, a children's day and the Gum-Boot Golf Tournament are part of the fun. Held mid-March to mid-April.

Location: Various venues in Ucluelet, Tofino, and the native villages.

Information: InfoCentre, 725-3414.

Tofino

Information on the attractions and festivals of Tofino:
Seasonal InfoCentre, 351 Campbell St., Box 476, Tofino,
V0R 2Z0. Phone: 725-3414, FAX: 725-3296.

■ **Coast Guard Station Visit:** The Coast Guard
Rescue Station at Tofino welcomes visitors for an informal
open house every day between 10:00 a.m. and 2:00 p.m. Visitors
can view the station, a 13-m (43-ft.) self-righting rescue vessel,
and two rubber-hulled craft used in combined search and rescue
operations.
Location: On main street in Tofino.
Information: 725-3231.

■ **Forest Tour:** Harvesting began here in 1889, and present-day
forestry operations are centred around Kenny Lake. This tour covers
the transport of trees to Port Alberni for manufacture into specialty
paper, newsprint, and pulp; smaller operators use the trees to make
shake and shingles or yellow cedar cants. Guided tours available
in summer; phone ahead to see if still available.
Location: MacMillan Bloedel Office, Kenny Lake. Inquire about
start point.
Information: 726-7712.

■ **Art Gallery:** This building, owned by native artist
Roy Vickers, was inspired by the traditional form of a west-
coast longhouse. The artist's style has evolved from traditional west-coast native art to a unique blend of traditional and contemporary forms.
Location: Eagle Aerie Gallery, Main street of Tofino.
Information: 725-3235, FAX: 725-4466.

■ **Summer Festival Presentations:** Mini-concerts by the raging sea? Performances such as the Maori Dance Theatre of New Zealand and the Summer Pops Youth Orchestra can be seen in a spectacular setting. Contact the festival office for a listing of this year's performances of "Music on the Edge." Some concerts are free, some for a fee.
Location: Various venues in Tofino.
Information: Festival Office, 726-4488.

Qualicum Beach

Information on the attractions and festivals of Qualicum Beach: InfoCentre, 2711 West Island Highway, Box 103, Qualicum Beach, V0R 2S0. Phone: 752-9532, FAX: 752-2923.

■ **Big Qualicum and Little Qualicum Hatcheries:** Two facilities deal with millions of fish, both salmon and trout, that return here each season. Both are most interesting in the autumn, when the salmon fight upriver. There are educational displays and self-guiding paths around the hatcheries. "Big" and "Little" are the names of the rivers and do not reflect the size of the hatcheries.
Location: Big Qualicum: 16 km (10 mi.) past Qualicum Beach, watch for a sign on the west side of the highway indicating the road to the site; Little Qualicum: take the Parksville cutoff towards Port Alberni, turn right on Melrose Rd. and follow the signs to the site.
Information: Big Qualicum Hatchery, 757-8412; Little Qualicum Hatchery, 752-3231.

■ **Horne Lake Caves Park:** Formed as a result of the solvent action of water and the compounds in it, caves are often found in regions with high rainfall. Surface water reacts with the constituents in the soil to create an acidic mixture that attacks underground limestone. Over time, subterranean chambers form. Several caves here are available for casual exploration. Regular guided public tours of the main cave are scheduled July and August; phone ahead. Tours leave from the end of the parking lot. Respect the formations and do not bring home chipped-off souvenirs; obey all signs. **Location:** Turn west off Highway 19 at Horne Lake Rd., travel north through Qualicum Beach to the Horne Lake Store. Turn at the store and travel 11 km (7 mi.) to the lake. The caves are 8 km (5 mi.) along the shore road. Before venturing out, get exact directions from an InfoCentre. **Information:** Rathtrevor Park, 248-3931. No children under the age of 6 are allowed in the caves. Wear long pants and long sleeves. A flashlight per person and rubber-soled waterproof shoes are compulsory in order to explore.

■ **Marshall Steveson Wildlife Preserve and Bird Sanctuary:** A wide range of wildlife inhabits this marshy zone where shore wanderers and land dwellers meet. The network of trails are opened or closed depending upon the season. Opening hours are limited and a call should be made to be certain there is a supervisor on-site. Guided tours may be available; phone ahead. **Location:** From Highway 19, a "Canadian Wildlife" sign indicates the turnoff. Located at the mouth of the Little Qualicum River. **Information:** 752-9611.

■ **Old School House Gallery and Arts Centre:** This busy centre for artists, jewellers, weavers, sculptors, woodworkers, photographers, and craftspeople is located in a refurbished school. Continuous demonstrations, such as wood carving, stained-glass construction, batik, and pottery making take place during opening hours. The public gallery features local and regional artists whose works reflect the natural beauties of the area. Opening hours are variable; phone ahead. **Location:** 122 Fern Rd. West. **Information:** 752-6133.

Denman and Hornby Islands

Ferry from Fanny Bay: A car-passenger ferry crosses to Denman Island. On the far side of Denman Island, at Gravelly Bay, a second car-passenger ferry travels to Hornby Island; each ferry crossing takes about 10 minutes. Phone: B.C. Ferries, 629-3215; Fanny Bay ferry, 386-3431.

Information assistance: Tourist services and General Store, Denman Island, V0R 1T0. Phone: 335-2293.

■ **Museum Society Activity Centre:** This small facility features shells, fossils, native artifacts, and the prized work of the Denman Lace Club. Open daily in summer; open by arrangement year-round.
Location: In the senior's hall on Denman Island.
Information: Supervisor's residence, 335-0985.

■ **Celebrations:** Yearly events include: Celtic Festival in April every second year; Hornby Ringside Fair craft market all summer every day; Hornby Festival of the Performing Arts, Summer Fair and Games, Mountain Bike Races in August.
Location: Various venues on Hornby Island.
Information: Hornby Island General Store, 335-1121.

Comox Valley Area

Information on the attractions and festivals of Courtenay and Comox: InfoCentre, 2040 Cliffe Ave., Courtenay, V9N 2L3. Phone: 334-3234, FAX: 334-4908.

Information on the attractions and festivals of Cumberland: InfoCentre, 2755 Dunsmuir Ave., Box 74, Cumberland, V0R 1S0. Phone: 336-8313, FAX: 336-2455.

Information and maps on B.C. parks in the Comox Valley: Ministry of Parks, Miracle Zone, Miracle Beach Park, Site 11, Box 1, Highway 19, Black Creek, V0R 1C0. Phone: 337-5121; FAX: 337-5659.

■ **Puntledge Hatchery:** This salmon hatchery provides stock for the Puntledge River system. Best viewing: adult chum in November; chinook in September and October; spawning steelhead in February and March; juveniles from February through June.
Location: From Courtenay take Lake Trail Rd., turn right on Powerhouse Rd. Follow the signs.
Information: 338-7444.

■ **Seal Bay Regional Nature Park and Trumpeter Swan Viewing:** Large numbers of the once-endangered trumpeter swan pass through this region, and the InfoCentre will detail the best viewing locations. Most visitors travel to this park to see a distant but permanent colony of seals which can always be sighted offshore. Trails on the ocean side of the road are wheelchair accessible.
Location: Take Island Highway, turn west on Ryan Rd., then north on Anderton Rd., which changes into Waveland Rd. Follow the signs.
Information: InfoCentre, 334-3234.

■ **Courtenay Museum:** Reputed to be the world's largest vertical log cabin, this facility highlights native artifacts, logging and farming equipment, fossils, local Chinese and Japanese artifacts, a doll collection, and archives of regional history. Nestled among the mountains of the Beaufort Range, the natives called this abundant area *komuckway,* meaning "plenty." Guided tours may be available; phone ahead.
Location: 360 Cliffe Ave.
Information: 334-3611.

■ **Comox Airforce Museum:** Indoor displays feature 100 years of police and military history, including a scale model of a 1950 RCAF station. Outdoors, several airplanes are on display: the DC-3 Dakota, CF-100 Canuck, CF-101 VooDoo Fighter, CF-104 Starfighter, and CP 107. Opening hours are limited. Guided tours may be available; phone ahead.
Location: Take Ryan Rd. off Island Highway 19 from the Courtenay Bypass. The Airforce Museum is at the entrance to the Canadian Forces Base in Comox.
Information: 339-8635.

■ **Cumberland Museum and Chinatown Reminders:**
Token admission. Cumberland was an important coal-mining town, but when the company refused to improve conditions after more than 300 men were killed in various accidents between 1884 and 1912, the miners rioted and a thousand soldiers were sent to keep the peace. Here, a 13-m (43-ft.) model mine shaft with rock samples and photographs recalls those times. Guided tours may be available; phone ahead. In the 1880s, when labourers came off railway crews to work in the mines, Cumberland's Chinatown was the largest on the continent. One of the historic Chinatown shacks stands alone at the old approach to the mines.
Location: 2680 Dunsmuir Ave., Cumberland; old shack located on the road out of Cumberland, past the row of similar company homes, along the road to Comox Lake. The Chinese and Japanese cemeteries can be found at the north end of Union Rd.
Information: Museum, 336-2445; InfoCentre, 336-8313, FAX: 336-2455.

■ **Filburg Lodge, Gallery, and Park:** This elegant 19th-century manor house and 3.6-ha (9-ac.) estate were the private domain of Robert J. Filburg, president of the Comox Logging Company; today, it is a public centre for the arts. Although the area was primarily a simple farming community, Filburg tried to build an estate that would capture "elegance in the wilderness." Built of local materials in a semi-English style, the interior features an impressive stonework fireplace and a yew staircase hand rail. A 4-day Festival of the Arts is centred here in early August, with booths nestled among the trees overlooking Comox Bay; more than

75 craftspeople sell high-quality pottery, weaving, and jewellery against a backdrop of continuous stage entertainment. On the way to the Filburg Lodge, watch for the exterior of the old Lorne Hotel built in 1878, located on Comox Ave. After a visit to Filburg, continue along Comox Ave. to "Shakeside," the home of local naturalist Mac Laing (1883-1982), and today the site of a park with a pleasant waterfront walk in a cedar forest.
Location: 61 Filburg Rd., Comox.
Information: Filburg Arts and Music Festival, 338-6211; Filburg Lodge, 339-2715.

■ **Forestry Tour:** This guided timber tour features scenic views from Mount Washington, active logging operations, and a review of forestry operations such as pruning, spacing, and research. Scheduled tours are held in the summer; phone ahead. The tour takes 7 hours and requires a great deal of walking. Wear sturdy footwear and bring a lunch.
Location: Fletcher Challenge; ask for start point.
Information: 334-1923. Not suitable for persons under the age of 12. For safety, no open-toed footwear or shorts are allowed, and participants should wear clothing which covers the arms.

■ **Miracle Beach Interpretive Programs:** The visitor centre at Miracle Beach is the start point for naturalist programs that run throughout the summer months. Interpretive programs include nature walks or the identification of seashells and intertidal creatures. The Nature House has displays on sea life and the changing forest. A sand-castle competition is held in June.
Location: Take Highway 19 about 20 km (12 mi.) north of Courtenay.
Information: B.C. Parks, Miracle Zone, 337-5121.

■ **Arts Festival and Summer Recitals:** Some performances and displays are free. The city of Courtenay, its streets decked with flowers, is home to a Festival of the Arts for young people which is growing in scope each year.

A wide range of literary, visual and musical arts are planned for, practised for, and performed with care and enthusiasm. The Courtenay Youth Music Centre brings together gifted students with top-notch teachers from around the world; phone for a complete recital program.

Location: Recitals from March to September; Festival, first weekend in July.

Information: Arts Alliance, 338-7463.

■ **Celebrations:** Yearly events include Courtenay Winter Carnival in January; Courtenay Snow to Surf Race in May; Courtenay Canada Day Celebrations, Comox Tri-K Triathlon, Comox Windsurfing Regatta, Courtenay Market Day in July; Courtenay Youth Music Camp during July and August; Comox Nautical Days, C.F.B. Comox Air Show every second year in August; Comox Valley Annual Fall Exhibition in September.

Location: Various venues in the Comox Valley.

Information: InfoCentre, 334-3234.

Campbell River

Information on the attractions and festivals of Campbell River: InfoCentre, 1235 Shopper's Row, Box 400, Campbell River, V9W 5B6. Phone: 287-4636, FAX: 286-6490.

■ **Ripple Rock Lookout:** Tides in Seymour Narrows, site of the largest non-atomic blast in peacetime history, run up to 16 knots. Adding to that hazard until 1958 was a dual-peaked underwater mountain called Ripple Rock, less affectionately called "the rip." It caused more than two dozen major shipwrecks and claimed 114 lives. The problem was solved with one calculated dynamite blast, the largest non-nuclear detonation to that time. The photograph made front pages all over the world. Approximately 11 m (36 ft.) was blown off each underwater peak;

today, the destruction has almost ceased but the tides remain treacherous. The rest area by the side of the road has a panoramic view of the narrows.
Location: 12 km (7 mi.) north on Highway 19.
Information: InfoCentre, 287-4636.

■ **Quinsam River Hatchery:** A self-guided tour, especially appropriate because of the sports fisheries' heavy usage of the area, is found here. Best viewing: pinks in September; coho and chinook from October to November; steelhead from November through April; chinook fry from March through May. There are picnic tables and walking trails on-site.
Location: 5 km (3 mi.) west of Campbell River. Take Highway 28 towards Gold River, past the junction to Port Hardy, and turn left on Quinsam River Rd. Watch for signs.
Information: 287-9564.

■ **Campbell River Museum:** Token admission. As this has long been an area noted for salmon fishing, native populations were active here. The exhibits cover culture of native peoples, coastal exploration in the 18th century, and the settlers of the 18th and 19th centuries. Guided tours may be available; phone ahead.
Location: 1235 Island Highway, Tyee Plaza.
Information: 287-3103.

■ **Discovery Fishing Pier:** Token admission. This is Canada's first fully equipped saltwater fishing pier. Extending 180 m (600 ft.) from the shore, the wide pier has fishing facilities for adults, children, and the handicapped, shelters for cover in poor weather, fish-cleaning stations, plenty of seating, and lighting for night fishing. Opened in 1987 at a cost of $1.3 million, in its first season alone it was utilized by an estimated 67,000 visitors.
Location: On the downtown waterfront.
Information: InfoCentre, 286-4636.

■ Painter's Lodge Memorabilia and the Tyee Club:

The unofficial headquarters for the renowned Tyee Club has always been Painter's Lodge. The old lodge's public rooms were filled from floor to ceiling with photographs of movie stars, politicians, world-famous figures, and ordinary people alike, who had each landed a tyee-king salmon. Unfortunately, the lodge and collection were destroyed by fire on Christmas Eve, 1985. In June 1988, a new lodge opened in its place and since then, memorabilia is being slowly accumulated again. In the meantime, the new pub here features the first and only "salmon-skin bar" in the world. Back in 1895, perched in an Indian dugout, Sir Richard Musgrave landed a 70-pound tyee-king; then in 1896, he published an account in an English journal, "The Field"; his preserved fish was displayed in London as the "largest salmon ever taken on a rod" and British readers began to arrive. By 1924, the Tyee Club was open to anyone who could land a giant salmon under restrictive rules, still in operation to the present. The record tyee-king to date is a 32-kg (71-lb.) fish landed in 1968. Whenever a 14-kg (30-lb.) or heavier tyee-king is officially recorded, a bell is rung in the pub for a round of drinks "on the house."

Location: Painter's Lodge Lobby, 1625 MacDonald Rd.
Information: 286-1102.

■ Timber Tour or Pulp and Paper Tour:

Lasting 6 to 7 hours and beginning early in the morning, Fletcher Challenge offers an extensive tour of logging sites, forestry operations, and a walk through a 75-year-old second-growth forest. Bring lunch; wear walking shoes. Tours available from May to October; book ahead. In addition, there are short summer tours of the Elk Falls Pulp and Paper Mill weekday afternoons from June through August. Allow 90 minutes. No cameras are allowed on the tour.

Location: Fletcher Challenge Canada Forest Industry Information Centre, at Tyee Plaza, or start points as specified.
Information: 286-3872. Not suitable for persons under the age of 12. For safety, no open-toed footwear or shorts are allowed, and participants should wear clothing which covers the arms.

■ **UBC Experimental Farm Tour:** This farm is a research facility for dairy operations. Visitors can see the barns, followed by the automated milking of up to 150 cows at one time. Milking takes place in the early afternoon. Guided tours are available year-round; phone ahead. Wear rubber-soled footwear that can be cleaned.
Location: Located 15 minutes from Campbell River, south on Highway 19.
Information: 923-4219.

■ **Celebrations:** Yearly events include Raft Races, Mining Sports in July; Loggers' Sports, Eagle Fishing Derby in August.
Location: Various venues in and around Campbell River.
Information: InfoCentre, 286-4636, FAX: 286-6490.

Quadra Island

Ferry from Campbell River: A car and passenger ferry runs from downtown Campbell River to Quathiaski Cove on Quadra Island, a distance of 3 km (2 mi.) by sea with a crossing time of 10 minutes. Phone: B.C. Ferries, 629-3215.

Information on Quadra: Travel Information, P.O. Box 90, Quathiaski Cove, Quadra Island, V0P 1N0.

■ **Eagle Feeding:** From May 1 to the middle of June, eagles congregate on Quadra Island. When they are prevalent, staff of the Heriot Bay Inn dump buckets of fish heads onto the beach every day at 3:00 p.m. From 8 to 10 eagles usually arrive for the feeding—talons extended for hunting. These birds are wild. Remain at a safe distance and bring a camera.
Location: Heriot Bay Inn, on the east side of the island at Heriot Bay.
Information: 285-3322.

■ **Kwagiulth Museum and Cultural Centre:** Small admission. Inside the museum is a comprehensive collection of ceremonial regalia including masks, button blankets, rattles, coppers, speaking sticks, and cedar baskets. The museum presents a series of summer workshops open to the public. Subjects include petroglyph rubbing, the technology of cedar, and native food gathering and preparation; there is not usually an additional fee except for the material required for petroglyph rubbing. Ask for a program outline available in May each year. Several petroglyphs have been moved from the beach to a small park near the museum for preservation.
Location: Cape Mudge Village.
Information: 285-3733.

■ **Remains of the Lucky Jim Mine:** This gold and copper mine that operated from 1903 to 1910 is now in shambles; a few scattered pieces include an iron flywheel, the pit shafts (now covered) and some deteriorating bunkhouses.
Location: Take the Granite Bay Rd. turnoff to a sharp left; the road to the mine joins in a T; the road is rough. Park, then walk in from a trail; take the first left fork and then the middle trail. Get precise directions from a knowledgeable local before setting out.
Information: Campbell River InfoCentre, 286-4636.

■ **Cape Mudge Lighthouse Tour:** Using an electric light focused through a Fresnell lens, this 17-m-high (55-ft.) lighthouse can cast a beam about 21 km (13 mi.) out to sea. The guided tour covers the station grounds, the engine room, foghorn compressers, generator, weather instruments, seismograph, and a trip up into the tower. Guided tours are available April to late fall, weather permitting, from 10:00 a.m. to 2:00 p.m. by appointment; phone ahead.
Location: 15-minute drive south from the Quadra Island ferry; follow signs to the Cape Mudge Light Station.
Information: 285-3352.

■ **Nature Walking-Tour:** A natural history club maintains
several trails on Quadra Island. Amateur naturalists lead free walks
for different levels of physical fitness to various areas of the island.
Tours depart Saturday, May through September, 7:30 a.m. Phone
in advance; ask for tour duration and difficulty of the walk. Wear
sturdy walking shoes.
Location: Meet in the lobby of Heriot Bay Inn, on the east side
of the island at Heriot Bay.
Information: 285-3322.

■ **Petroglyphs:** Several petroglyphs, most now fad-
ing, are located in accessible areas along the beaches.
Location: The location of petroglyphs and pictographs
throughout B.C. is protected due to vandalism; for exact directions,
inquire at the InfoCentre in Campbell River or ask knowledgeable locals.
Information: Kwagiulth Museum, 285-3733.

■ North Vancouver Island ■

Planning kit for travel to the North Island: North Island
Travel, Regional District of Mount Waddington, P.O. Box 729,
Port McNeill, V0N 2R0.

**Information and maps on B.C. parks on northern
Vancouver Island:** Strathcona District, B.C. Parks, Box 1479,
Parksville, V0R 2S0. Phone: 755-2483. FAX: 248-8584.

Side Trip to Strathcona Park, Gold River

Information on the attractions and festivals of Gold River:
Seasonal InfoCentre, Box 610, Gold River, V0P 1G0. Phone:
283-2202, FAX: 283-7500.

Information and maps on Strathcona Provincial Park:
Ministry of Lands, Recreation Division, 1019 Wharf St.,
Victoria, V8W 2Y9. Phone: 387-1067.

Information on exploring caves: B.C. Speleological
Federation, Box 993, Gold River, V0P 1G0. Phone: 283-7144,
Fax: 284-2461.

■ **MV *Uchuck III*:** Outstanding value; adults $35 to $45, children under 12 years free. Reservations are required. This boat ride is rich in historical and cultural connections to British Columbia's past. Yuquot, also known as Friendly Cove, is the place Captain James Cook landed in 1778. Searching for a spar to replace a broken mast, he found the natives to be hospitable; in turn, the story goes, the natives found the sailors to be unpleasant-looking with "hooked" noses like old salmon. According to another story, Captain Cook pointed to their dwellings, asking, "What is the name of your village?" The native responded, "That? Over there?" (*"Noot? Ka?"*) The name remains and the area and its people are known as Nootka. This encounter was certainly not their first contact with whites; they knew Russian words and were skilled at bargaining with sea-otter skins. The sailors who bought a few to warm their hammocks received a surprise—in China, the pelts caused a sensation, starting a trade in sea-otter skins that almost wiped out this animal. Today, there is a only a church and a few old buildings to be seen of this historic meeting place, but Tahsis Inlet has many historical connections. The *Uchuck III,* a freight-passenger-mail boat, chugs up the inlet, stopping at isolated communities, most still unserviced by commuter roads. The public can join the crew on the converted 1943 minesweeper, but this is a working boat. Ask about food services. Time required for the return cruise: 6 hours.

Location: Departs from the head of Muchalat Inlet, 12 km (7 mi.) south of Gold River.

Information: Nootka Sound Service Boat, 283-2515, 283-2325. Write: Uchuck III Nootka Sound Service, Box 57, Gold River, V0P 1G0.

■ **Strathcona Park Nature Walk:** The shores of the Campbell Lakes and Buttle Lake wind along to Strathcona Park, B.C.'s oldest provincial park, covering almost 202,000 ha (500,000 ac.). Much of the park is wilderness, with canoe routes and remote hiking trails, but at Lupin Falls, near the Ralph River Campground, a self-guided nature walk is an easy way to appreciate the wilder-

ness. Strathcona Park is also noted for a concentration of Roosevelt elk and for alpine and subalpine meadows only minutes away from parking areas.
Location: Information tent at Buttle Lake during July and August.
Information: B.C. Parks, Zone Manager at Black Creek, 337-5121, FAX: 337-5695.

■ **Tlupana-Conuma Hatchery and Chinook Project:** This year-round facility replenishes salmon stocks, including steelhead. Best viewing: adult chum mid-September to October; coho mid-October to November; chinook, November; juveniles from April through June. Camping and picnicing facilities are nearby.
Location: Midway between Gold River and Tahsis. Watch for signs.
Information: Vancouver Radio Operator 9-0711 N710-215.

■ **Upana Caves:** Become a spelunker and take a self-guided tour through the Upana Caves, which are safe for careful amateurs. Four public caves feature a walk through narrow passages and caverns, out into the sunlight, then down and between narrow passageways again. A signpost marks the entrance; obey all signs. Allow about 1 hour. The Caveman Days Festival is held during the last 2 weeks of June.
Location: 17 km (11 mi.) west of Gold River on Head Bay Forest Road west. Turn at Branch H27. Parking lot provided.
Information: Gold River Chamber of Commerce, 283-2202; cave information, 283-2283. Not suitable for children under the age of 10. For each person, a flashlight and rubber-soled waterproof shoes are compulsory.

■ **Ore-Processing Tour:** Copper, zinc, and other riches are extracted through a preliminary ore process and shipped elsewhere for further extraction. The method, known as froth flotation, is a chemical bubbling that floats valuable ores to the surface. Scheduled surface tours are held on weekdays in the summer; phone ahead. Allow 90 minutes.
Location: Westmin Resources, accessible from Campbell River on Highway 28, 12 km (7 mi.) beyond the Ralph River Campground, around the south end of Buttle Lake.
Information: 287-9271.

Sayward

■ **Cable House Restaurant, Steel Totem, Link and Pin Museum:** Token admission to the museum. Three unusual structures are found side by side: the Cable House Restaurant is constructed of 2700 m (8,860 ft.) of steel cable rope, weighing 24 tonnes (26 tons), wrapped around a steel frame; a totem pole made of steel honours B.C. loggers; the Link and Pin Museum displays a jumble of artifacts from pioneer logging days. "Snoose" is an oversized wooden lumberjack carved by chainsaw artist Henry Stadbouer.
Location: About 1 km (.6 mi.) from Sayward junction on Highway 19.
Information: Cable House Restaurant, 282-5532.

■ **Valley of One Thousand Faces:** Token admission. This one-of-a-kind outdoor gallery is set among the trees. Hetty Fredrickson has painted the faces of more than 1000 creatures, human and otherwise, on cedar slabs and alder logs. "May you go home with a smile" is their motto, and after a look at more than 1000 puckered faces, there are usually a few smiles. Noah's Ark, the newest exhibit, is now reinterpreted with North American animals. Open every day from May 15 to September 1, but check in advance.
Location: 75 km (47 mi.) north of Campbell River, at the Sayward Junction of Highway 19.
Information: 282-3303.

Port McNeill and Area

Information on the attractions and festivals of Port McNeill: Seasonal InfoCentre, Box 129, Port McNeill, V0N 2R0. Phone: 956-3131.

■ **Little Hustan Cave Park:** Myriads of caves and unusual rock formations await the explorer in the Nimp-kish Valley. The Regional District has opened Little Cave Park, providing ready access to limestone caves within a few kilometres of the paved highway. Along the way, a swift-flowing river, called the Vanishing River, appears and disappears. The Cave Park includes trails, directional signs, and viewing platforms. The caves are not particularly challenging or fragile, but all signs should be strictly obeyed. A map of other interesting geological forma-tions, such as the Never-ending Fountain, is available.
Location: About 23 km (14 mi.) north of Woss junction, take the gravel logging road to Zeballos. Follow the signs to Little Hustan Cave Park. This road is not suitable for large campers or oversize vehicles.
Information: Regional District, 956-3301; InfoCentre, 956-3131. Not suitable for children under the age of 10. For each person, a flashlight and rubber-soled waterproof shoes are compulsory. Map of Little Hustan Cave Park is available from Regional District of Mount Waddington, P.O. Box 729, Port McNeill, V0N 2R0.

■ **Telegraph Cove:** Looking like a movie set, the charming buildings form a picturesque community standing on stilts in the water. Summer visitors can stroll the boardwalk decorated with tidy flower boxes, and browse the stores. Whale-watching tours depart from here to Robson Bight in Johnston Strait. The "Cove" was once the northern terminus of a telegraph line strung from tree to tree along the coast of Van-couver Island; morse code messages were relayed onward to Alert Bay and then transmitted forward on foot. The present owners are dedicated to preserving village life for the 20-some people who winter over. During the summer and fall, the population swells as hundreds of visitors camp near here to take advantage of the fishing. Near Telegraph Cove, across the Kokish River Bridge, is

one of the north island's largest fish farms.
Location: Take the Beaver Cove turnoff on Highway 19 near Port McNeill and follow the signs.
Information: Port McNeill InfoCentre, 956-3131.

■ **World's Largest Burl:** Weighing in at 20.5 tonnes (22.5 tons) and measuring 14 m (46 ft.) around, this "knot" was discovered in 1976 by a group of MacMillan Bloedel surveyors. It was growing at the base of a tree that towered to 87 m (285 ft.) and was estimated to be 351 years old; check the Guiness Book of Records, 24th edition, under World's Biggest Burl. Burls result from abnormal development in the size of wood cells following a disturbance to the cambium layer; they are commonly debarked, varnished, and used as decorative signposts. This record-breaking spruce burl is far too large for that purpose.
Location: At the entrance to the MacMillan Bloedel logging company office, just outside of Port McNeill.
Information: InfoCentre, 956-3131.

■ **North Island Forestry Centre and Tours:**
Take in the displays and videos at the North Island Forestry Centre, operated by five forest companies. Each day in summer, a different company sponsors a tour featuring a look at second-growth forests, an active logging site, or a log dumping and sorting operation. One popular tour features a ride on a logging railway through about 25 km (16 mi.) of the Nimpkish Valley to the booming ground at Beaver Cove. Scheduled tours are held in the summer; phone ahead. Allow 6 hours. Visitors can also drop in to the centre, without taking a tour.
Location: Near the junction to Beaver Cove, just south of Port McNeill on Highway 19. Each tour may have a different start point; inquire.
Information: Forestry Centre, 956-3844. Not suitable for persons under the age of 12. For safety, no open-toed footwear or shorts are allowed and participants should wear clothing which covers the arms.

■ **Port Alice Pulp Mill Tour:** This tour covers the operation of a pulp mill producing a product later used in the manufacture of high-quality papers. Phone ahead.
Location: Port Alice Mill; inquire about start point and time when booking.
Information: 284-3331. Not suitable for persons under the age of 12. For safety, no open-toed footwear or shorts are allowed, and participants should wear clothing which covers the arms.

■ **Logger's Sports Day:** A fee is charged. Join the gathering of the biggest, the best, and the toughest loggers on the fringe of deep logging country. This event attracts thousands who come to watch log-scaling and log-splitting events of speed and dexterity. Professional and non-professional loggers concentrate here for the day. Find out about the free events surrounding this festival. Held in July.
Location: Various venues.
Information: InfoCentre, 956-3131.

Alert Bay and Sointula

Ferry from Port McNeill: Car-passenger ferries run a triangular route across Broughton Strait to Alert Bay on Cormorant Island, and Sointula on Malcolm Island. Phone: B.C. Ferries, 629-3215; Alert Bay-Sointula Ferry Terminal, 956-4533.

Information on the attractions and festivals of Alert Bay: InfoCentre, 116 Fir St., Box 28, Alert Bay, V0N 1A0. Phone: 974-5213, FAX: 974-5470.

■ **Gator Gardens Ecological Park:** A 225-m (738-ft.) boardwalk meanders among cedar snags, hemlock, and pines draped with moss. Ravens perch in photographic readiness among the spires of dead trees. The eerie swamp was created by damming a stream, which resulted in the drowning of some trees,

and a new aquatic environment for other species. Allow 30 minutes.
Location: Up the hill from the ferry, Alert Bay.
Information: InfoCentre, 974-5213.

■ **Alert Bay Library and Museum:** Admission by donation. Housing a small display of artifacts and old photographs in a glass cabinet, the museum also pays tribute to the life and art of one of the last hereditary west-coast chiefs, Chief Henry Speck.
Location: 199 - 1st St.
Information: 974-5721.

■ **Christ Church Exterior:** Behind a white picket fence stands a church built in 1879. The commemorative stained glass windows can be seen from the outside and visitors are welcome.
Location: Fir St., Alert Bay.
Information: InfoCentre, 974-5213.

■ **Sointula Museum:** Utopia is defined as a visionary scheme for an ideally perfected society. In the early 1900s, Matti Kurikka, Finnish author and playwright, started a utopian colony named Sointula, meaning "harmony" in Finnish. He chose Malcolm Island for its proximity to the sea and apparently fertile farmland. After an enthusiastic start, the community suffered a number of setbacks: fire in the community hall killed 11 people, there was a housing shortage, the community was unable to fulfill outside contracts by which it generated income for its dreams. By 1905, the colonization company had folded and the property reverted to the government. Today, Sointula is a fishing village noted for its worn, but tidy appearance, well-maintained cemetery, peaceful atmosphere, and Finnish culture. The museum features a collection of artifacts reflecting the Finnish farming roots; it must be booked to be opened.
Location: The village is just a few blocks long. Ask local residents for directions.
Information: Sointula Museum, 973-6353.

■ **Nimpkish Burial Grounds:** Memorial poles overlooking the water stand as a tribute to the ancestors of the native people here.
Location: Located next to the museum, Alert Bay.
Information: InfoCentre, 974-5213. Do not enter the graveyard; view from the road or the sidewalk.

■ **U'Mista Museum:** Small admission. A showpiece longhouse houses an authoritative collection of Kwakiutl ceremonial regalia, masks of the potlatch collection, copper and prehistoric artifacts. In large part, these items were returned to the people after being seized in the 1920s during a period when potlatches were illegal. In much earlier times, on the rare occasion of the return of a long-lost relative, a *u'mista* celebration was held. Today, the word marks the return of lost treasures. Visitors to the museum can watch a videotape relating the story of the potlatch and the return of these items to their rightful owners.
Location: At the end of Front St., right next to the old St. Michael's School, Alert Bay.
Information: 974-5403.

■ **World's Tallest Totem Pole:** At 53 m (174 ft.) high, the pole features 22 figures topped by the sun and is reputed to be the tallest totem pole in existence. The intricate figures depict the history of the Kwakwak'awakw nation. It has been noted by one native scholar that the more tightly packed the figures, the more complex the story.
Location: On Park St., near the Big House.
Information: InfoCentre, 974-5213.

■ **Celebrations:** Yearly events include June Sports Day (974-5556) and the Cormorant Sea Festival in August.
Location: Various venues in Alert Bay.
Information: InfoCentre, 974-5213.

Port Hardy and Area

Information on the attractions and festivals of Port Hardy: InfoCentre, 7250 Market St., Box 249, Port Hardy, V0N 2P0. Phone: 949-7622, FAX: 949-6653.

■ **Quatse River Tidal Marsh:** This marsh environment is home to several varieties of geese, ducks, herons, and other shorebirds. The sanctuary has a number of birdwatching trails for better views of natural nesting areas. The influence of saltwater tidal action interacts with the dynamics of a freshwater marsh, a fertile area for wildlife.

Location: Located at the head of Hardy Bay and flanked by the mouths of two rivers; access through the Sunny Sanctuary Campground, 1 km (.5 mi.) north of ferry junction and Highway 19, by the Quatse River.

Information: Campground, 949-8111. Phone ahead.

■ **Quatse River Hatchery and Nature Trail:** This salmon enhancement facility is operated by a local society producing coho, chinook, and chum; the facility takes partial credit for the weighty fish for which the area is noted. Nearby are picnic areas and nature trails along the river. Guided tours may be available; phone ahead.

Location: From Highway 19, follow the entrance way to Quatse River Campsite to Hardy Bay Rd.

Information: 949-9022. Write: Northern Vancouver Island Enhancement Society, Box 1409, Port Hardy, V0N 2P0.

■ *Queen of the North*: Outstanding value; adult one-way around $80. The land of the killer whale, seal, and eagle is the highlight of a 15-hour, one-day trip on the modern car-passenger ferry, the *Queen of the North*. This special B.C. ferry has a sumptuous buffet dining room, pleasant lounges equipped with video and recliner passenger chairs, a children's playroom, day cabins, a small shop, a cafeteria, and a piano-bar lounge. The route follows the green forests and snow-capped mountains of British Columbia's scenic Inside Passage. Cabins on the *Queen of the North* are extra, but take note—they have no windows and scenery is the prime interest on this trip. In summer: allow 15 hours; 1 sailing every second day; reservations compulsory. Cabins are optional and extra. In winter: allow 20 hours; 1 sailing each week; reservations requested. Cabins optional and extra. If hotel or campground accommodations are required in Port Hardy the night before, always book ahead. Facilities are often totally full.

Location: British Columbia's Inside Passage from Port Hardy to Prince Rupert.

Information: B.C. Ferries, 669-1211 or 386-3431. Write: B.C. Ferry Corporation, 1112 Fort St., Victoria, V8V 4V2.

■ **Carrot Park:** A carved wooden carrot and a heritage plaque here reads "Mile 0 Trans-Carrot Highway." As late as the 1970s, the northern third of Vancouver Island was without a paved road. Isolated by 160 km (100 mi.) of wilderness known as the incredible gap, the residents wanted a proper blacktop highway. Finally, North Island clamour overwhelmed budgetary restraints and contracts were let for half the distance. In 1976, with work barely started, the highways ministry suddenly cancelled further work; the carrot was snatched away. Visitors can now see the sporting reaction of the angry citizens; there is a restaurant with the "Carrots" name and there are references to "carrots" throughout the town. The highway was finally constructed a few years later—after it became a national debate going all the way to Ottawa.

Location: On Market St. at Island Highway terminus in Port Hardy.

Information: InfoCentre, 949-7622.

■ **Coal Harbour Whaling Station and W.W.II Reconnaissance Outpost:** The jawbone of a blue whale and an early harpoon gun stand as a reminder of the community's whaling station days—1947 to 1967. During W.W.II, Coal Harbour was a Royal Canadian Airforce base; vestiges of 1940s hangars and military huts remain. A small museum, open by appointment, features memorabilia from that time. En route, at the BHP Minerals Canada

turnoff, visitors can see the ongoing work at an open-pit copper mine.
Location: On Coal Harbour Road, 14 km (8.4 mi.) south of Highway 19 near the mouth of Holberg Inlet.
Information: Museum, 949-7622; BHP Minerals Canada, 949-6326.

■ **Old H.B.C. Chimney:** A crumbling chimney at Fort Rupert is the only remnant of an historic Hudson's Bay Company coal-mining operation. In 1835, bemused natives were surprised to discover the blacksmith importing coal, when there was so much of it lying loose at Beaver Harbour. At the smith's behest, the steamship *Beaver* arrived with a team of H.B.C. experts. A stockade and bastion were established and in 1849, mining commenced under the direction of two Ayrshire men. Unfortunately, a few years into the project, a disagreement over terms in their contract flared into an open controversy, resulting in the Scots' imprisonment and an abrupt closure of the mine. The two Scots somehow escaped and apparently lived out their days in San Francisco. H.B.C. never re-opened the mine.
Location: Between the road and the shore of Beaver Harbour, take the airport turnoff, on the road through the Fort Rupert Indian Reserve.
Information: InfoCentre, 949-7622.

■ **Port Hardy Museum:** Admission by donation. This museum features historic photographs and mementos of pioneer settlers, including a pioneer's kitchen, and a selection of native artifacts. A large landscape mural on the north side of the building was painted by the late David Courtenay. Guided tours may be available; phone ahead.
Location: 7110 Market St.
Information: 949-8143.

■ **Wooden Sign Scavenger Hunt:** Several chainsaw-carved sculptures, carved wooden signs, and totem poles are found in this community. Visitors can start at the entrance to the town, with the much photographed wooden "bear and salmon" welcome sign. An intricate eagle is placed outside of the Glen Lyon Inn (6435 Hardy

Bay Rd.) and grizzly bears are found at Jessie's Gallery (5710 Hardy Bay Rd.). The RCMP station features a salmon-sign and the Airport Inn, a bear. Totem poles are located at the turnoff to Coal Harbour, the nearby Fort Rupert Indian Reserve, the airport, and Bear Cove ferry terminal.
Location: Various locations. Ask for a wood carving locator map at the InfoCentre, 7250 Main St.
Information: InfoCentre, 949-7622.

■ **Workshop and Gallery Visit:** Calvin Hunt is a world-renowned native carver who creates his own distinctive style of poles and masks; his family produces silver and gold jewellery. Visitors can phone ahead for an appointment to visit their combined workshop and gallery. While in Fort Rupert, take in other aspects of the native community, including the Fort Rupert Bighouse, residential area, and Stories Beach, which has "spitting clams" at low tide.
Location: Copper Maker Shop; east off Highway 19, take the airport turnoff (Byng Rd.), then left on Harbour Rd. Located at Fort Rupert.
Information: 949-8491.

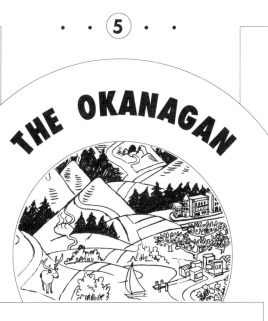

THE OKANAGAN

The Okanagan valley is an arid region surrounding three long lakes. These waters, lying between steep dry valleys, create their own mini weather systems—perfect for growing the fruit and grapes of this bountiful agricultural belt. Lingering elusively within the watery depths of Okanagan Lake is reputed to lurk Ogopogo, a distant cousin of the Loch Ness monster. The region has much to keep visitors busy—that is, if they can resist the temptation to drop a towel onto a mound of sand and relax on the beach. The Okanagan boasts more than 2,000 hours of sunshine annually, the highest in Canada.

Over 30 percent of Canada's apples are

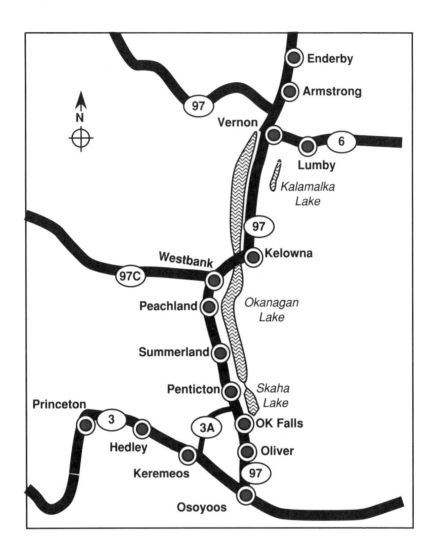

grown in the Okanagan region along with 100 per cent of its apricots, 60 percent of its cherries, 20 percent of its peaches and 50 percent of its pears and prunes. Experienced travellers pay attention to Okanagan seasons: fruit tree blossoms, mid-April to the first week of May; cherries, June 25 to July 20; apricots, July 15 to August 10; raspberries, July 20 to August 7; peaches, August 1 to September 1; apples, August 1 to October 30; pears, August 15 to

September 15; and wine, grapes and wine festivals, September 5 to October 10.

Wine is sold from one of three types of facility. The commercial winery buys its grapes from various farmers, produces the wines, and distributes them to government liquor stores and private wine outlets. An estate winery does everything itself, from planting vines to marketing the finished product on-site and through selected outlets. The farm-gate winery is a relatively new concept in wine production that does everything itself, but sales are limited to an on-site tasting room. Estate and farm-gate wineries produce notable vintages which bring out the potential of the grapes grown on their own particular hillsides.

Numerous guided tours and tastings are scheduled throughout the valley, but the hours change from season to season and year to year, so visitors should phone ahead to avoid disappointment. Groups of 6 or more must book in advance to allow the facility time to prepare extra samples or set out extra chairs. Some facilities are willing to present guided tours in the off-season by prior arrangement. Visitors should be aware that tours of alcoholic facilities are not suitable for children.

The Okanagan region includes the Similkameen and Spallumcheen. The Similkameen is an area of mountainous wilderness on the route between the Lower Mainland and the Okanagan, from Princeton to Oliver. This region experienced a flurry of mining activity within the last 100 years, during which some mines were quickly exhausted, while others remain active to the present. The area is a mecca for rock hounds and those who like to explore ghost towns or pan for a little gold dust.

The Spallumcheen begins at Armstrong and offers a glimpse of the rolling terrain that was familiar to fur traders, early explorers, and those pressing onward to the gold fields of the Cariboo. The Shuswap Highlands rise to merge with the Monashee Mountains; to the west grow dry ponderosa pine contrasting with the moist coastal forests where Douglas fir thrives. Today the Spallumcheen is mainly farmland and has won a measure of fame with its ploughing competitions.

General Information

Information on the attractions and festivals of the Okanagan and Similkameen: Tourist Association, #104 - 515 Highway 97 South, Kelowna, V1Z 3J2. Phone: 769-5959, 1-800-663-5052, FAX: 492-0237. Specify interests: winery tours, tennis, golf, road maps, skiing, outdoor adventures, fruit stands, camping, fishing, or summer schools for the fine arts.

Information and maps on B.C. parks in the region: Ministry of Parks, Okanagan Lake Parks, Box 399, Summerland, V0H 1Z0. Phone: 494-0321, FAX: 494-9737.

Map and guide to wineries in the Okanagan: British Columbia Wine Institute, #5 - 1864 Spall Rd., Kelowna, V1Y 4R1. Phone: 762-4887 or 1-800-661-2294, FAX: 862-8870.

■ The Similkameen ■

Princeton and Area

Information on the attractions and festivals of Princeton and Hedley: InfoCentre, 57 East, Highway 3, Box 540, Princeton, V0X 1W0. Phone: 295-3103, FAX: 295-3255.

■ Recreational Gold-Panning Reserve: Princeton is ripe with stories of lost gold mines and abandoned gold caches. Some of the creeks that bore gold in pioneer days continue to produce in small amounts up to the present day. Visitors who bring their own pans can slosh the gravel around at a gold-bearing creek set aside as a recreational reserve by the provincial government. No large or automated equipment is allowed.
Location: For information on recreational reserves, contact: Government Agent, P.O. Box 9, Princeton, V0X 1W1.
Information: Government Agent, 295-6957 or 1-800-663-0637;

Public Information Unit of Energy and Mines, 356-2824, for general information.

■ **Cement Factory Remains:** The B.C. Portland Cement factory no longer exists, but back in 1910, when it cost $150,000 to build, it brought great optimism to the region. It closed after less than a year of operation due to a poor financial climate and a lack of limestone and coal. Today the remains of the manufacturing plant and its 7-m-high (23-ft.) walls made of cement and rocks are all set in 44 ha (108 ac.) of meadows and streams. Visitors should register at the Castle Park office on-site, prior to exploring.
Location: Castle Park, east of Princeton. From Highway 5A, turn east on Old Hedley Rd., turn north onto Highway 4, known to locals as Five Mile Rd. Continue about 6 km (4 mi.).
Information: InfoCentre, 295-3103.

■ **Ghost Towns and Ruins:** In its day, Granite City was the third-largest city in British Columbia. It was reputed to have been discovered by cowboy John Chance, who stopped for a drink of water only to stumble upon gold nuggets at the bottom of Granite Creek. Not much of the town is left today, but it is interesting to imagine the 13 saloons, 9 general stores, 2 jewellery stores and the shoemaker's shop that once thrived here. The historic buildings at Coalmont are mostly gone, with the exception of the Coalmont Hotel (circa 1911), still active as a pub. Blakeburn, on the slopes of Lodestone Mountain, was closed in 1940 after a short career as a coal mine. Today visitors can view parts of the old railway system, the open pit mine, and loading chutes. Some of these ghost towns are sure to be refurbished and restored some day, but purists prefer the dilapidated versions.
Location: Granite City, Coalmont, and Blakeburn, Ghost town trails map available through the Princeton InfoCentre, 57 East, Highway 3.
Information: InfoCentre, 295-3103, FAX: 295-3255. Wear sturdy shoes and use common sense.

■ **Hedley and Area:** Rock hounds may find jasper, agate, and opal in the sagebrush hills here. Explorers can see the remains of an historic 3-km (2-mi.) cable tramway used by the Mascot Mine clinging precariously to Lookout Mountain. In the early 1900s, some $47 million in gold was removed; however, the claim was exhausted by the 1930s. The Heritage House at Hedley features displays of mining history and a small garden of drought-resistant plants.
Location: Hedley is about 40 km (24 mi.) east of Princeton; ghost town trails map available through the Princeton InfoCentre, 57 East, Highway 3.
Information: Government Agent, 295-6597, for advice on exploring the ruins of the Mascot mine; Public Information Unit of Energy and Mines, 356-2824, for rock-hounding information. Historic information and rock-hounding suggestions available through Hedley Heritage Arts and Crafts Society, Box 218, Hedley, V0X 1K0.

■ **Princeton and District Pioneer Museum:** Admission by donation. The mining days of Granite Creek live on in Princeton's pioneer museum. On display are examples of Victoriana and artifacts from Chinese gold miners and interior Salish natives. Guided tours may be available; phone ahead.
Location: 167 Vermilion Ave.
Information: Museum, 295-7588.

■ **Forestry Tour:** This tour covers active forestry operations, the spacing of new growth, the care and understanding of the forest at various stages of its development, selective harvesting methods, areas devastated by mountain pine beetle, plantations, naturally regenerated areas, and spaced areas. Transportation is by old school bus. Scheduled tours are held in the summer; phone ahead. Allow 6 hours. A second tour of a sawmill that produces dimensioned lumber is also available; phone ahead. Allow 90 minutes.
Location: Weyerhauser Canada, Old Hedley Road, Princeton. Ask for specific start-point instructions.
Information: 295-3281. Not suitable for persons under the age

of 12. For safety, no open-toed footwear or shorts are allowed, and participants should wear clothing which covers the arms.

■ **Petroglyphs:** Tales of the past are told in Indian rock paintings on the cliffsides here. About 5 to 10 paintings can still be seen along the roadside, but they are disappearing quickly; one seems to represent a hunter shooting a large animal. The Princeton library has a petroglyph map.
Location: Along Old Hedley Rd. from Princeton. The location of petroglyphs and pictographs throughout B.C. is protected due to vandalism; for exact directions, inquire at the local InfoCentre or ask knowledgeable locals.
Information: InfoCentre, 295-3103; Princeton library, 295-6495.

■ **Celebrations:** The "Snooshing" championship in January features "foot-strapped" snowshoeing around an obstacle course and other hilarious winter sports competitions. Other yearly events include Snowfest in February; Spring Fair in March; the Princeton Rodeo in late May, a celebrated Raft Race in July; Horse Racing, June through July; the Princeton Fall Fair in September.
Location: Various venues in and around Princeton.
Information: InfoCentre, 295-3103.

Keremeos

Information on the attractions and festivals of Keremeos:
Seasonal InfoCentre, 415 - 7th Ave., Box 452, Keremeos, V0X 1N0. Phone: 499-5225, FAX: 499-2252.

■ **Fruit Stands:** The area surrounding Keremeos has earned the title: "Fruit Stand Capital of Canada." Springtime brings in the first tender sprigs of freshly picked asparagus. Summer starts off with plump cherries, continues with perky apricots, progresses to luscious peaches and ends with crisp apples. Stop at one of the dozens of fruit stands here and browse for honey, fruit syrups, cider and fresh produce. Especially notable is fresh-squeezed cherry juice in season. Not quite free, but worth it.

Location: Various venues along Highway 3 and 3A. Maps of fruit stand locations are published in the Okanagan-Similkameen tourist booklet distributed through Okanagan InfoCentres.

Information: InfoCentre, 499-5225.

■ **Keremeos Museum:** Admission by donation. Displays here focus on photographs and reminders of the former provincial police force that kept order in the early rough and tumble days of gold mining. There are also pioneer artifacts and mementos of native Indian history. Open June through August or by arrangement; phone ahead.

Location: 6th Ave. and 6th St.

Information: 499-5802.

■ **Grist Mill Walking Tour:** Small admission. This flour mill was established in 1877, served the ranching community here for almost 20 years, producing flour from wheat that was grown in the Similkameen Valley, and is now the scene of a total "history" experience. During the summer, animators in historic costume illustrate the water-powered equipment and show visitors what life was like in the 1870s. The mill's own flour is available in the gift shop. Visitors can stroll through an orchard and vegetable garden. The site is restored and managed by British Columbia Heritage Trust.

Location: Upper Bench Rd., beside Keremeos Creek.

Information: Grist Mill, 499-2888.

■ **St. Lazlo Estate Winery:** Estate wineries are dedicated to improving the flavour of B.C. wines and lead in producing "specialty" products from particular varieties of grapes. The winemaker here maintains that the Similkameen produces just as good or better white wines than any European country. Guided tours are held year-round; tastings and retail store hours vary seasonally.

Location: Take Highway 3A out of Keremeos and turn east on Richter Pass Rd. Ask for exact directions before heading out.

Information: 499-2856, FAX: 499-5600.

■ **Celebrations:** One of the highlights of the year is the Chopka Rodeo on Easter weekend that features, not professional competitors, but real "working" cowboys. Other yearly events include a Craft Show in March; Elks Rodeo, Indian Pow Wow at Ashnola on the May long weekend; All-Indian Rodeo in June; B.C. Softball Championships in late June; Lion's Community Picnic and Fun Day in August.

Location: Various venues in and around Keremeos.

Information: InfoCentre, 499-5225.

■ The Okanagan ■

Osoyoos

Information on the attractions and festivals of Osoyoos: InfoCentre, Junction of Highways 3 and 97, Box 227, Osoyoos, V0H 1V0. Phone: 495-7142, FAX: 495-6161.

■ **Fernandes Banana Farm:** Small admission. The sweet, tree-ripened bananas of this indoor banana farm, originally started as a hobby, are sold along with pieces of sugar cane. Unfortunately, the owner does not wear a panama hat and a white suit, but is more often seen in overalls or blue jeans. Guided group tours require a fee.

Location: On the east side of Osoyoos, on Highway 3, 1 km (.6 mi.) east of the Highway 97 junction.
Information: 495-6678.

■ **Mount Kobau Stargazing:** "Heavens Above" is the name of an annual international star-gazing party held in August. But amateur astronomers can scan the starry skies from the tip of the highest peak in the Okanagan-Similkameen on any clear night of the year. Drive your car almost to the top, park in the lot provided, then it's a 10-minute walk to a "star-watching" tower. No telescopes are provided.
Location: 11 km (7 mi.) west of Osoyoos. Ask for exact location at the InfoCentre.
Information: InfoCentre, 495-7142.

■ **Pocket Desert Ecological Reserve:** Nicknamed the "vest-pocket desert," this area is an arid strip of land that records the lowest rainfall in British Columbia. During the last 100 years, the Okanagan has been systematically irrigated and altered. This dry portion of remaining desert is a Federal Ecological Reserve with species rarely seen elsewhere in Canada: prickly pear cactus, antelope bushes, and the world's smallest hummingbird—the calliope. An active burrowing owl re-establishment program is underway and turkey vultures can sometimes be sighted. The prickly pear cactus blooms in June and July. Removal of wildlife, vegetation, rocks, or soil is strictly prohibited.
Location: On the northeast side of Lake Osoyoos, 7.5 km (5 mi.) north of Osoyoos. Ask at the InfoCentre for the best route to enter the desert. Note: the sand dunes are part of the Osoyoos Indian Reservation and permission must be obtained to enter the Inkameep Campsite and beyond.
Information: InfoCentre, 495-7142, FAX: 495-6161; Osoyoos Indian Band Office, 498-4906.

■ **Spotted Lake:** The muds which make up this unusual lake contain epsom salts, calcium, magnesium, and trace minerals. In summer, evaporation creates white mineral-salt circles on the lake bed as the water dries out. The natives named the oddity *klikuk,* meaning "medicine lake," and warring enemies were known to

come here to soothe their wounds. Even today the minerals are reputed to relieve aches and pains. Good photographs can be obtained from the vantage point of the road. The area is privately owned; do not trespass.
Location: Visible from Highway 3, 9 km (6 mi.) west of Osoyoos, along Richter Pass Rd.
Information: InfoCentre, 496-7142.

■ **Osoyoos District Arts Centre:** During the winter, the arts council sponsors Class Acts; a program of comedy, music and drama. In the summer, buskers perform at the centre and in the surrounding area. All year round, there are art shows mounted by local and regional artists, as well as other cultural presentations. Phone for a list of events.
Location: Located in the Cultural Centre on Main St. North.
Information: 495-7142.

■ **Osoyoos Museum:** Admission by donation. The displays here include preserved bird specimens, native artifacts, and some historic photographs. The facility also features the archives of the B.C. Provincial Police, a force that kept order in the early days of the province. Its central exhibit is a liquor-making still said to be one of the few intact stills on display anywhere. Guided tours may be available; phone ahead.
Location: In Community Park.
Information: 495-6723.

■ **Haynes Point Interpretive Programs:** Presentations are held in the summer here in a natural amphitheatre. A park naturalist conducts public programs explaining wildlife, plants, and the sagebrush and sand features of the area; phone for current programs.
Location: On Highway 97, a few kilometres north of the U.S. border.
Information: B.C. Parks Okanagan District, 494-0321.

■ **Windmill Tour:** Token admission for the guided tour. This building is a full-sized replica of a Dutch windmill copied by a Dutch couple from an old-country original. The tour covers the process of milling wheat into flour.
Location: Beside Highway 3, .5 km (.3 mi.) east of town.
Information: 495-7818.

■ **Celebrations:** Annual events include the Warm Water Open, a water-ski and leisure tournament in May; Horse racing, Osoyoos Lake Sailing Regatta in June; Canada Day Celebrations, Cherry Fiesta in early July; International Power Boat Races on Labour Day.
Location: Various venues in Osoyoos.
Information: InfoCentre, 495-7142, FAX: 495-6161.

Oliver

Information on the attractions and festivals of Oliver:
InfoCentre, CPR Station, 93rd St., Box 460, Oliver, V0H 1T0.
Phone: 498-6321, FAX: 498-3156.

■ **Vaseux Lake Wildlife and Bird Sanctuary:** The area features trails, bird-watching blinds, and the opportunity to glimpse a herd of California bighorn sheep. There is no visitor's centre. The shallow, weed-filled lake, bordered by sandy beaches, is one of the best places in Canada to sight migrating bird species. Sightings include: the white-throated swift, the white-headed woodpecker, and the canyon wren. Wildlife is protected under the Federal Wildlife Sanctuary Program.
Location: 16 km (10 mi.) north of Oliver.
Information: InfoCentre, 498-6321, FAX: 498-3156.

■ **Oliver Heritage Museum:** Admission by donation. Outside the museum is a preserved jailhouse. Exhibits inside include interpretive displays and specimens from the nearby pocket desert, as well as artifacts and photographs from the era of early mining. Guided tours may be available; phone ahead.
Location: 106 West 6th Ave.
Information: 498-4027.

■ **Brights Wines:** Occupying arid land leased from the Osoyoos Indian Band, the new $2-million facility was constructed in 1981 by the band and now employs many band members. One of Canada's oldest companies will take visitors through the process of winemaking to illustrate how research programs have resulted in an award-winning cellar. Brights emphasizes an understanding of the quality of the grapes and the micro-climates around the lakes which produce them. Guided tours from May to September every opening hour starting at 10:00 a.m. on selected days; phone ahead. Guided tours from October through April by appointment; tastings and retail store hours vary seasonally.
Location: Drive 6 km (4 mi.) north of Oliver on Highway 97. Watch for signs.
Information: 498-4981, FAX: 498-6505.

■ **Gehringer Brothers Estate Winery:** Several variables determine the quality of a given wine in a given year: the pruning of the vines, the suitability of the soil for optimal nourishment, the relative amounts of sunshine and rainfall, the timing of the harvest, the precision and skill of the wine-making process, and the storage of the immature wine. This winery specializes in making clear, clean-tasting wine by carefully analyzing the grape and using stainless-steel tanks. Established in 1981, with their first vintage 1985, they have been consistent medal winners. They have no agents or distributors and are strictly a family operation. Guided tours are held year-round by appointment; tastings and retail store hours vary seasonally.

Location: Drive 4 km (2.5 mi.) south of Oliver Highway 97, then west on Road 8. Watch for signs.
Information: 498-3537, FAX: 498-3510.

■ **Inkameep (Grape) Vineyards:** Wine grapes and juice are for sale here during September and October. Depending upon the timing, visitors can learn about growing, spacing, culling, pruning or harvesting grapes at vineyards operated by members of the Osoyoos Indian Band. Grapes must be protected from sudden temperature drops, particularly in the evening; the lake here acts as a modifying influence on temperature shifts. Visitors should phone ahead to be certain to be allowed on the property. Allow 90 minutes.
Location: Drive north on Highway 97 and turn east on Tuc El Nuit Dr.
Information: 498-3552.

■ **Okanagan-Similkameen Cooperative Growers Association Packing House Tour:** "Soft" fruits such as cherries and peaches are packed from June 15 to the beginning of September; apples or "hard" fruits are packed to the end of October. This tour of Oliver's packing house covers the arrival of the fruit by truck, the unloading and identification of the grower and the process by which fruits are pregraded, presized, and placed in bins. An automatic packing system places fruits in tray packs and a second packaging line is used for special packaging requirements. Guided tours are available in summer; phone ahead. Groups only may request an apple-packing tour year-round. Allow 1 hour.
Location: East 9th St. Ask for start point directions.
Information: 498-3491. For safety, no open-toed footwear or shorts are allowed, and participants should wear clothing which covers the arms.

■ **Okanagan Vineyards Estate Winery:** A truly meritorious wine will specify both the vineyard of origin and the year of the vintage; ask about this winery's finest wines. These wine-makers say that British Columbia is on its way to opening up a new chapter not only within Canada but within the global wine industry. Guided tours are held in season by appointment; phone ahead. Tastings and retail store hours vary seasonally.

Location: Drive 5 km (3 mi.) south of Oliver on Highway 97, turn west on Road 11. Watch for signs. **Address:** R.R. 1, S24, C5, Oliver, V0H 1T0. **Information:** 498-6663, FAX: 498-4566.

■ **McIntyre Bluff Pictographs:** Native pictographs and undeciphered hieroglyphics can be viewed on the rock faces in this area; symbols depict both human and animal profiles. Access is on foot, about a 10-km (6-mi.) hike. **Location:** South end of Vaseux Lake. McIntyre Canyon is located 3 km (2 mi.) beyond Vaseux Lake campsite, south of Okanagan Falls on Highway 97. The location of petroglyphs and pictographs throughout B.C. is protected due to vandalism; for exact directions, inquire at the local InfoCentre or ask knowledgeable locals. **Information:** InfoCentre, 498-6321, FAX: 498-3156.

■ **Celebrations:** Oliver sponsors several festivals and special events, including Blossom Time, April through May; Fairview Mining Heritage Days in June; School of Baseball, July to August; Wine Festivals from September to October; Alpenfest wine and German sausage-tasting in October. **Location:** Various venues, Oliver. **Information:** 498-6321, FAX: 498-3156.

Okanagan Falls ("O.K." Falls)

Information on the attractions and festivals of Okanagan Falls: Use the Oliver InfoCentre: CPR Station, 93rd St., Box 460, Oliver, V0H 1T0. Phone: 498-6321, FAX: 498-3156.

■ **Basset House Museum:** Admission by donation. The pioneer Basset family furnished their dream home from the 1909 Eaton's catalogue. Today the house

sits on its original site overlooking Skaha Lake and consists of one level with a living room, kitchen, 2 bedrooms and no bathroom. Its furnishings are restored to original condition. It is said that the first whites to winter over (Hudson's Bay Co. scouts) were reduced to eating their dogs. Skaha, a beautiful, blue, deep-water lake, was originally named Dog Lake; Okanagan Falls was first called Dogtown. The Shuswap native name, *skaha,* sounds prettier, but is simply translated as "dog." Limited opening hours. Guided tours may be available; phone ahead.
Location: South end of Okanagan Falls on Highway 97.
Information: Residence of curator, 497-5205.

■ **Astrophysical Radio Telescope Observatory Tour:** The huge radio telescopes located here gather minute waves from deep space and assemble data on the stars. Signs in the Visitor Centre explain the functioning of radio telescopes and why they are set up at this point on the earth. Self-guided tours take the form of recorded messages that move visitors through the outdoor facility. Guided tours are held Sunday afternoons in summer; phone ahead. Operated by the National Research Council of Canada as part of the Herzberg Institute of Astrophysics.
Location: Take Highway 97 south of Penticton, about 1.6 km (1 mi.) past the 3A junction, and turn right at White Lake Rd. Follow the signs.
Information: 493-7505.

■ **Le Comte Estate Winery:** Many wines are named for the type of grape from which they are pressed: Riesling, Pinot Noir, Zinfandel. Unless the point of origin of such wines is specified, these terms have little meaning, as the same type of grape grown in different locales will produce very different wines. This winery will tell visitors many more interesting facts about grapes and wine. Guided tours are scheduled 3 times a day, July to October; phone ahead. Tours off-season by appointment; tastings and retail store hours vary seasonally.
Location: Take Green Lake Rd. for 5 km (3 mi.) southwest of Okanagan Falls. Watch for signs and turn before crossing the bridge.

Address: P.O. Box 498, Okanagan Falls, V0H 1R0.
Information: 497-8267, FAX: 497-8267.

■ **Dried Fruit Product Demonstration:** This company processes fresh fruit into a dried fruit leather called Sunshine Kids Fruit Snacks. Visitors watch a video, then view the factory from a safe distance. Based on an ancient method of preserving food, this drying and rolling process has been reinvented and commercialized in an era of increased health consciousness. Demonstrations are held at regular intervals; sampling and gift shop 9:00 a.m. to 5:00 p.m., 7 days a week in season. Allow 15 minutes.
Location: O.K. Dried Fruits Ltd., 1406 Maple St.
Information: 497-8051.

■ **Wild Goose Farm-Gate Winery:** Modern wine-making methods here specify the use of glass-lined or stainless-steel tanks and substitute strains of cultured yeasts for the random yeasts normally present at harvest. Guided tours are welcome year-round by appointment; tastings and retail store hours vary seasonally.
Location: From Okanagan Falls, take 10th Ave., turn south on Maple St., and west on Sun Valley Way.
Information: 497-8919.

Penticton and Area

Information on the attractions and festivals of Penticton: InfoCentre, Jubilee Pavilion, 185 Lakeshore Dr., Penticton, V2A 1B7. Phone: 492-4103, 1-800-663-5020; FAX: 492-6119.

■ **Floating Channel:** A 6-km (4-mi.) man-made channel meanders between Skaha Lake and Okanagan Lake. Bring an inner tube and slowly roll along with the gentle current on any sunny afternoon. Allow 2 hours for the float. As there is no public transportation in the area, the trick is to return to your vehicle without walking. Participants can either arrange for a friend to pick them up, or check with Coyote Cruises, 215 Riverside Dr., phone 492-2115. For a fee, they rent inner tubes and provide transportation back.

Location: Water channel pathway, between Okanagan and Skaha lakes.

Information: InfoCentre, 1-800-663-5052, 492-4103, FAX: 492-6119.

■ **Munson's Mountain:** The Ogopogo has been the subject of intense searches. In 1991, a film crew from Japan brought over high-tech underwater equipment to film the monster's lair. They apparently spotted the beast immediately upon setting up but were unable to repeat the electronic sightings on a second visit. Said to be related to the Loch Ness monster, these giant creatures may be left over from prehistoric times. From this 16-ha (40-ac.) undeveloped park and viewpoint, the city and lake are spread out below. This is said to be a good place to hunt for the elusive Ogopogo. Bring binoculars.

Location: Road access from the corner of Middle Bench Rd. and Munson Ave.

Information: InfoCentre, 1-800-663-5052, 492-4103, FAX: 492 6119.

■ **Analemmatic Timepiece:** Designed by Vancouver sculptor Gwen Boyle, this "do-it-yourself" timepiece is on display outdoors. Visitors stand on the platform and the sun and shadows do the rest; the sculpture is said to be the world's largest sundial.

Location: Situated at Skaha Lake beach by the concession stand.

Information: InfoCentre, 492-4103, FAX: 492-6119.

■ **Leir House Cultural Centre:** Admission by donation. This heritage house was built in 1927 and in its day accommodated a family of 11 offspring. It is now used for local arts and crafts displays, music and theatre recitals, and is home to the Okanagan Summer School of the Arts; classes are held in piano, opera, and various artistic pursuits. Visitors can drop in and browse through the art gallery and small museum year-round. Guided tours may be available; phone ahead.

Location: 220 Manor Park Ave.

Information: Okanagan Summer School of the Arts, 493-0390; Leir House Museum, 492-7997.

■ **R.N. Atkinson Museum:** Admission by donation. Displays here include Interior Salish native artifacts and pioneer memorabilia, plus a collection of taxidermy specimens and military mementos. The taxidermy collection is said to be the largest in Canada and features large animals such as a grizzly bear, moose, and bobcat, as well as small specimens such as the fetus of a kangaroo. Travelling displays from the Royal British Columbia Museum complement the permanent displays. The museum is part of a community arts centre and library complex. Guided tours may be available; phone ahead. Allow 2 hours. **Location:** 785 Main St., across from the Penticton High School. **Information:** 492-6025.

■ **SS *Sicamous*:** Admission by donation. The SS *Sicamous,* a retired sternwheeler that plied the waters of Okanagan Lake, was retired in 1935 and beached here in 1954. Inside, interpretive displays outline the boat's history. To take a good photograph of the sternwheeler, head along the beach to the Kiwanis Walking Pier opposite the vessel, or walk to the adjacent rose garden. **Location:** Riverside Park and Riverside Dr., on the west end of Lake Okanagan. **Information:** InfoCentre, 492-4103, FAX: 492-6119.

■ **South Okanagan Art Gallery:** This gallery is reputed to be the only passive solar art gallery in North America. Skylights have been strategically placed to illuminate selected art with natural light and the gallery is warmed by a solar heating system. Lectures, workshops, and demonstrations held on a regular basis are designed to give an understanding of art materials as well as an appreciation of the end product; phone ahead. Afternoon tea is served Saturday and Sunday from 2:00 to 4:00 p.m. As a fundraiser for the gallery, during the annual Ironman Biathlon in August, athletes are recruited as models and participants bid on tee-shirts acquired from sports competitions around the world. **Location:** 11 Ellis St., on the shore of Okanagan Lake. **Information:** 493-2928.

■ **Cartier Wines:** This commercial winery produces a "private label" wine for customers in addition to its other vintages. Guided tours are scheduled three times a day in July and August and once a day from September to June; phone ahead. Group visits are welcome by appointment year-round. Tastings and retail store hours vary seasonally.
Location: 2210 Main St.
Information: 492-0621, FAX: 492-6990.

■ **Hillside Cellars Farm-Gate Winery:** The winemaker here is interested in developing wines and in promoting a regional cuisine to accompany B.C. wines. Guided tours are welcome year-round by appointment; phone ahead. Tastings and retail store hours vary seasonally.
Location: 1350 Naramata Rd.
Information: Phone or FAX: 493-4424.

■ **Lang Farm-Gate Vineyards:** Winery owners have their own special ideas about which grapes to grow and how to bring out the best in their own hillside. Additionally, wineries periodically change their vintages to reflect shifts in consumer taste. A few years ago red wines were popular, but in the last two decades there has been a trend away from the reds to whites and now to varieties of white so light they are compared to alcoholic soda pop. This winery will answer questions about their wines and future trends in the industry. Guided tours are welcome year-round by appointment; tastings and retail store hours vary seasonally.
Location: 2493 Gammon Rd., Naramata.
Information: 496-5987, FAX: 496-5706.

■ **Boar-raising Ranch:** This ranch raises gourmet wild game products, uses no commercial feeds or medication and produces an "authentically finished" game product. Their specialty is European wild boar, ancestor of present breeds of domestic pigs. Their gamey taste is considered very desirable. Occasionally, demonstrations are held during which participants can determine the difference in taste between the female sow and the male boar; phone ahead for times.

Location: Surprise Ranch, R.R. 2, Oliver. Take Highway 97. Drive for about 20 minutes south of Penticton. Turn on White Lake Rd.
Information: 498-2698.

■ **Celebrations:** Yearly events include Penticton Mid-Winter Breakout in February; B.C. International Highland Games, Okanagan Summer School of the Arts (493-0390), Big Peach Festival, Jaycees Raft Race in July; Ironman Canada Triathlon, a grueling 17-hour competition, Canadian Square-Dance Jamboree in August; Okanagan Harvest and Grape Fiesta from September to October.
Location: Various venues in and around Penticton and Okanagan Falls.
Information: InfoCentre, 492-4103, FAX: 492-6119. Applications for the Ironman Triathlon competition: 522 Dawson Ave., Penticton, V2A 3N8. Phone: 490-8787, FAX: 490-8788.

■ **Scenic Bike Ride:** For an activity that is out of the ordinary, ride a bike along an old rail bed, across 16 breathtaking railway trestles and through the tunnels of the historic Kettle Valley Railway (no longer operative). The railroad ties have been removed in several places and the grade is relatively gentle. Participants start at Chute Lake and travel through the Myra Canyon as far as Ruth Station at Naramata. This stretch of railway was used in the CBC production of "The National Dream" for its spectacular scenery and heart-stopping views atop the trestles. For a fee, organized group tours and bike rentals are also available. Allow 2 to 3 hours for the ride.
Location: Start point details and maps from the InfoCentre.
Information: Mountain bike tour, 493-4662; InfoCentre, 492-4103, FAX: 492-6119.

Summerland and Peachland

Information on the attractions and festivals of Summerland and Peachland: InfoCentre, CNR Highway 97 and Thompson Rd., P.O. Box 1075, Summerland, V0H 1Z0. Phone: 494-2686, FAX: 494-4039.

■ **Giant's Head Park and Mountain:** This rock formation was once an active volcano. Its outline resembles the profile of a man and the mountain lends its image to Summerland's coat of arms: mountains encircled by sunflowers and the motto, "A Giant in Stature." From the top is a panoramic viewpoint of the lake with interpretive signs explaining each portion of the 360-degree view. Under the cairn is a time capsule scheduled to be opened in 2067.
Location: Near Highway 97, Summerland.
Information: InfoCentre, 494-2686.

■ **Trout Hatchery:** For many years natural trout populations were able to reproduce on their own, but today hundreds of lakes are dependent upon hatchery stock. Visitors first see maps and interpretive posters, then go downstairs to view the trough-room where fry are present from September to December. Outside, large ponds teem with fingerlings until they are liberated in April and May. Guided tours may be available; phone ahead. Allow 1 hour. Operated by the B.C. Ministry of the Environment.
Location: 13405 South Lakeshore Dr., Summerland.
Information: 494-0491.

■ **Eight-Sided Church and Museum:** Admission by donation. Built in 1910, this former Baptist Church now contains historic photos of orchard development in the region. Guided tours may be available; phone ahead.
Location: 5890 Beach Ave.
Information: InfoCentre, 767-3441.

■ **Silver Lake Forestry Centre:** This Visitor's Centre familiarizes the public with the practice of forestry. On display are artifacts from the pioneering era of forestry and interpretive displays on the story of logging, tree harvesting, and forest-fire fighting

in B.C. Open May to October, dawn to dusk. Sponsored by the B.C. Forestry Association.
Location: Drive Highway 97 west of Peachland for 16 km (10 mi.). Follow directional signs.
Information: 860-6410.

■ **Summerland Museum:** Admission by donation. On display here is a collection of pioneer memorabilia, small farming implements, some of the early equipment used on the old "canning" lines, and historic photographs. There is also an interpretive display of the former railway station and its telegraph equipment. Guided tours may be available; phone ahead.
Location: 9521 Wharton St., Summerland.
Information: 494-9395.

■ **A&H Farm-Gate Vineyards:** In Germany, travelling from vineyard to vineyard and sampling wine is known as "finding God in the grape." The story goes that since the vineyards were once tended by monks, the more pure the monks, the better the wine. Visitors who constantly sample wines are merely attempting to ascertain the "holiness" of the monks who work these fields. While monks do not work the fields here, visitors to the Okanagan do seek to expand their knowledge of the grape and this winery is available for testing. Guided tours are welcome year-round by appointment; tastings and retail store hours vary seasonally.
Location: Take Highway 97 north. Turn west on Trepanier Bench Rd. Follow directional signs.
Information: 767-9250.

■ **Agricultural Research Station Tour:** Established in 1914, this facility does research into the improvement of more than 100 varieties of fruits and vegetables. A short video outlines research on pesticide management, tree fruits, wine grapes, soils, and the breeding of fruits; visitors then tour the labs, food-processing pilot plant, and growth chambers, where research is monitored. Allow 1 hour to this point in the tour. Finally, visitors are ushered into ornamental gardens and a manicured picnic area that includes a small interpretive display for those who wish more information; it is suggested that visitors bring a picnic lunch. A scheduled tour for the public is held once a day during July and August; phone ahead. Groups should phone ahead for an appointment. Operated by the Federal Department of Agriculture.

Location: Take Highway 97 south to the Trout Creek Bridge; follow signs.

Information: Agricultural Research Station, 494-7711.

■ **Chateau St. Claire Estate Winery:** Estate wineries seek to be leaders in improving the quality of British Columbia wines through the careful choice of grapes; this was B.C.'s first estate winery. Guided tours three times a day in season; phone ahead. Tastings and retail store hours vary seasonally.

Location: Take Highway 97 north. Turn west on Trepanier Bench Rd. Follow directional signs.

Information: Phone or FAX: 767-3113.

■ **Hainle Vineyards Estate Winery:** Featuring dry wines and "ice wine," a very light wine, this winery focuses on a taste as pure, unobtrusive, and natural as possible. Light wines have become increasingly fashionable in the '90s, adding a new dimension to white wines. Guided tours are welcome year-round by appointment; tastings and retail store hours vary seasonally.

Location: Drive Highway 97 north. Turn west on Trepanier Bench Rd. Follow directional signs.

Information: 767-2525, FAX: 767-2525.

■ **Sumac Ridge Estate Winery:** The B.C. Wine Institute today supports the best of home-grown wines with a black and gold label which reads "VQA" for "Vintners Quality Assurance." This winery is just one of several wineries which qualifies for the label. It features a restaurant which is open for lunch. Guided tours three times daily from late May to early October; phone ahead. Guided tours from October through April by appointment; tastings and retail store hours vary seasonally.

Location: On the west side of Highway 97, just north of Summerland.

Information: 494-0451, FAX: 494-3456.

■ **Syrup and Jam-Making Demonstration:** This manufacturer produces fruit candy, fruity pancake syrups, gourmet jams, and wine pulp. Visitors start with a video that outlines the history of fruit growing in the Okanagan, see the machinery and operations on the plant floor, and move into a tasting room to sample products. Scheduled viewings are held in the summer; group visits are welcome year-round by appointment. Allow 45 minutes.
Location: Summerland Sweets, 6206 Canyon View Dr., Summerland.
Information: 494-0377. For safety, no open-toed footwear is allowed.

■ **Celebrations:** Yearly events include the Junior Hockey Tournament in April; Summerland Junior Horse Show in May; Art Club Council Show, Action Athletic Festival, Okanagan Express Relay Runners Race, Man of Steel Family Triathlon, 4 WD Mud Bog Contest in June; Canada Day Celebrations (Peachland), Soap Box Derby, Trail Horse Rider's Rodeo (Summerland) in July; Invitational Regatta in August; Summerland Fall Fair, Peachland Fall Fair on Labour Day; Hallowe'en Spooktacular (Summerland) on October 31.
Location: Various venues in Summerland and Peachland.
Information: InfoCentre, 494-2686, FAX: 494-4039.

Westbank

Information on the attractions and festivals of Westbank:
Seasonal InfoCentre, 2375 Pamela Rd., Box 571, Westbank, V0H 2A0. Phone: 768-3378, FAX: 768-3465.

■ **Mission Hill Wines:** Since its establishment in 1981, Mission Hill has won over 200 national and international awards and is interested in small releases of wine made from particularly notable grapes. One of its wines, Semillon, has been chosen for inclusion on the Canadian ambassadorial wine list. In

addition to the process of making wine, the tour guide may demonstrate the proper technique of "tasting." The setting features a panoramic view of the valley. Families are welcome here; bring a picnic lunch. Guided tours are scheduled twice a day, April to Victoria Day and hourly from Victoria Day to October; phone ahead. Off-season tours by appointment; tastings and retail store hours vary seasonally.
Location: Drive Highway 97 south of Kelowna or north of Westbank. Turn east on Hudson Rd., south on Bouchere Rd., then west on Mission Hill Rd. Follow the signs.
Information: 768-5125 for general information; 768-7611 for group tour bookings; FAX: 768-2044.

■ **Quail's Gate Estate Winery:** Wine is classified into three broad categories: table wines that are consumed mainly with meals; sparkling wines that are distinguishable by their effervescence and often consumed on festive occasions; and fortified wines, such as sherry or vermouth, that have been altered by the addition of grape-distilled brandy and are usually drunk after meals. Many more interesting facts about wine may be discussed during a tour at this winery. Guided tours every hour on the half hour, May through August; phone ahead. Off-season tours by appointment; evening tours also available by appointment. Tastings and retail store hours vary seasonally.
Location: Drive Highway 97 south of Kelowna or north of Westbank. Turn east on Hudson Rd., then south on Bouchere Rd.
Information: 769-4451, FAX: 769-3451.

Kelowna

Information on the attractions and festivals of Kelowna: InfoCentre, 544 Harvey Ave., Kelowna, V1Y 6C9. Phone: 861-1515, 1-800-663-4345, FAX: 861-3624.

Information on programs, tours, and educational publications on regional forests: British Columbia Forestry Association, #105 -2417 Highway 97 North, Kelowna, V1X 4J2. Phone: 860-6410. FAX: 860-8856.

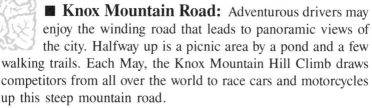 ■ **Knox Mountain Road:** Adventurous drivers may enjoy the winding road that leads to panoramic views of the city. Halfway up is a picnic area by a pond and a few walking trails. Each May, the Knox Mountain Hill Climb draws competitors from all over the world to race cars and motorcycles up this steep mountain road.
Location: Access from the north end of Ellis St.
Information: InfoCentre, 861-1515.

■ **Kokanee Salmon Run:** The kokanee is a unique species of salmon that long ago became trapped inland and has no exit to the sea. The species has adapted its lifestyle to preclude the need for salt water. Migrating kokanee can be seen at Sutherland Hill Regional Park, in a major spawning stream complete with a fish ladder to assist returning adults to their spawning beds. College students hired by the regional park periodically provide commentary on the run in season; phone for details. Best times: mid-September to mid-October.
Location: In Rutland, along Mission Creek. Access off Springfield and Benvoulin Rd.
Information: InfoCentre, 861-1515; North Okanagan Regional District, 545-5368.

■ **B.C. Orchard Industry Museum:** Admission by donation. Housed in a 1917 building originally used as a fruit-packing house, the exhibits tell about the story of orchard development. The refurbished brick building was opened in 1989 to coincide with the 100th anniversary of the B.C. Fruit Growers Association, the 50th Anniversary of B.C. Tree Fruits, and the 75th Anniversary of the Summerland Agricultural Research Station. Visitors can see a large model of a railway, displays on the cultivation of fruit, interpretive displays, artifacts from the valley's first farmers, and the general history of the fruit industry. Guided tours may be available; phone ahead.

Location: 1304 Ellis St.; located in the historic Laurel Packing House.
Information: 763-0433.

■ **Benvoulin Church:** Admission by donation. The Earl and Countess of Aberdeen lived in Kelowna for a time near the end of the 1800s and were convinced of the area's potential to be a major fruit-producing region. An enduring testimony to the community spirit of the Countess of Aberdeen is this very small wooden church, constructed around 1892 to provide a spiritual home for local Presbyterians. This well-proportioned church with pews arranged in a typical curved style is now the oldest standing church in Kelowna. Visit during daylight hours, except when it is in use for weddings.
Location: 2279 Benvoulin Rd.
Information: InfoCentre, 861-1515.

■ **Father Pandosy Mission:** Admission by donation. Father Pandosy, a pioneer Oblate priest, ministered to natives and whites for over 30 years until his death in 1891. His log mission, with its church, school, farm, and orchard, was established in 1860 and formed the first white settlement in the Okanagan Valley; there is some controversy as to whether he is buried here. The site has been restored to its original condition. Groups should phone ahead for an appointment. Nearby are several stands that sell fruits and vegetables straight from the orchards and farms.
Location: Benvoulin and Casorso roads.
Information: InfoCentre, 861-1515; Father Pandosy Mission, 860-8369.

■ **Guisachan Heritage House:** This century-old India-style colonial house was owned by English royalty, the Earl and Countess of Aberdeen. They were sponsors of the first serious attempts to turn Kelowna's land into fruit orchards and the Earl later went on to become Canada's governor general. Visitors can see the grounds and house exterior, now in use as a restaurant.
Location: 1060 Cameron Ave.
Information: 862-9368.

■ **Kelowna Centennial Museum and Art Gallery:** Admission by donation. This museum recalls a time when there

were no highways here, and the flow of people and goods was all in the direction of lakes—the natural transportation corridors. There is a display about an historic hotel and a model of the landmark Kelowna floating bridge and its engineering specifications. The art gallery, located in the same building, chronicles the lifestyles of the Okanagan through works painted mainly by regional artists. Guided tours may be available; phone ahead. Presentations at the gallery are held at regular intervals; inquire in advance.
Location: 470 Queensway.
Information: Museum, 763-2417; Kelowna Art Gallery, 762-2226.

■ **Calona Wines:** This is the most-awarded winery in B.C. Established in 1932, the largest commercial winery in western Canada is a pioneer in wine-making in this valley. Guided tours every hour daily, commencing at 9:00 a.m., from late May to early October; guided tours from October through April, 3 times per day; phone ahead. Tastings and retail store hours vary seasonally.
Location: 1125 Richter St.
Information: 762-3332, FAX: 762-2999.

■ **Cedar Creek Estate Winery:** This winery is found in a picture-book setting within a white stucco, flat-roofed building reminiscent of California architecture. The lovely view of Lake Okanagan is an added bonus. Guided tours on the hour from April through October; phone ahead. Guided tours from November through March by appointment. Tastings and retail store hours vary seasonally.
Location: 5445 Lakeshore Rd; located 12 km (7 mi.) south from downtown Kelowna. Take Pandosy St., which becomes Lakeshore Rd., and watch for signs.
Information: 764-8866, FAX: 764-2603.

■ **Gray Monk Cellars Estate Winery:** This multi-award-winning estate winery specializes in producing varietals from several types of grapes. Guided tours vary seasonally; phone ahead. Tastings and retail store hours also vary seasonally.

Location: Take Highway 97 in the direction of Winfield. Just south of Winfield take Okanagan Centre Rd. Turn west on Camp Rd. Follow the signs.

Information: 766-3168, FAX: 766-3390.

■ **Distillery Tour:** Located on a well-groomed 85-ha (210-ac.) site, this is the second-largest distillery complex in Canada, second only to its mother plant in Ontario. The tour covers the blending process, then moves from the bottling plant to the automatic warehouse. Visitors can see the oak barrels which are still a vital part of the aging process. Scheduled tours are held in the summer; phone ahead. Allow 2 hours. Pre-booking is recommended.

Location: Hiram Walker; travel 5 km (3 mi.) north of the airport, take Jim Bailey Rd. in Winfield.

Information: General information, 766-2431; group tours, 766-5805. Tour not available for those 12 and under. For safety, no open-toed footwear or shorts are allowed, and participants should wear clothing that covers the arms.

■ **Okanagan Mountain Park Interpretive Program and Bike Trails:** This wilderness park encompasses more than 10,000 ha (24,700 ac.). There is no internal road network, so the park can retain its relatively wild state. Sheer cliffs, granite ridges, deep canyons, and spring-fed mountain lakes are set against dry grasses on open slopes. The wild horses are gone, but the arid ground does support deer, elk, mountain goats, cougars, bobcats, coyote and the odd rattlesnake. The park is recommended for mountain bikes; horses are allowed on designated trails. Guided walking tours for different levels of expertise are held periodically throughout the summer; phone ahead.

Location: At the end of Lakeshore Rd.

Information: B.C. Parks, 494-0321, FAX: 494-9737.

■ **Sawmill and Plywood Plant Tour:** This tour covers the operation of a plant that produces lumber mainly used in the new-home-building industry. On site is a second facility that produces plywood sheets. Guided tours are available in summer; phone ahead.

Location: Riverside Forest Products, 820 Guy St.

Information: 762-3411. Not suitable for persons under the age of

12. For safety, no open-toed footwear or shorts are allowed, and participants should wear clothing that covers the arms.

■ **Fruit-Juice Plant Tour:** Owned for many decades by a cooperative of fruit growers, this manufacturing plant produces juices, cocktails, nectars, apple sauce, "sparklers"—carbonated juices—and granola bars. Visitors begin with a video and taste a sample, followed by a look at the active manufacturing floor. Guided tours are available; phone ahead.
Location: Sun Rype Products, 1165 Ethel St.
Information: 860-7973, FAX: 762-3611.

■ **Truck Manufacturing Tour:** Hundreds of local people are involved in the manufacture of specialty trucks. The tour follows the manufacturing process starting with the chassis, followed by the addition of rear and front axles, the engine, cab, wiring, and the optional sleeper cab. These powerful vehicles are used as hauling trucks, dump trucks, or logging trucks in Canada, the U.S.A., New Zealand, Australia, and worldwide. A shipment of 11 right-hand trucks was sent to Zambia and 47 trucks went to Kuwait. Each vehicle is customized to particular specifications. Scheduled tours are held every Wednesday in the late afternoon; phone ahead. Allow 45 minutes.
Location: Western Star Trucks Ltd., 2076 Enterprise Way.
Information: 860-3319. Not suitable for persons under the age of 5. For safety, no open-toed footwear or shorts are allowed, and participants should wear clothing that covers the arms.

■ **Working Honey Farm Visit:** Token admission. All tours visit the "honey house," where participants can see bee-keeping equipment and taste a specialty honey—fine flavored honeys produced when bees visit a single variety of flower. Allow 40 minutes for the demonstration to this point. When it is safe to do so, a limited number of participants can request a visit to a live brood hive, but children must be dressed in a protective suit and adults must heed strict precautions. Allow an additional 45 minutes. These informal presentations on bee-keeping are held by appointment, except during the days when the bees are being attended to (and thus disturbed) by work teams. Guided tours may be avail-

able April through September; phone ahead. Year-round tours for special-interest groups, by appointment. Specify your interests when you call—either honey house only, or honey house plus brood hives—so the owner can set aside the appropriate amount of time. Note: regardless of booking requests, the owner determines when the bees are too aggravated for public tours.
Location: The Honey Farm; Glemore Rd. Ask for exact directions when booking an appointment.
Information: 762-8156.

■ **Celebrations:** Yearly events include Kelowna Snowfest Winter Carnival in January; Ski-to-Sea Race in March; Knox Mountain Hill Climb, Chili Cookoff, Black Mountain Rodeo, Blossom Time Sailing Regatta in May; Oyama Days on the last Saturday in May; Knox Mountain Hill Climb for Cars and Motorcycles on Victoria Day; Sunshine Theatre, June through August; Folkfest and Westside Days, Ogopogo Golf Tournament, Lake Country Days held at Okanagan Centre in July; Kelowna Apple Triathlon in August; 1920s Garden Party held at Okanagan Centre on Labour Day weekend; Septoberfest and Okanagan Wine Festival, September to October.
Location: Various venues in Kelowna.
Information: InfoCentre, 861-1515, 1-800-663-4345, FAX: 861-3624.

Vernon and Lumby

Information on the attractions and festivals of Vernon: InfoCentre, 6326 Highway 97 North, Box 520, Vernon, V1T 6M4. Phone: 542-1415, FAX: 542-3256.

Information on the attractions and festivals of Lumby: Seasonal InfoCentre, 2400 Vernon St., Box 534, Lumby, V0E 2G0. Phone: 547-2300.

■ **Shuswap River Hatchery:** Visitors see fish incubation and rearing facilities for salmon. Fish stock is at the site in September, fry are on display from September through May and the fish are released during the summer. If they are not too busy, staff will conduct guided tours by request; phone ahead.
Location: At Lumby, take Mabel Lake Rd. north to Shuswap Falls, a distance of 13 km (8 mi.).
Information: 547-6673.

■ **Swan Lake Bird Sanctuary:** This undeveloped sanctuary protects birds such as white swans, geese, and herons. The reserve is located in a swampy area at the north end of Okanagan Lake. There is no visitor centre, but there are a few primitive trails for bird viewing. Ask for information at the Vernon InfoCentre.
Location: About 5 km (3 mi.) east of the O'Keefe Ranch on Highway 97 about 3 km (1.8 mi.) beyond Salmon River Rd. West of Highway 97A junctions.
Information: InfoCentre, 545-0771.

■ **O'Keefe Historic Ranch and Buildings:** Small admission. This property was one of the biggest pioneer ranches in British Columbia. Today, visitors can take a wagon ride around the perimeter, enjoy a picnic lunch on the grounds, or take in the children's petting zoo. The ranch was active until it was purchased from its second-generation owners by the Devonian Foundation; it is now administered by Vernon and the province of British Columbia for heritage purposes. Open from May to Thanksgiving. Scheduled tours of the buildings are held at selected times each day; phone ahead.
Location: Drive north of Vernon, on Highway 97, a distance of 12 km (7 mi.).
Information: 542-7868.

■ **Sports Hall of Fame:** This informal outdoor museum housed in glass showcases is located beneath a stand of maple trees. Featured are the uniforms and photographs of local "greats" who have dedicated themselves to the healthy pursuit of sports. **Location:** At Jubilee Cenotaph Park, across from the Greyhound Station, Vernon. **Information:** InfoCentre, 542-1415.

■ **Vernon Museum and Public Art Gallery:** Admission by donation. The newly remodeled museum contains exhibits of pioneering history, agricultural research, displays of historic bridal wear, and a showcase of minerals. The art gallery features changing exhibits that interpret the area through the eyes of local artists. Nearby Lake Kalamalka is called the "lake of a thousand colours" and its elusive beauty is a frequent subject for local painters and weavers. **Location:** Museum located in the Civic Centre, 3009 - 32nd Ave.; art gallery located above the museum. **Information:** Museum, 542-3142; art gallery, 545-3173.

■ **Brewery Tour:** This tour covers the intake of grains and hops, the importance of the taste of the water, the mixing of the amber brew in giant kettles, fermentation, and bottling. Visitors are provided with a small sample at the end of the tour. Scheduled tours are held in summer on Fridays; phone ahead. Group visits by appointment. Allow 1 hour. **Location:** Okanagan Springs, 2801 - 27A Ave., Vernon. **Information:** 542-2337. Not suitable for persons under legal age; for safety, no open-toed footwear is allowed.

■ **Ellison Park Interpretive Program:** On select summer days, a park naturalist presents public lectures or demonstrations on local flora and fauna. Within the park are two sandy beaches, barbecue pits, a picnic area, a freshwater park for scuba divers, plus six unmarked archaeological sites. **Location:** On the east shore of Okanagan Lake, 10 km (6 mi.) southwest of Okanagan Landing, southeast of Vernon. **Information:** B.C. Parks, 494-0321, for the times of interpretive programs. For information on archaeological sites, write: The Archaeological Society of B.C., P.O. Box 520, Station A, Vancouver, V6C 2N3.

■ **Equestrian Academy:** The tour covers the carriage room and outlines the qualities of the Halflinger horse breed. Depending upon timing, visitors can see students involved in riding, jumping, dressage, carriage driving, or horse grooming. Groups only, by appointment.
Location: Fohlenhof Equestrian Academy; 7 km (4 mi.) south of Vernon. Ask for exact location when an appointment is accepted.
Information: 542-4274.

■ **Paydirt and Historical Tour:** Outstanding value at $5 each. Participants receive a bag of paydirt guaranteed to contain a few flakes of gold. After a demonstration of gold-panning techniques, they can separate out their own nuggets. Participants then board an old bus for a rough, dusty ride to see the remains of Chinese mine workings, water canals, sluice boxes and rocker boxes on a privately owned site first recorded as "Cherryville" in 1863. There is also an outdoor assembly of antique mining and farming equipment at the campground. Groups of five or more only; phone ahead. An appointment may be necessary.
Location: Gold Panner Campground, 423 Highway 6, Site 9A, Comp. 6. Take Highway 6 east of Lumby for 22 km (14 mi.).
Information: 547-2025.

■ **Wood Manufacturers' Tours:** This tour starts at a Visitor's Centre at Lumby with information on forest industry activities. Participants may drive to one of two facilities within the area for a first-hand look at a manufacturing operation. Weyerhauser produces lumber and Riverside Forest Products produces veneer. Scheduled tours are held in the summer; phone ahead. Allow 2 hours.
Location: Start point: Tourist Information Centre at Lumby. Take Highway 6 east of Vernon for 25 km (16 mi.).
Information: Weyerhauser Canada, 547-2141; Riverside Forest Products, 547-2111.

■ **Celebrations:** Yearly events include Vernon Winter Carnival (largest in the west), "Over the Hill" Downhill Ski Race in February; Molson's Old-timers Hockey Tournament in March; Vernon Home Show in April; Head of the Lake Rodeo in May; Creative Chaos Craftshow in June; Vernon Horse Racing Days over the summer months; Kennel Club Dog Show, Regatta Watersports, Landing Regatta in July; Vernon Silver Star Triathlon, Cadet Camp Sunset Ceremony, Old-Time Fiddler's Contest in August; Horseshoe Tournament, Gymkhana in August; "Suds, Cider and Stuff" Festival in late September; Carling O'Keefe Curling Bonspiel in October; Rotary Carol Festival in December.
Location: Various venues in and around Vernon.
Information: InfoCentre, 542-1415.

■ The Spallumcheen ■

Armstrong

Information on the attractions and festivals of Armstrong: InfoCentre, Box 118, Armstrong, V0E 1B0. Phone: 546-8155, FAX: 546-8868.

■ **Armstrong-Spallumcheen Museum:** Admission by donation. Interpretive displays and artifacts place an emphasis on farming—particularly ploughing. In 1892, a London banker supported the building of a railway to this farming community. Today, the railway still traverses the centre of town and several downtown buildings have been restored to a western motif. Limited opening hours.
Location: Railway Ave. and Bridge St.
Information: 546-8318.

■ **Cheesemaking Demonstration:** Individuals can observe the cheesemaking process, but no tour leader is provided. Cheesemaking days are usually Saturdays, Mondays, and Thursdays. Visitors watch the factory floor through viewing windows, then taste a few samples. Phone ahead for confirmation that cheesemaking is proceeding as scheduled, as the milk supply varies from season to season.
Location: Armstrong Cheese, two blocks north of Railway Ave. on Pleasant Valley Rd.
Information: 546-3084 for demonstration times.

■ **Celebrations:** Yearly events include Asparagus Week in May; Caravan Theatre Productions (546-8953) all summer long; Kinsmen Rodeo in August; Interior Provincial Exhibition, Ploughing Match in September; Ploughing Match, Fish-Game Derby, Demolition Derby in October.
Location: Various venues, Armstrong.
Information: InfoCentre, 546-8155.

Enderby

Information on the attractions and festivals of Enderby: Seasonal InfoCentre, Shuswap River Park, Old Vernon Rd., Box 1000, Enderby, V0E 1V0. Phone: 838-6727, FAX: 838-0123.

■ **Cliffs and Rock Hounding:** The rock face here reflects a surprising number of colours, particularly at sunset. The elevation of the cliffs is 610 m (2000 ft.) and they are the subject of numerous paintings and photographs. Rock hounds will find particularly good specimens of jasper and agate in the general area between here and Vernon, and along the cliffs.
Location: Cliff viewing: in the townsite, off Brash Rd. Cliff explor-

ing and rock hounding: travel east across the Enderby Bridge, following Mabel Lake Rd. for approximately 2 km (1.2 mi.) before turning left on Brash Allan Rd. Follow this road, as it becomes gravel, to the end, until you drive into a farmyard. Ask permission from the owner to cross his property. The trail is challenging, approximately 3 hours to the top. Ask for exact instructions at the InfoCentre before setting out.

Information: InfoCentre, 838-6727; Public Information Unit of Energy and Mines, 356-2824, for rock-hounding information.

■ **Deep Creek Tool Museum:** Admission by donation. Features a large collection of tools, including hand tools, mechanical devices, pumps, chain saws, stationary engines, and cast-iron collectibles.

Location: Between Salmon Arm and Enderby, 1 km (.6 mi.) off Highway 97B on Deep Creek Rd.

Information: InfoCentre, 838-6727.

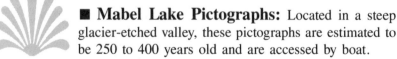

■ **Enderby District Museum:** Admission by donation. This museum features pioneer artifacts, including a model kitchen set up for the era of the 1930s with an old battery radio set, hand-activated rocker washing machine, an icebox, egg preservation equipment, and a utility room. Also on permanent display is a blacksmith shop with a forge, anvil, and pioneer tools. The museum features a children's "touching" corner and rotating displays of B.C. heritage. Guided tours may be available; phone ahead.

Location: 901 George St., off Highway 98.

Information: 838-7170.

■ **Mabel Lake Pictographs:** Located in a steep glacier-etched valley, these pictographs are estimated to be 250 to 400 years old and are accessed by boat.

Location: Located 37 km (23 mi.) east of Enderby. The location of pictographs throughout B.C. is protected due to vandalism; for exact directions, inquire at the local InfoCentre or ask knowledgeable locals.

Information: InfoCentre, 838-6727.

MOUNTAIN HIGHS

Shaped by massive underground pressures, British Columbia's mountains and valleys are composed of several spines or ranges, each with their own character. Beyond the Coastal Range and Fraser Plateau lie the vast ranges of the Shuswap Highlands, the Monashees, the Selkirks, the Purcells, and, of course, the celebrated Rockies. Most nations on earth would be pleased to lay claim to the beauty contained in just one mountain grouping; British Columbians take range after glorious range in easy stride. On the British Columbia side of the continental divide are three national parks—Glacier, Yoho, and Kootenay—as well as numerous

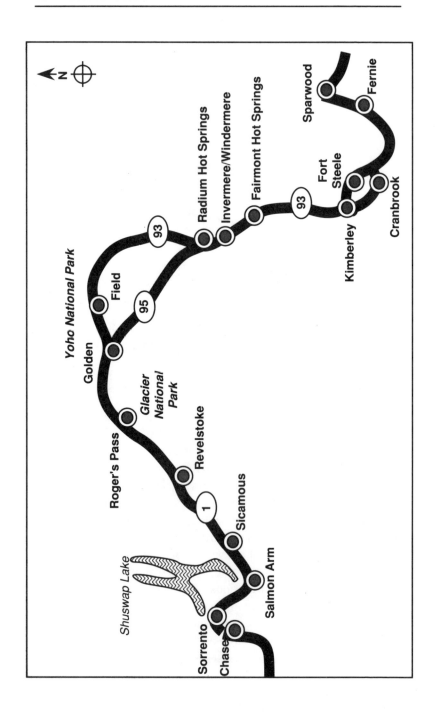

provincial parks and protected areas.

Emerald-coloured lakes and alpine flowers today beckon in an area that 100 years ago was legendary among railway-builders for its unyielding rock and lack of passable valleys. Road construction has changed all that, and travellers will find that attaining solitude within a beautiful mountain setting is simple: leave the main road and take a short walk along a path. "Yoho" is a Cree word meaning "astonishment or wonder" and this sentiment continues to reflect the common feeling of visitors to these craggy heights.

This chapter is divided into three sections. It begins in the area of the Shuswap Lakes and follows the Trans-Canada Highway east to the heart of the Rocky Mountains. The second section turns south along the Rocky Mountain Trench, following Highway 95 from Golden to Fernie, with the Rockies to the east and the Purcells to the west. The third section meanders the S-shaped roads of the Kootenays, entering from the west side at Greenwood and Grand Forks and taking in Trail, Nelson, Creston, and several hot springs.

General Information

Information on the attractions and festivals of High Country: High Country Tourism Association, #2 - 1490 Pearson Pl., Kamloops, VIS 1J4. Phone: 372-7770, FAX: 828-4656.

Information and maps on B.C. parks in the Shuswaps: Ministry of Parks, Southern Interior Region, #101 - 1050 West Columbia St., Kamloops, V2C 1L2. Phone: 828-4501, FAX: 828-4737.

■ East to the Rockies—Shuswap ■ Lakes to the Rocky Mountains

Information on the attractions and festivals of the Shuswap Lakes: Tourism Shuswap, P.O. Box 1670, Salmon Arm, VIE 4P7. Phone: 832-5200, FAX: 832-8382.

Information and maps on the provincial parks and lakes of the Shuswap: Shuswap Lake Park, Site 12, Comp. 4, Chase, V0E 1M0. Phone: 955-2217, FAX: 955-2524.

Safety information and navigational indicators for
houseboat renters: The Institute of Ocean Sciences, Patricia
Bay, P.O. Box 6000, Sidney, V8L 4B2. Phone: 363-6517.

North Shuswap—Chase and Sorrento

Information on the attractions and festivals of North
Shuswap: InfoCentre, 124 Chase St., Box 592, Chase,
V0E 1M0. Phone: 679-8432, FAX: 679-3120.

■ **Adams River Sockeye Run:** This river is the site
of British Columbia's most famous salmon run. There is
good viewing every year in early October, as bright red
sockeye at the end of a 17-day, 485-km (300-mi.) odyssey upstream
from the ocean return to their stream of origin to spawn. The returning salmon can be seen from observation decks and riverside
viewing trails. Park naturalists give interpretive talks only during
the major run of the 4-year cycle, next occurring in 1994. Pamphlets are always available to explain the run. The river is located
within the Roderick Haig-Brown provincial recreation area, which
also contains the ruins of flumes used by pioneer loggers to transport timber, some native pictographs, and 20 km (12 mi.) of trails.
Location: From Highway 1, turn north onto Anglemont Rd. at Squilax Bridge.
Information: B.C. Parks Shuswap Zone, 955-2217, FAX: 955-2524.

■ **Bighorn Sheep Viewing:** Bighorn sheep are often present
on the sides of Squilax Mountain or in the immediate area. For
recent information on the whereabouts of the herd, ask the Chase
InfoCentre. Note: these wild animals range freely, and sightings
cannot be guaranteed. However, since the Fish and Wildlife Association track the herd via radio collars, the InfoCentre can usually
give visitors an estimation of their last noted position. The animals
were originally imported from Banff, Alberta, and the village of
Chase has chosen the bighorn sheep as its emblem. Bring
binoculars.
Location: One viewing area is from the Squilax Bridge, near

Little River which joins Shuswap and Little Shuswap Lake. Ask for other likely locations at the InfoCentre.
Information: InfoCentre, 679-8432, FAX: 679-3120.

■ **Kekuli Pit House:** Next to the Visitor's Centre is a replica of an early native Kekuli pit house reconstructed with the assistance of the B.C. Museums Association and native people. A periodic naturalist program in the summer provides additional insights on water safety, natural history, and native history; phone for program details.
Location: Shuswap Lake Provincial Park, Anglemont Rd. Drive 19 km (12 mi.) northeast of the Squilax Bridge.
Information: B.C. Parks Shuswap Zone, 955-2217, FAX: 955-2524.

■ **Squilax Pow Wow:** Outstanding value; separate charges for individual events. The Little Shuswap Indian Band, an interior Salish tribe, sponsors an annual gathering featuring a teepee encampment, drum competition, and dancing. Natives dress in traditional costume and invite other native groups from Canada and the U.S.A. to participate. All visitors are welcome. Held in July.
Location: Chase and area. Inquire as to exact location.
Information: Little Shuswap Band Office, 679-3203.

■ **Celebrations:** Yearly events include North Shuswap fishing derby in late May; Chase Days Canoe Regatta, Chase Annual Fun Fly of Scale Model Aircraft (955-2306) in June; Chase Daze Rubber Ducky Race on the July 1st weekend; Shuswap Festival of the Arts (Sorrento, 675-2546), Squilax Indian Pow Wow and Rodeo, Shuswap Bluegrass Festival in July; Chase Craftarama in August; Chase Fall Fair on Labour Day weekend; "Salute to the Sockeye" in October.
Location: North Shuswap region.
Information: InfoCentre, 679-8432, FAX: 679-3120.

Salmon Arm and Area

Information on the attractions and festivals of Salmon Arm: InfoCentre, 70 Hudson Ave., Box 999, Salmon Arm, V1E 4P2. Phone: 832-6247, FAX: 832-8382.

■ **Ghost of Margaret Falls:** This place of beauty and mystery is said to harbour a ghost within a waterfall. For years, the falls were named Reinecker Falls, but the spirit of "Margaret" was too pervasive; in 1980, the Provincial Parks authority switched the name back to the 19th-century original. The elusive "Margaret" may have been the first adventurous white woman to visit here, but her true identity has been lost over time. Perhaps she too is quietly enjoying this little bit of heaven.
Location: 1 km (.6 mi.) from Herald Provincial Park on Sunnybrae-Canoe Point Rd., 37 km (23 mi.) west of Salmon Arm. The falls are a 10-minute walk through a massive cedar grove.
Information: InfoCentre, 832-6247, FAX: 832-8382.

■ **Wharf and Nature Enhancement Area:** Walk a long curved wharf out into the bay. The area to the east and west of the wharf allows bird watching. Trails and blinds permit amateurs or professionals to catch a glimpse of some of the 150 species that have been noted in the area.
Location: Arriving from the east, turn right on 4th St. to Lakeshore Dr., cross tracks on Marine Dr. to wharf.
Information: InfoCentre, 832-6247.

■ **Haney Heritage Village:** Small admission. A long wooded driveway leads to a reconstructed village circa 1900, complete with a schoolhouse, church, fire hall, log homes, and farm buildings. The main house, originally owned by R.K. Haney, is now restored and tours of the interior are held in summer. The site covers 16 ha (40 ac.) and trails are surrounded with 70 varieties of unusual plants, including orchids and rare fungi. During the summer various pioneering activities, such as weaving or spinning, are held here; phone for the times of demonstrations. Guided tours may be available; phone ahead. **Location:** At the junction of Highway 1 and Highway 97B, 2 km (1.2 mi.) east of Salmon Arm. **Information:** 832-5243.

■ **Dairy and Cheese-making Visit:** Visitors first watch the cheese-making process through glass partitions as workers create gouda rounds ranging from 300 grams (10 ounces) to 15 kg (33 lb.) in size; samples are provided. The dairy also makes quark, a fresh uncured cheese that is frozen. Participants view the barn, milking equipment, cows and calves. Individuals may drop in Tuesdays and Fridays at 2:00 p.m. Groups should phone ahead for an appointment. Allow 45 minutes. **Location:** Gort's Dairy. Take Highway 1, west of Salmon Arm, for 1 km (.6 mi.) to Silver Creek Rd. **Information:** 832-4274.

■ **Plywood and Sawmill Plant Tour:** Participants first see an overview of this company's operations and then continue with a guided tour of a sawmill that produces finished lumber and a plywood plant that manufactures rolled sheets of wood. Scheduled tours may be available; phone ahead. **Location:** Federated Co-op Plywood and Sawmill, 7 km (4 mi.) east of Salmon Arm, near Canoe Public Beach. **Information:** 832-2194. Not suitable for persons under the age of 12. For safety, no open-toed footwear or shorts are allowed and participants should wear clothing that covers the arms.

■ **Celebrations:** Yearly events include Kesli-Salmi Cross-country Ski Marathon in January; Sonnet Contest in June; Annual Shuswap Rodeo in late June; Shuswap Theatre from June through July; Klahanie Strawberry Festival and Teddy Bear Picnic at South Canoe Beach in July; Chariot Races

and Salmon Arm Triathlon (832-7242) in August; Salmon Arm Agricultural Fall Fair and Horse Pull in September.
Location: In and around Salmon Arm.
Information: InfoCentre, 832-6247, FAX: 832-8382.

■ **Salmon Arm Farmer's Market:** The Farmer's Market is held every Tuesday and Friday in season from 8:00 a.m. to 1:00 p.m. Merchants sell crafts, canned goods, bedding plants, flowers, fruits, vegetables, and baked goods. A reminder of the Salmon Arm fruit season: blossoms, mid-April through May; strawberries, late June through July; cherries, June 10 to July 10; plums September 5 to 15; corn, September; apples, pumpkins, squashes, October 5 onward.
Location: At Picadilly Place Mall.
Information: InfoCentre, 832-6247, FAX: 832-8382.

■ **Sonnet Contest:** Participants who complete a sonnet are eligible to win cash. Write for this year's starting line and a correct rhyme scheme; all are welcome to participate. Deadline is usually late March. Prizes are awarded on Canada Day.
Information: The Annual Sonnet Contest, P.O. Box 999, Salmon Arm, V0E 2T0.

Sicamous and Area

Information on the attractions and festivals of Sicamous: InfoCentre, Main St. and Riverside Ave., Box 346, Sicamous, V0E 2V0. Phone: 836-3313, FAX: 836-4368.

■ **Eagle River Salmon Hatchery:** This hatchery enhances the reproductive survival rate of chinook, coho salmon, and rainbow trout. Best viewing times for adults, August through December; juveniles, January through May. Guided tours may be available; phone ahead.
Location: 32 km (19 mi.) east of Sicamous, ask for instructions before setting out.
Information: 836-4291.

■ **Craigellachie: Site of the "Last Spike":**
A famous black and white photograph chronicles a great
moment in Canadian history: the last spike of Canada's
first transcontinental railway was set on November 15, 1885, sig-
nifying the uniting of the nation from sea to sea. The photograph
shows a bearded man in a top hat, mallet in hand, surrounded by
dour onlookers and one small boy. Today, a simple grass clearing
by the track, a commemorative cairn, and a small information booth
mark one of the greatest achievements in Canadian history. Pamphlets are available here for a Heritage Driving Tour of railway points
of interest. Costumed assistants are periodically in attendance in
summer.
Location: 30 km (19 mi.) east of Sicamous beside Highway 1.
Information: On-site information building, 836-2244. Historical
Information: Craigellachie and Malakwa Community Hall Association, Box 101, Malakwa, V0E 2J0. Phone: 836-4379.

■ **Three Valley Gap Pioneer Village:** Admission charged
to view building interiors. This interesting collection of old wood-
en buildings was gathered and reassembled by members of the
Bell family. Western buildings perch in a spectacular setting at the
meeting of three valleys in Eagle Pass. Visitors can browse a refurbished saloon, barber shop, and old schoolhouse; wedding
ceremonies are periodically performed at historic St. Stephen's
Church. The valley itself is significant: there had been grave doubts
that a trans-Canada railway was possible, prior to its discovery by
railway surveyors in 1885. Guided tours may occasionally be available; phone ahead.
Location: On Highway 1, 48 km (30 mi.) from Sicamous, or 19
km (12 mi.) west of Revelstoke.
Information: Three Valley Gap, 837-2109, FAX: 837-2109.

■ **Dairy Visit:** Visitors can walk around this facility
and see the calf barns as well as a children's zoo with a camel
and a llama. Cheese is made periodically, and during these times

visitors can watch the process through windows. Occasionally, samples of cheddar are available. Dozens of flavours of home-made, creamy-smooth ice cream, fresh milk, cream, butter, and farm-made yogurt are for sale here. Drop-in tours anytime in summer. **Location:** D Dutchman Dairy, on Highway 1, 1 km (.6 mi.) east of Sicamous. **Information:** 836-4304.

Revelstoke

Information on the attractions and festivals of Revelstoke: Chamber of Commerce, 300 First St. West, P.O. Box 490, Revelstoke, V0E 2S0. Phone: 837-5345 year-round; 837-3522 in summer, FAX: 837-4223.

Information on hiking or walking trails in Mount Revelstoke or Glacier national parks: Environment Canada, Parks Service, P.O. Box 350, 301 Campbell Ave., Revelstoke, V0E 2S0. Phone: office, 837-7500; information, 837-6867; FAX: 837-7536.

■ **Depot Remains and Canyon Hot Springs:** This roadside mineral-water pool is located in the Selkirk Mountains. The steaming waters were discovered by a railway worker about 1900; he and a few others built a timber enclosure and the railway judiciously established a maintenance depot here. Today visitors can explore the remains of the buildings, just south of the present pool site. There is a charge for use of the pool. River rafting is also available from this location. **Location:** On Highway 1, 35 km (22 mi.) east of Revelstoke. **Information:** Canyon Hot Springs pool, 837-2420.

■ **Revelstoke Railway Museum:** Token admission. An impressive new structure interprets the history, machinery and personal intrigues that combined to complete a national railway through Canada's most challenging terrain. On display are the 5468 Mikado engine and Business Car No. 4 used by the superintendent of the CPR until 1992. Three tracks alongside the museum hold rolling stock. Guided tours are available; phone ahead. Open in summer. **Location:** 719 Track St. West, downtown Revelstoke. **Information:** 837-6060.

■ **Mica Dam Tour:** Mica, the last of three Columbia River Treaty dams to be completed reached a height of 244 m (800 ft.) above bedrock and 198 m (650 ft.) above the riverbed in the autumn of 1972. Containing more than 33 million cubic meters (43 million cubic yards) of fill, it is one of the largest earth-fill structures in the world. Completed with the help of financial support from the United States to prevent damaging floods in Washington and Oregon, the underground powerhouse is capable of holding 6 generators. Visitor Centre is open select hours in summer; guided tours are scheduled twice a day in summer. Groups welcome year-round with two weeks' notice. Allow 2 hours. **Location:** 136 km (85 mi.) north of Revelstoke. The Visitor Centre is located adjacent to the switch-gear building at the top of the dam. **Information:** Tour guide office, 834-7382.

■ **Revelstoke Dam Tour:** Each visitor is provided with a headphone upon arrival. The automated tour leads participants through the dam complex, providing interesting facts about electricity and British Columbia's connections to the U.S.-Canada interdependent electricity grid. The tour includes an elevator ride to the dam crest viewpoint and views of the main powerhouse gallery, circuit breaker gallery, tailrace area, and powerhouse control room. The dam looms more than 175 m (575 ft.) above the canyon floor. Visitor Centre open select hours most of the year; automated tours are available anytime during opening hours. Allow 2 hours. **Location:** North on Highway 23, about 5 km (3 mi.) from Revelstoke. **Information:** B.C. Hydro, 837-6515 or 837-6211.

■ **Celebrations:** Yearly events include Snow Festival in February; Canada Day Celebrations on July 1; Provincial Water Skiing Championships in mid-July; Eva Lake Yearly Pilgrimage to Mt. Revelstoke in early August; Labour Day Golf Tournament, Fall Fair in September.
Location: Various venues, Revelstoke.
Information: InfoCentre, 837-5345 year-round; 837-3522 in summer.

Glacier National Park

■ **Rogers Pass Visitor Centre:** Videos and displays show the construction of the mammoth Mount MacDonald railway tunnel, completed in 1988 to allow the railroad (begun in 1885) a grade of under 1 percent. Before its construction, 6 3,000-horsepower "pusher" locomotives per train were required to move freight through the pass. Visitors can see pictures of historic killer avalanches that buried whole railway work crews, and a continuous film showing of *Snow Wars*—the story of how avalanches are "shot down" by the military every winter. Allow at least 1 hour for a stop here. Around the back of the centre are trail entrances for self-guided nature walks. A red-suited R.C.M.P. officer is on duty in summer, at the Best Western Glacier Park Lodge next door; he is periodically available for "mountain-mountie" pictures.
Location: At the summit of the pass, Highway 1.
Information: Glacier Park information line, 837-7500.

■ **Glacier National Park Interpretive Program:** Conducted hikes are led by a park naturalist daily during limited periods in July and August. Participants learn about the massive steep-walled mountains with narrow valleys which

characterize the Columbias. This is an excellent opportunity for beginners, or those who are ill-prepared to go into wilderness areas alone. Note: climbers, walkers, and hikers in this park may find unexploded howitzer shells; do not touch. Hiking season is very short due to the high altitudes and heavy snowfall. Tours are conducted by the Federal Parks Service; phone ahead. Wear sturdy shoes.
Location: Start at the Illecillewaet Campground, 3.4 km (2 mi.) west of the Roger's Pass Information Centre.
Information: Canadian Parks Service, 837-5155.

Yoho National Park

Information and maps on Yoho National Park: Environment Canada Parks Service, P.O. Box 99, Field, V0A 1H0. Phone: 343-6324. Note: periodically, groups can ask to arrange for the services of a park interpreter while visiting the park.

■ **Field Visitor Centre:** Stop by for informative pamphlets and maps of local hiking trails. The attractions in this park that are accessible by car and a short walk include Wapta Falls, Kicking Horse River, hoodoos, a natural rock bridge at Emerald Lake, viewpoint for the spiral railway tunnels, Takakkaw Falls, and the Burgess Shales displays.
Location: InfoCentre is just off Highway 1 near the town of Field, Yoho National Park.
Information: 343-6324.

■ **Yoho Park Interpretive Service:** Between mid-June and Labour Day, park interpreters present guided walks, campfire programs, slide talks, and special events designed to share the history and natural features of the park. Program subjects in past years have included "the mystery of the Burgess Shale"; "beavers, the animals that built a country"; and "Field, the gentle place." Most programs originate from the campgrounds; check the bulletin boards there or phone ahead.

Location: Hoodoo Creek Campground Theatre, 7 km (4 mi.) beyond the park entrance.
Information: 343-6324.

■ The Rocky Mountain Trench— ■ Golden to Fernie

Information on the attractions and festivals on the western side of the Rockies: Rocky Mountain Visitors Association, P.O. Box 10, 495 Wallinger Ave., Kimberley, V1A 2Y5. Phone: 427-4838, FAX: 427-3344.

Information and maps on B.C. parks located on the western side of the Rockies: Ministry of Parks, District Manager, Box 118, Wasa, V0B 2K0. Phone: 422-3212. Specify Mount Assiniboine Park, Elk Lakes, Top of the World Provincial Park or Bugaboo Glacier.

Golden

Golden Highways Conditions Report: 1-800-665-8001.

Information on the attractions and festivals of Golden: InfoCentre, 10th Ave. North, Box 677, Golden, V0A 1H0. Phone: 344-7125, FAX: 344-6688.

■ **Golden and District Museum:** Admission by donation. Interpretive displays on regional and local history include the building of the highway through the Kicking Horse Pass and its evolution beyond a narrow cliff-hugging byway to a somewhat wider cliff-hanging highway. There is an excellent collection of photographs as well as printing presses from the historic newspaper office. Guided tours may be available; phone ahead.
Location: 1302 - 11th Ave.
Information: 344-5169.

■ **Celebrations:** Yearly events include "Willy Forrest" Snow Festival, Logger's Sports Day in February; Columbia River Raft Race in May; Western Canada Small Bore Championship in July; Firemen's Hose-Laying Competition in August; Golden Rodeo Days, Softball Tournament on Labour Day weekend; Parson Fall Fair in September.
Location: Various venues, Golden.
Information: InfoCentre, 344-7125, FAX: 344-6688.

Kootenay National Park

Information and maps on Kootenay National Park: Environment Canada Parks Service, Box 220, Radium Hot Springs, V0A 1M0. Phone: 347-9615, FAX: 347-9980.

■ **Natural Wonders:** The attractions in this park that are accessible by car and a short walk include: Sinclair Canyon, Redwall faults and the Iron Gates Tunnel, the Kootenay viewpoint, animal licks, Paint Pots ochre beds, Marble Canyon, Vermilion Pass nature trail, and the Continental Divide. Marble Canyon is an exceptionally narrow canyon that has been cut deep by a mountain stream. In some places, the soft limestone canyon walls have metamorphosed into dolomite marble. Explanatory pamphlets are available at park literature kiosks, at the campgrounds, or from Environment Canada Parks Service in advance.
Location: Various locations in Kootenay National Park.
Information: Parks Service, 347-9615.

■ **Kootenay National Park Interpretive Program:** Park interpreters lead guided walks or give short talks in the early evenings. In past years, children have been invited to drop by the Redstreak Campground on select days for 3 free hours of nature activities. Ask for a copy of this year's program of activities and nature walks. Presentations are held in the summer; check the bulletin boards in the campgrounds or phone ahead. **Location:** Redstreak Campground Amphitheatre or McLeod Campground Theatre or Marble Canyon Campground. **Information:** Parks Service, 347-9615.

Radium Hot Springs

Information on the attractions and festivals of Radium Hot Springs: Seasonal InfoCentre, St. Joseph St., Box 225, Radium Hot Springs, V0A 1M0. Phone: 347-9331, FAX: 347-6459.

■ **Hot Springs:** Small admission. In these odorless, therapeutic mineral waters, temperatures average 39°C (102°F). A cooler pool is available for those who wish to do laps. Rocky Mountain bighorn sheep are frequently sighted on the mountainside behind the pool and the red cliffs of Sinclair Canyon can be seen beyond the pool-house. The Kootenay natives drew spiritual inspiration from these waters which were first introduced to European settlers in the late 1800s. A second hot springs resort is located nearby at Fairmont. **Location:** Radium Hot Springs Aquacourt. Follow the signs in Radium. **Information:** 347-9485.

■ **Celebrations:** Yearly events include Columbia Valley Marathon in February; Radium Days, "The Biggest Little Parade In the World" on Victoria Day weekend; Classic Car Show and Shine in September; Fall Fair in late October; "Christmas Tree Capital of the World" Celebration during the month of December. **Location:** Various venues in and around Radium Hot Springs. **Information:** InfoCentre, 347-9331 in the summer only.

Invermere and Windermere

Information on the attractions and festivals of Invermere and Windermere: Seasonal InfoCentre, 6th St. and 7th Ave., Box 2605, Invermere, V0A 1K0. Phone: 342-6316, FAX: 342-2934.

■ **St. Peter's Stolen Church:** The church with the bright red roof has the unusual distinction of being "stolen." Built in 1887 in the railway community of Donald, the CPR changed the railway divisional point to Revelstoke. Most residents literally moved their homes and commercial buildings. In the flurry of relocating the town, when it came time to transport the church residents found it was gone. A local couple had dismantled the building and shipped it to where it stands today. They left the bell behind. Limited opening hours.
Location: On Victoria Ave. in Windermere.
Information: InfoCentre, 342-6316.

■ **Windermere Valley Pioneer Museum:** Token admission. This log museum features displays on mining history, the story of the railway, the history of the Upper Columbia Valley, and artifacts from native life. One building is furnished as a pioneer cottage and another as a 1906 schoolhouse. Guided tours may be available; phone ahead.
Location: 622 Seventh Ave.
Information: 342-9769.

■ **Celebrations:** Yearly events include Curling Bonspiel, held on the lake in January or February; Kinsmen Trade Fair in May; Windermere Team Triathlon, Canadian Native Fastball Championship, Windermere Loop Team Triathlon in July; North American Native Fastball Championship, Lakeside Hang-Gliding Competition in August; Fall Fair in September.

Location: Various venues, Invermere and Windermere.
Information: InfoCentre, 342-6316, FAX: 342-2934.

Fairmont Hot Springs Area

■ **Lussier Undeveloped Hot Springs:** Where there are commercially developed hot springs, there is likely to be an undeveloped outlet somewhere in the area. Adventurers can soak in a natural hot springs; it is accessed with some difficulty, but is beside a gravel road.
Location: In Whiteswan Lake Provincial Park on the way to Top of the World Provincial Park. Ask for exact directions from the Kimberley InfoCentre. It is 17 km (11 mi.) along gravel roads.
Information: InfoCentre, 427-3666, FAX: 427-5378.

Kimberley

Information on the attractions and festivals of Kimberley:
InfoCentre, 350 Ross St., Box 63, Kimberley, V1A 2Y5.
Phone: 427-3666, FAX: 427-5378.

■ **Cominco Gardens:** Admission by donation. More than 50,000 bedding plants are cultivated here each year as a demonstration of one of Cominco's products—Elephant Brand Fertilizer. As well as the carefully tended flower beds, there is a small teahouse open in the summer, where "high tea" is served from 3:00 to 5:00 p.m. daily (for a charge).
Location: Take the footpath from the Platzl (town centre); about a 10-minute walk.
Information: Gardens, 427-2293; Tea Room reservations, 427-4885.

■ **Platzl:** The pedestrian-only main street of Kimberley, called the "platzl," is storybook-pretty with brightly painted buildings, a painted bridge over a chuckling stream, European-style shops, and sidewalk cafés. Characters in costume, such as accordionists in lederhosen, periodically walk the streets to create the impression of a happy Bavarian village. "Adi" is Kimberley's yodelling woodcarver and "Urs" is the friendly wandering minstrel. Kimberley is reputed to possess the world's largest cuckoo clock—a device so large it needs its own house; the cuckoo bird named "Happy Hans" yodels loudly. The International Arts centre, located one block away, is periodically open for demonstrations of old-world craftsmanship. Special presentations are held almost every weekend in summer and periodically in winter; phone ahead for details. Nearby is a Bavarian railway (small admission charged).
Location: The Platzl is in the Kimberley town centre.
Information: InfoCentre, 427-3666.

■ **Kimberley Heritage Museum:** Admission by donation. This museum offers interpretive displays of the history of the Cominco mining industry, artifacts from the Sullivan mine, and the stories of local sports heroes, such as Gerry Sorenson—the world's fastest downhill skier in 1982. Guided tours may be available; phone ahead.
Location: 105 Spokane St. in the Library Building.
Information: 427-7510.

■ **Celebrations:** Yearly festivals include Marysville Daze Fun in June; Old-Time Accordion Championships, Julyfest Music and Dancing in July; Songfest Gospel Music, Elk Bugling Championships and Dance, Volksmarch Trail Walking in August; Alpine Folk Dance Festival and Yodeling on the Labour Day weekend; Hallowe'en Howl in October; Wintertime Fests on various snowy weekends in winter.

Location: Various venues in and around Kimberley.
Information: 427-3666, FAX: 427-5378.

Cranbrook and Area

Cranbrook Highway Conditions Report: 426-1500.

Information on the attractions and festivals of Cranbrook: InfoCentre, 2279 Cranbrook St., Box 84, Cranbrook, V1C 4H6. Phone: 426-5914, FAX: 426-3873.

■ **Kootenay Trout Hatchery:** Fish and Wildlife's second-largest facility is designed to enhance the level of natural spawning trout in the region. From 5 to 8 million trout fry are hatched here each year. Special viewing areas are provided for self-guided tours; groups only can phone ahead for an appointment.
Location: Located 8 km (5 mi.) north of Wardner on the east side of the Kootenay River, approximately 40 km (25 mi.) southeast of Cranbrook.
Information: 429-3214.

■ **Aasland Taxidermy Museum:** On display are distinctive mounted animal heads, as well as many varieties of birds and typical Canadian animals, both large and small. At select times, visitors can view a taxidermist at work; phone ahead. Visitors to the taxidermy demonstration should be emotionally prepared for the fact that the animals are dead.
Location: North of Cranbrook on Highway 95A.
Information: 426-3566.

■ **Cranbrook Railway Museum:** Small admission. The vintage luxury train on display here cost a million dollars to build—when it was constructed back in the 1920s. Nine restored cars of the sumptuous 1929 Trans-Canada Limited now display inlaid black walnut and mahogany panels, silverware, china, glass, and other aspects of railway elegance. It is possible to tour the dining car, sleeping car, and parlour cars; a model railway is in operation in the baggage car. Guided tours may be available; phone ahead. **Location:** 1 Van Horne St., on Highway 3-95. **Information:** 489-3918.

■ **St. Eugene Mission Church:** Admission by donation. This mission church was built in 1897 with the funds from the sale of two high-grade mining claims. A native Indian named Pierre discovered the ore; with the assistance of his benefactor, Father Coccola, Pierre got a new house, and Father Coccola built this church featuring hand-painted Italian-made stained-glass windows. Along with a native residential school built in 1912, the Kootenay Area Indian Council now uses the buildings as a cultural centre, office complex, and archive collection. Guided tours may be available; phone ahead. **Location:** Follow Highway 95A towards Kimberley. Approximately .5 km (.2 mi.) from the city overpass, turn right on Mission Rd. Continue 4.5 km (3 mi.). Address: 15 Mission Rd. **Information:** 489-2464.

■ **Wildlife Museum:** Small admission. Life-sized displays, typical of the wildlife of the area, are presented here in natural settings. The East Kootenay Hunters' Association has sponsored conservation projects ranging from the rehabilitation of critical wildlife wintering ranges to the displays in this museum. **Location:** Chamber of Commerce Building, 2279 Cranbrook St. **Information:** 426-5914.

■ **Heritage Self-Guided Tour:** Cranbrook's finest older buildings date from 1888 to 1929. The home of the founder of the community celebrated its 100th birthday in 1988. Several dignified residences, the old fire hall, and the CNR superintendent's home can be seen. Self-guided tours anytime with a map; groups only can book a guided tour. **Location:** Heritage map available at the InfoCentre, 2279 Cranbrook St., or at the Railway Museum.

Information: InfoCentre, 426-5914, FAX: 426-3873. Groups only contact: The Landmarks Foundation, Box 400, Cranbrook, V1C 4J4.

■ **Raptor Rescue-and-Rehabilitation Society Visit:** Admission by donation. This society helps wild birds of prey, nurtures burrowing owls, barn owls and offers hope of survival to injured or orphaned birds, such as hawks, falcons, ospreys, and eagles. Guided tours may be available; visiting hours are scheduled on a regular basis in the summer.
Location: On Wycliffe Parkway Road. Take Highway 95A, turn left at Old Kimberley Highway and it is on the left side.
Information: 489-2841.

■ **Celebrations:** Yearly events include Cranbrook Wintertainment in January; Kinsmen Trade Fair in May; Wheelchair races, "Sam Steele" Days in June; Canada Day Celebration on July 1; Professional Rodeo in August; Santa Claus Parade in December.
Location: Various venues in and around Cranbrook.
Information: InfoCentre, 426-5914, FAX: 426-3873.

Fort Steele

For historic or visitor information: Visitor Services, Fort Steele, V0B 1N0. Phone: 489-3351, FAX: 489-2624.

■ **Fort Steele Heritage Town:** Outstanding value at $5, good for 2 days; admission fees in effect from the end of June to the beginning of September, 9:30 a.m. to 5:30 p.m. Grounds are open off-season at no charge. Fort Steele includes 60 original restored buildings on an 11-ha (27-ac.) site. They include Kershaw's General Store, Mrs. Spague's Confectionery, Prospector Printshop and a bakery that still produces fresh-baked goods daily in a wood-fired oven. Once visitors enter the grounds they become part of history; historical animators dressed in period costumes re-create the year 1897. For example, two women may hurry past talking loudly of the trial at the local courthouse or participants can help to bake fresh bread. Fort Steele is probably as lively as the days when the Kootenay gold rush attracted the first residents and a contingent of law-enforcement officers to this area. Professional entertainment (extra cost) takes place in the Wildhorse Theatre. Allow a full day at this historic attraction. Best days to be here: Dominion Day on July 1; the Annual Hose Reel Races in early July; Thanksgiving Sunday harvest and hot potato bake. Operated by the B.C. Ministry of Municipal Affairs, Recreation and Culture.

Location: 16 km (10 mi.) northeast of Cranbrook on Highway 93-95.
Information: 489-3351.

Fernie and Area

Fernie Highway Conditions Report: 423-6896.

Information on the attractions and festivals of Fernie:
InfoCentre, Highway 3, Dicken Rd., Fernie, V0B 1M0. Phone: 423-6868; FAX: 423-3811.

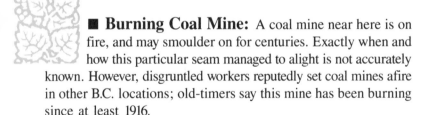

■ **Burning Coal Mine:** A coal mine near here is on fire, and may smoulder on for centuries. Exactly when and how this particular seam managed to alight is not accurately known. However, disgruntled workers reputedly set coal mines afire in other B.C. locations; old-timers say this mine has been burning since at least 1916.

Location: Located 6 km (3.5 mi.) from Fernie on the north side of the city. Ask for exact directions at the Fernie InfoCentre.
Information: InfoCentre, 423-6868, FAX: 423-3811.

■ **Ghosts of Hosmer Mountain:** Local legend says that every evening, when the sun is just so, the ghosts of a high-ranking native princess and her father ride across the slopes of Hosmer Mountain, approximately 10 km (6 mi.) to the north. The two phantoms continue their never-ending search for William Fernie, who long

ago spied a necklace made of coal pieces worn by the comely maiden. With cunning charm, he extracted information about the location of a certain coal deposit, in return for a firm promise of marriage. She was jilted and her father placed a curse upon the entire valley. In 1902, an explosion at Fernie's coal mine killed 128 men; in 1904, there was a fire, and 4 years later, a more disastrous fire. Floods have ravaged the town and finally, in 1964, at the request of the town's citizens, Chief Red Eagle ceremonially lifted the curse on Fernie; he died the following year. According to the same legend, prospects for Fernie have vastly improved. **Location:** The ghosts appear regularly on the slopes of Hosmer Mountain as the summer sun sets. Ask for the best viewing area and times at the InfoCentre.
Information: InfoCentre, 423-6868, FAX: 423-3811.

■ **Akamina No. 2 Cable Tool Rig:** When pioneers first explored the streams around Fernie, they found slicks of pure, straw-coloured oil. Natives had been using the gooey oil for trading and grooming purposes. Gold and coal prospectors eventually heard of the seeps and descended on the area about 1892. As many as 23 rigs were installed; no oil was found. As late as 1980, Shell Canada drilled several wells. The source of the oil slicks remains a mystery. The rig was restored by Shell Canada, the Fernie Chamber of Commerce, Heritage Trust, B.C. Lotteries, Tom Wark, Canada Employment, and the City of Fernie.
Location: Located beside the Fernie InfoCentre on the north side of town.
Information: InfoCentre, 423-6868, FAX: 423-3811.

■ **Fernie and District Museum:** Admission by donation. On display are interpretive signs and artifacts on local mining history and the story of a coal town at the turn of the century. The building was originally a Roman Catholic rectory; original doors, kitchen cupboards, and 1905 linoleum remain intact. Guided tours may be available; phone ahead.

Location: Corner of 5th Ave. and 5th St.
Information: 423-6512.

■ **Fernie Art Station:** This building is a restored railway station serving the needs of the arts and crafts community, the theatre crowd, shoppers, and visitors. Restaurant patrons are requested to hold onto their dishes as the occasional train clatters past. The most difficult activity is the famous summer "sundeck-train-watching-cheesecake-eating" feat. Take note that Fernie has the only untreated mountain spring water in Canada. Savour a drink of pure water—right out of the tap.
Location: 601 First Ave.
Information: 423-4842.

■ **Historic Fernie Courthouse:** Those who do not have time for the entire Fernie Heritage Walking Tour can visit the historic Fernie Courthouse. Constructed between 1909 and 1911 of British Columbia granite and Alberta limestone, the Edwardian-style edifice stands majestically on a hill as a stately symbol of law, justice and order. The cost of construction raised eyebrows in its day, at a mammoth $70,000. Visitors entering the building notice the spacious vestibule of oak and a floor of fret tiles. A maximum of 6 prisoners could be placed in lock-up facilities in the basement. Guided tours may be available; phone ahead.
Location: 401 - 4th Ave.
Information: InfoCentre, 423-6868, FAX: 423-3811.

■ **Heritage Walking or Driving Tour:** Fernie features turn-of-the-century architecture unlike any other community in the Rockies. In 1908, a major fire left 23 buildings standing and the town enacted a bylaw enforcing the use of brick and stone as primary building materials; the result is a number of sturdy and unique heritage buildings. Self-guided tours anytime with a map; groups only may book a guided tour.
Location: The map for the self-guided tour is available from Fernie Travel InfoCentre, on the north side of town.
Information: InfoCentre, 423-6868, FAX: 423-3811.

■ **Elk Valley Educational Forest Trail:** This interpretive trail focuses on the forest and wildlife. Participants occasionally see elk here: the Elk Valley claims to have the highest concentration in North America; also present in large numbers are bear, deer, and bighorn sheep. On this walk, opportunities abound for photographers: a fish-supporting creek, beaver pond, meadows and fields, wetland forest, and coniferous and deciduous forests. Cooperative project of Crow's Nest Resources and Crestwood Forest Industries. Self-guided tours with a brochure anytime during opening hours; groups only can book a guided tour. Manual available for teachers from address below.
Location: The Elk Valley Educational Forest is found along Coal Creek Rd. Map and directions are available at the InfoCentre.
Information: InfoCentre, 423-6868, FAX: 423-3811. Group contact: British Columbia Forestry Association, Kootenay Region, P.O. Box 845, Cranbrook, V1C 4J6. Phone: 489-1113.

■ **Celebrations:** Yearly events include Curling Bonspiel in January; "Griz the Mountainman" Days Winter Celebration in February; Fernie and Area Trade Fair in April; Pedal-Paddle-Power Competition in May; Snow Valley Wrangler's Rodeo in August; Annual Craft Fair in November.
Location: Various venues in Fernie.
Information: InfoCentre, 423-6868, FAX: 423-3811.

Sparwood

Information on the attractions and festivals of Sparwood: InfoCentre, Highway 3 and Aspen Dr., P.O. Box 1448, Sparwood, V0B 2G0. Phone: 425-2423, FAX: 425-7130.

■ **Sparwood Mining History Murals:** Three giant wall murals are painted on downtown buildings in Sparwood; all depict historical scenes from the local mining industry. Dan Sawatzky, a Chemainus mural artist, created these scenes and portraits from archival photographs and composites of actual residents who worked in the mines here over 60 years ago. One is of a coke oven worker; one depicts miners waiting for the whistle that signified work was available; and one depicts a resident in a street scene from 1919 (note that the outhouses were in the middle of the street).

Location: Various locations in the downtown of Sparwood: Red Cedar Drive; Centennial Square, Express Mart Building; Express Mart Building Pharmacy.

Information: InfoCentre, 425-2423, FAX: 425-7130.

■ The Kootenays—Wandering ■ Mountain Valleys

Information on the attractions and festivals of Kootenay Country: Kootenay Country Tourist Association, 610 Railway St., Nelson, V1L 1H4. Phone: 352-6033, FAX: 352-1656.

Information on touring dams in the Kootenays: Public Relations Department, B.C. Hydro, 970 Burrard St., Vancouver, V6Z 1Y3. Phone: 663-2212.

Information and maps on B.C. parks in the Kootenays: Ministry of Parks, Kokanee Creek Park, R.R. 3, Site 8, Comp. 5, Nelson, V1L 5P6. Phone: 825-4421, FAX: 825-9509.

Information on programs, tours, and educational publications on regional forests: British Columbia Forestry Association, P.O. Box 845, Cranbrook, V1C 4J6. Phone: 489-1113, FAX: 426-5505.

Midway, Greenwood and Area

Information on the attractions and festivals of Greenwood and area: Seasonal InfoCentre, 214 South Copper St., Box

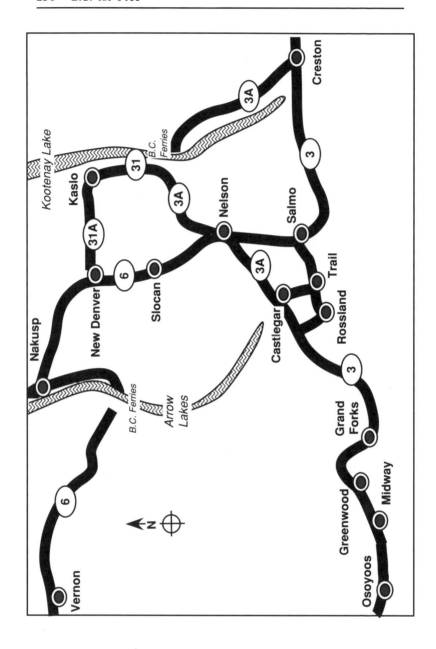

399, Greenwood, V0H 1J0. Phone: 445-6355 in summer; 445-6323 year-round; FAX: 445-6166.

■ **Greenwood Museum:** The museum features displays on the railway, the Japanese community, and pioneer mining. At the turn of the century, pioneers came with dreams of finding wealth in the rich ore deposits that were scattered throughout the hillsides. Guided tours of Greenwood's Heritage Buildings periodically originate here in the summer by arrangement; phone ahead. Closed in winter.
Location: On Copper St., Highway 3.
Information: 445-6355.

■ **Greenwood Historic Courthouse:** Built in 1903 and now being revitalized, this wooden building served as the centre for law and order in Canada's smallest city. The boom town had 3,000 itinerant residents, and served as a gambling and supply centre for people with names like "Pie-Biter" Smith, "Two Fingered" Jack, and "Dirty" George. With the collapse of mining around 1920, Greenwood became a ghost town but is now a growing community. The stained-glass windows at the Old Courthouse represent the original provinces of Canada. Self-guided tours of the exterior anytime; groups only can visit the interior by appointment. Other historic buildings include the Post Office and McArthur Centre.
Location: Building now used as the City Hall. On Copper St.
Information: InfoCentre, 445-6263, FAX: 445-6166.

■ **Smelter Stack:** There are several remnants of smelters and mines in the area. Most prominent is the smelter stack that towers 40 m (131 ft.) over the city and a huge slag heap of once-molten tailings.
Location: Remnants of the B.C. Copper Co. stack at Lotzbar Park within walking distance of Greenwood.
Information: InfoCentre, 445-6355, FAX: 445-6166.

■ **Kettle Valley Railway Station Museum:** This small railway station was the terminus for the railway known as "McCulloch's

Wonder." One of the greatest engineering feats in railroad history is hidden far away among majestic coastal mountains and pristine waterways—the abysmally challenging terrain that this ambitious railway crossed. After avalanches, mud slides, rock slides, and declining demand, "the little railway that could" gave up in 1960. The station was taken over by the CPR, and is now designated as a CPR heritage building. It is presently combined with the new museum and there are displays of interest to railway buffs. On the grounds is a collection of railway handcars, and old agricultural, mining, and logging equipment. Those who wish to walk or bicycle the abandoned railway bed should ask locals how to access the nearest point.

Location: On Highway 3 in Midway, 13 km (8 mi.) west of Greenwood.

Information: Chamber of Commerce, 449-2222.

■ **Old Phoenix Mine Site:** This huge open-pit mine operated until the mid-1970s. Two cemeteries and the remains of the open-pit mine evoke an eerie feeling, but it is a pleasant nature walk in the summertime.

Location: Directions available from the Greenwood InfoCentre, on Copper St., near Highway 3.

Information: InfoCentre, 445-6263, FAX: 445-6166.

■ **Historic   Greenwood   Walking-Driving   Tour:** In its heyday, about 1900, Greenwood boasted 3 banks, 16 hotels, 15 general stores and innumerable gambling and drinking establishments. Today, it remains the smallest incorporated city in Canada (July 12, 1897). It was the service centre for a number of mines, including one known as the Mother Lode. When the mining boom collapsed, it became a ghost town until thousands of Japanese-Canadians were interned here in the early 1940s. Under a heritage program, many historic buildings have been revitalized. Self-guided tours anytime; occasionally tours originating from the museum are scheduled in the summer; phone ahead.

Location: Heritage Walking Tour map from the InfoCentre.

Information: InfoCentre, 445-6263, FAX: 445-6166.

Grand Forks

Information on the attractions and festivals of Grand Forks: InfoCentre, 7362 Fifth St., P.O. Box 1086, Grand Forks, V0H 1H0. Phone: 442-2833, FAX: 442-5688.

■ **Boundary Museum:** Token admission. Outside the museum are displays of transportation artifacts, including a turn-of-the-century fire pumper, stagecoach, and original buggies. Inside is a display and tribute to Grand Forks' status as a long-established Canada-U.S. border town, plus interpretive displays on natives, agriculture, and smelting. There is a scale model of the original copper smelter that was touted in its day as the largest smelter in the British Empire. Guided tours may be available; phone ahead.
Location: 7370 - 5th St.
Information: 442-3737.

■ **Grand Forks Art Gallery:** Four galleries in one building feature works by local artists who interpret the region known as the Sunshine Valley. This broad, inviting valley with its two-storey brick houses and barns invites artistic interpretation.
Location: 7340 - 5th St.
Information: 442-2211.

■ **Mountain View Museum:** Open only by request; admission by donation. Russians fled religious persecution in their native homeland, first to Saskatchewan and then to this area about 1908. One radical sect, called the Sons of Freedom, became known for sensational demonstrations, but the majority of Doukhobor sects were quiet-living pacifists. This museum is an example of Doukhobor architecture circa 1912—the historic communal farm home of the Gritchen family. In the 1920s there were almost 100 Russian communes in British Columbia, each achieving a high level of self-sufficiency, making their own clothing, and farm tools. The tightly knit communities began to break down after the unfortunate death of their charismatic leader, Peter Verigin, in 1924.

Location: North off Central Avenue, Highway 3 to 19th St. and then along Hardy Mountain Rd. for 5 km (3 mi.).
Information: 442-8855.

■ **Grand Forks Milling Cooperative Visit:**
This milling cooperative, constructed in 1915 to supply flour to the communes around Grand Forks, is still in use today. It produces flour without additives or preservatives from locally grown wheat. Guided tours may be available; phone ahead.
Location: West of Grand Forks alongside Highway 3.
Information: 442-8478.

■ **Heritage Self-Guided Tour:** The architecture of this turn-of-the-century town, with the Russian communal influence, has been restored and revitalized. Visitors can obtain a map with background information on each of the historic buildings; self-guided tours anytime.
Location: Heritage map available from the InfoCentre, 7362 - 5th St.
Information: InfoCentre, 442-2833.

■ **Celebrations:** Yearly events include Phoenix Ski Hill "Spring Thing," Rocker Reynolds Bonspiel in March; River Raft Race in June; Canada Week Biathlon in July; Sunshine and Borscht Festival in July; Children's Fishing Derby in August; Fall Fair, B.S.H.A. Rodeo in September; International Baseball Tournament, featuring teams from Japan, on the Labour Day weekend; the Borscht Russian Hearty Soup Festival and Songfest in early October.
Location: Various venues, Grand Forks.
Information: InfoCentre, 442-2833.

Rossland and Area

Information on the attractions and festivals of Rossland:
Seasonal InfoCentre, Junction of Highways 3B and 22, Box
26, Rossland, V0G 1Y0. Phone: 362-7722, FAX: 362-5379.

■ **Nancy Greene Lake Nature Trail:** Named after
Rossland's skiing heroine who won Olympic gold in 1968,
this small subalpine lake features a special trail that cir-
les the lake and doubles as a cross-country ski trail in winter. In
season, the trail is noted for wild huckleberries; wildlife encounters are frequent.
Location: Take Highway 3 to the summit between Christina Lake
and Castlegar; at the junction with Highway 3B watch for signs.
Information: InfoCentre, 362-7722.

■ **Historic Miner's Union Hall and Can-
Can Dancers:** This was the first union hall in British Columbia, built at a time when miners were forced
to endure unsafe working conditions and little consideration. Erected
by the Western Federation of Miners in 1897, it represents one of
the first successes in organizing workers. Since 1929, the mines
within the immediate area have run low on ore and today the city
is dependent on the nearby Cominco Smelting Operation. This
building now is the site of the annual "Gold Fever Follies"—a can-
can theatrical extravaganza held during July and August, twice a
day on select days. A small admission is charged for the show;
phone ahead for performance times. The building exterior can been
seen year-round; groups only, by appointment, can sometimes tour
the interior.
Location: 1854 Columbia.
Information: 362-7328.

■ **Heritage Self-Guided Tour:** When the first mineral strikes were made here around the turn of the century, Rossland quickly sprouted 5 banks, 7 newspapers, a stock exchange, and 30 saloons, complete with attached sleeping accommodations loosely called hotels. The town exploded from a small mining camp to a community of 7,000 with the discovery of gold on Red Mountain. Today, 30 interesting historical buildings, including the landmark Courthouse, the Bank of Montreal, and the Post Office, are in use and being restored. The Courthouse is a designated National Historic Site. Self-guided tours anytime with a map. **Location:** Map from Rossland Seasonal Travel InfoCentre at the junction of Highways 3B and 22. **Information:** InfoCentre, 362-7722; Chamber of Commerce, 362-5666.

■ **Le Roi Gold Mine Tour and the Rossland Museum:** Outstanding value at around $8. This complex is located on 2 ha (5 ac.) and features the B.C. Ski Hall of Fame, a museum, a geology building, a tour inside a mine, and outdoor displays of old mining equipment. A rich storehouse of gold was found inside the eroded crater of a long-extinct volcano. Visitors can take a guided tour 2676 m (8,780 ft.) into the depths of Red Mountain to an intersection with the Le Roi shaft, more than 100 m (328 ft.) below the surface. "Le Roi" means "the king" and investors from around the world were highly excited by the discovery of this so-called "Golden City" in 1890. Between 1900 and 1910, Rossland produced about 50 percent of all the gold that came from British Columbia. The Ski Hall of Fame showcases local contributions to the sport of skiing. A pioneer Scandinavian mine manager introduced skiing to the area before 1900, and the town eventually developed the first ski lifts in western Canada (1947). Nearby Red Mountain has produced more national ski team members than any other area in Canada and counts among its heroes Nancy Greene, an Olympic gold medal winner in 1968, and Karrin Lee-Gartner, who won gold in 1992. At the Geology Building, visitors can periodically learn how to pan for gold. Open only in summer.

Location: At the junction of Highways 3B and 22.
Information: 362-7722.

■ **Celebrations:** Yearly events include the Winter Carnival in January; Golden City Days featuring "dancing waiters," Fall Fair in September; Christmas Week Horse-Drawn Sleigh Rides in December.
Location: Rossland.
Information: Chamber of Commerce, 362-5666.

Trail

Information on the attractions and festivals of Trail: InfoCentre, 843 Rossland Ave., Trail, V1R 4S8. Phone: 368-3144, FAX: 368-6427.

■ **Alan Tognotti Sport Hall of Memories:** Displays here pay tribute to Trail's sports legends and champions through interpretive displays, photos, trophies, and equipment. The area has been home to legendary sports teams, including individual ski stars, and the famous Smoke Eaters, 1939 World Hockey champs.
Location: 1051 Victoria Ave., located in the Trail Memorial Centre.
Information: 368-6484.

■ **Champion Lakes Park Interpretive Programs:** These three warm-water lakes are nestled into a forest setting, with self-guided nature trails around and between the first two lakes. The park lies between the dry interior and moist coastal zones, which accounts for the wide disparity and profusion of plant species seen here. The first lake features two large developed swimming areas and the others are noted for their excellent canoe access. Motorboats are not permitted on the lakes. The lakes are stocked with rainbow trout reputed to grow 2.5 cm (1 in.) per month. In the summer, park interpreters deliver a number of naturalist programs on local flora and fauna; phone for details. **Location:** Off Highway 3B between Salmo and Trail, 10 km (6 mi.) along paved roads. **Information:** B.C. Parks West Kootenay District, 825-4421, FAX: 825-9509.

■ **Seven-Mile Generating Station Tour:** This powerhouse development consists of a concrete gravity dam, spillway, powerhouse, and switchyard. The powerhouse can accommodate 4 generators of approximately 200,000 kilowatts each and the reservoir extends some 15 km (9 mi.) across the American border. The diversion tunnel used during the 1975-1979 construction can still be seen. Most affected by the construction were the wintering grounds of the white-tailed deer. Following recommendations made by biologists, the deer were relocated. After construction, some 700,000 seedlings were planted for erosion control. Guided tours arc available in summer; phone ahead. **Location:** 11 km (7 mi.) upstream from the Waneta Powerhouse. Tourist building and viewpoint at the top of the rock cut above powerhouse access road. Ask for start point of tour at the time of booking. **Information:** B.C. Hydro, 367-7521. Not suitable for children under the age of 12.

■ **Smelter Tour or Waneta Dam Tour:** The first tour covers Cominco, a large smelter complex that produces refined lead, zinc, silver, and chemical fertilizers. Under the guidance of retired Cominco workers, visitors learn how the ores here are heated, melted, and processed. Allow 3 hours. No photography is allowed. Note: there are many stairs to climb and much walking. The second tour, held on separate days, visits the Waneta Dam on the confluence of the Columbia and Pend d'Oreille rivers. Visitors receive an explanation of power production and the cooperative venture between Canada and the United States in flood control and producing a power grid for use in both countries. Allow 2 hours. Guided tours are available; phone ahead. **Location:** Tours arranged only through the Trail District Cham-

ber of Commerce, 843 Rossland Ave. Ask for start point of each tour at the time of booking.
Information: Chamber of Commerce, 368-3144, FAX: 368-6427. Not suitable for persons under the age of 12. For safety, no open-toed footwear or shorts are allowed, and participants should wear clothing that covers the arms.

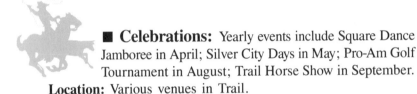

■ **Italian Community Archives:** The Italian heritage of this community is preserved in photographs and artifacts that tell about the story of the arrival of Italian immigrants in this region. Groups or individuals by appointment, in summer only.
Location: In Columbo Lodge, 584 Rossland Ave. Ask for exact directions when an appointment is scheduled.
Information: Residence of curator, 364-2052.

■ **Celebrations:** Yearly events include Square Dance Jamboree in April; Silver City Days in May; Pro-Am Golf Tournament in August; Trail Horse Show in September.
Location: Various venues in Trail.
Information: Chamber of Commerce, 368-3144.

■ **Silver City Days:** Primarily an Italian-theme festival, with sidewalk café happenings, grape stomping, bocca tournaments, and spaghetti-eating contests, as well as a midway and jet-boat river racing. Held on the second weekend in May.
Location: Various venues, Trail.
Information: 368-3144.

Castlegar

Information on the attractions and festivals of Castlegar: InfoCentre, 1995 - 6th Ave., Castlegar, V1N 4B7. Phone: 365-6313, FAX: 365-5778.

Information and maps on B.C. parks in the West Kootenay District: Ministry of Parks, West Kootenay District, Kokanee

Creek Park, R.R. 3, Site 8, Comp. 5, Nelson, V1L 5P6. Phone: 825-4421, FAX: 825-9509.

■ **Mel DeAnna Nature Walk:** This nature trail follows a 2.5-km (1.5-mi.) route around the Champion Ponds. The walk encompasses an area set aside for the environmental study of birds such as the ruffed grouse, the red-tailed hawk, and migratory waterfowl such as mallard ducks. Participants can also see the remains of an old miner's cabin and its shaft, excavated only to unearth fool's gold. Sponsored by Selkirk College and the West Kootenay Naturalist Club. Self-guided tours anytime with a map; groups can book a guided tour through the West Kootenay Naturalist Club. Inquire through the InfoCentre. Allow 2 hours.
Location: The InfoCentre provides an explanatory brochure and exact directions.
Information: InfoCentre, 365-6313.

■ **Merry Creek Self-Guided Nature Walk:** This trail, designed for nature interpretation, winds for 5.5 km (3.4 mi.) through forests, along streams, past scenic viewpoints and into wetlands. There is also the historic site of a pioneering homestead. For part of the way, the path follows old sleigh trails built for winter horse logging; the entire route is designed to require little uphill walking. Sponsored by B.C. Forest Service. Allow 2 hours.
Location: Stop by the InfoCentre for an explanatory brochure. Drive west on Highway 3; the turnoff is 3 km (2 mi.) from the overpass bridge. Turn right and continue on the Merry Creek Forest Rd. for 2.2 km (1.3 mi.).
Information: InfoCentre, 365-6313; Forest District, 365-2131.

■ **Yellow Pine Interpretive Trail:** This walk is designed to penetrate the habitat of wild birds and animals. The 45-minute walk includes 12 markers that explain the transplanting of bighorn sheep into the area, towering trees, deer yards, and native Indian dwelling remains. Note: stay on the trail, as the steep slopes are easily damaged. Sponsored by Selkirk College and B.C. Provincial Parks.
Location: Stop by the InfoCentre for an explanatory brochure.

Located in Syringa Creek Provincial Park, 19 km (11 mi.) from Castlegar at the southern tip of the Arrow Lakes, just south of Hugh Keenleyside Dam.
Information: B.C. Parks West Kootenay District, 825-4421.

■ **Castlegar Railway Station:** Token admission. This restored CPR station is now a museum. First built in 1902, and rebuilt after a 1907 fire. It was moved to its present location by the city of Castlegar in 1967. Today it offers interpretive displays that explain the importance of the coming of the railway to the community of Castlegar. Guided tours may be available; phone ahead.
Location: 400 - 13th Ave. on the corner of 13th Ave. and 3rd St.
Information: Heritage Office, 365-6440.

■ **West Kootenay National Exhibition Centre:** Changing exhibits of cultural, historical, scientific, archeological, and artistic interest are on display. The small centre assists and supports the local arts community by presenting solo and group exhibitions of West Kootenay artists. Past programs include "Clothmaking in Peru"; "Tapestries," by 4 B.C. artists; and "New Designs in Pacific Coast Hemlock," featuring the work of 25 woodcarvers. Works in glass, clay, metal, wood and fibre are displayed in a gift shop. Phone for an annual exhibition schedule.
Location: Across from the Castlegar Airport, off Highway 33A, about 6.5 km (3.8 mi.) beyond the city centre. Adjacent to the Doukhobor Museum, and downstairs.
Information: 365-3337. Write for a schedule: R.R. 1, S2, C10, Castlegar, V1N 3H7.

■ **Hugh Keenleyside Dam Tour:** This was the second of three Columbia River Treaty Dams completed in 1968. It is an earth-fill and concrete structure 50 m (164 ft.) high and controls a 3,650,000 ha (14,100 sq. mi.) drainage area. The reservoir is 232 km (144 mi.) in length and the dam features a navigation lock that lifts river traffic. Three entire communities had to be relocated to make way for the dam in 1968. Guided tours are available in summer only; phone ahead.

Location: 8 km (5 mi.) upstream from the town centre via Columbia Ave.

Information: B.C. Hydro Office at the Hugh Keenleyside Dam, 365-3115; tour leader, 365-5299, summer only.

■ **Syringa Creek Park Interpretive Programs:** In the summer, park naturalists hold nature interpretation programs along the long sandy beach at this popular provincial park. The program varies each year and may take the form of a nature walk or lecture; phone for this year's program. For sincere enthusiasts, there is an unmarked archaeological site in the park. An area resident has agreed to talk to those who wish more information on Indian pictographs or significant sites; contact the InfoCentre.

Location: South end of the Arrow Lakes Reservoir, south of the Hugh Keenleyside Dam.

Information: B.C. Parks West Kootenay District, 825-4421, FAX: 825-9509; InfoCentre, 365-6313.

■ **Doukhobor Historic Village:** Outstanding value at $5; meal is extra. This re-creation of an early Doukhobor communal village is designed to illustrate the philosophy of toil and the peaceful life. Visitors see arts and crafts, a wood-fired steam bath, fabric, clothing, tools; participants also receive either a guided tour or an audio-visual presentation. Presentations are scheduled in summer; phone ahead. For an additional fee, the visit periodically features a typical Doukhobor meal. This hearty offering usually consists of large dumplings and borscht, pyrahi, vareniki, galooptsi, and nalesniki. The food is vegetarian and no smoking is allowed. Reservations for the food service, if available, are suggested. Both services are open only in summer.

Location: Across from the Castlegar Airport, on Airport Rd. at the junction of Highway 3 and 3A.

Information: Village office, 365-6622; food reservations, 365-2625.

■ **Tomb of the Verigins:** Peter Verigin (b. 1858) was imprisoned in Russia for his pervasive pacifist influence—including his refusal to serve in the army. In 1902 he made his way to Canada, to lead the 100 communes and 7000 persons who made up the community. In 1924 he was killed by a bomb that exploded in his railway coach. Originally, his tomb was made of black marble, but after it was dynamited by fanatics, it was rebuilt of concrete. The rest of his family are also entombed here. Visitors can see the small mausoleum behind a locked gate.
Location: On Broadwater Rd., 800 m (2625 ft.) beyond Highway 3A. North side of the Kootenay River Bridge. The story of Peter Verigin is available on a sheet at the InfoCentre.
Information: Heritage Society Office, 365-6622.

■ **Zuckerburg Island Heritage Park:** The park is free; token admission to enter the home and chapel. Built in 1937 by Alexander Feodorovitch Zuckerburg, gentle teacher of Doukhobor children, this home is constructed of mitred logs. He died in 1961, but his carved masks and ornate windows live on. The island itself is considered important for its archaeological evidence indicating long-term human settlement. It is sometimes a peninsula and sometimes an island serviced by a 145-m (445-ft.) hand-built suspension bridge. Visitors to the island see a full-scale Kukuli pit house, a memorial to Hiroshima, a tiny cemetery, and Zuckerburg's Chapel House with its onion dome. Guided tours may be available; phone ahead.
Location: Drive Highway 22, turn east on the corner of 9th St. and proceed to 7th Ave.
Information: Heritage Society Office, 365-6440.

■ **Celebrations:** Yearly events include Curling Bonspiels from January to March; West Kootenay Trade Fair in April; Sunflower Open Golf Championship and Summer Sunfest Celebrations in June; Blueberry Craft Fair in early November.

Location: Various venues, Castlegar.
Information: InfoCentre, 365-6313.

Slocan, New Denver and Area

Information on the attractions and festivals of the Slocan area: Seasonal District InfoCentre, 903 Slocan St., Box 50, Slocan, V0G 2C0. Phone: 355-2282 or 355-2277, FAX: 355-2666.

■ **Sandon Ghost Town and Museum:** Once a thriving silver-mining community with 2 major railroads, a hydroelectric dam built before Vancouver had electricity, 3 newspapers, 24 hotels complete with one saloon each, an opera house and a brewery, this shadowy ghost town celebrated its centennial in 1991. Most of the present damage was caused in 1955 when a creek overflowed. Today visitors can still see the old city hall, a general store, and British Columbia's oldest operating hydroelectric powerhouse. Active mining is still carried out in the area. The Sandon City Museum (token admission), open daily from 9:00 a.m. to 6:00 p.m. from July 1 to October 1, features some of the smaller artifacts taken from the site, and a collection of old photographs. Open in winter by appointment. A 2-km (1.2-mi.) trail leads from Sandon to Idaho Mountain Lookout Point, famous for its wildflowers in late July and early August.
Location: 13 km (8 mi.) east of New Denver. Ask for exact directions at a nearby InfoCentre.
Information: Sandon Museum, 358-2247, in summer only; Sandon Historical Society curators' residences, 358-2631 or 358-2669. Write for pictograph information: Silvery Slocan Historical Society, 202 - 6th Ave., New Denver. Phone: 358-2201.

Nakusp

Information on the attractions and festivals of Nakusp: InfoCentre, 92 West 6th, Box 387, Nakusp, V0G 1R0. Phone: 265-4234, FAX: 265-3808.

■ **Halfway River and Halcyon Undeveloped Hot Springs:** Wherever there is a commercial hot springs located in British Columbia, it is likely there are hot waters at an undeveloped outlet nearby. Intrepid adventurers with a desire to soak in a natural hot springs can travel along rough logging roads to the outlet for these mineral waters. Both springs are extremely hot.

Location: Halfway River Springs: east off Highway 23, 26 km (16 mi.) north of Nakusp. Halcyon Springs: located on private lands on Highway 23, 34 km (21 mi.) north of Nakusp near the roadside. These directions are not complete. Before starting out for either of these springs, get exact directions, restrictions on travelling logging roads, and permission to venture onto private lands from the local InfoCentre.

Information: InfoCentre, 265-4234.

■ **Hill Creek Channel and Hatchery:** This man-made 1.5 km (1 mi.) spawning channel and hatchery with interpretive displays is best in late August. Guided tours may be available; phone ahead.

Location: Near Galena Bay, 50 km (31 mi.) northwest of Nakusp, 8 km (5 mi.) east on Highway 31. Ask for exact instructions at the InfoCentre.

Information: InfoCentre, 265-4234.

■ **Nakusp Hot Springs Pool:** Small admission. A commercial mineral springs pool in a somewhat remote mountain location is fun to visit in the winter, as well as the summer. Winter patrons, soaking in the hot pools, can sometimes experience the quiet drifting of large snowflakes into the steam-clouded pools. Open year-round except October, when it is closed for maintenance.

Location: 12 km (7 mi.) from Nakusp on a good all-weather road.

Information: Springs Resort, 265-4528.

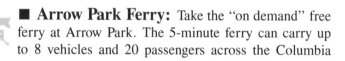

■ **Nakusp Museum:** Admission by donation. This small museum features the story of Columbia River steamboats plus historical artifacts and photographs on logging, mining, and native people. Open in summer; guided tours are available by arrangement in the off season.
Location: On Highway 23 in the Nakusp Village Hall basement.
Information: 265-3323.

■ **Arrow Park Ferry:** Take the "on demand" free ferry at Arrow Park. The 5-minute ferry can carry up to 8 vehicles and 20 passengers across the Columbia River.
Location: 25 km (15 mi.) south of Nakusp.
Information: Arrow Park Ferry, 837-7646. The ferry does not run 24 hours a day; phone ahead.

■ **Needles Ferry and Upper Arrow Lakes Ferry:** The upper and lower Arrow Lakes are too wide to bridge and too long to bypass, so these free car-passenger ferries do the job. One travels from Fauquier to Needles and the other from Galena to Shelter Bay. The scenery is considered outstanding.
Location: Needles Ferry, on Highway 6, 86 km (53 mi.) east of Cherryville or 60 km (37 mi.) south of Nakusp on Highway 6 at Fauquier, crosses Lower Arrow Lake. Upper Arrow Lakes Ferry, Shelter Bay to Galena Bay, on Highway 23, 49 km (30 mi.) north of Nakusp, crosses Upper Arrow Lake.
Information: 837-7646. The ferries do not run 24 hours a day; phone ahead.

Nelson and Area

Information on the attractions and festivals of Nelson:
InfoCentre, 225 Hall St., Nelson, V1L 5X4. Phone: 352-3433, FAX: 352-6355.

■ **Cody Caves:** Guaranteed to be cold, dark, and muddy, Cody Caves is a provincial park that offers about 800 meters (.5 mi.) of explorable passages. An interpretive display near the mouth of the caves illustrates the cave interior; visitors learn about formations called "soda straws," "bacon strips," and "moon-milk." The impressive calcite formations have taken centuries to grow; do not touch them. Bring a flashlight, hard hat and rubber-soled shoes; obey all signs. For a fee, guided tours of the caves, complete with the rental of coveralls, hard hats, and lights are available from a guide (hired by the parks department) who is periodically in attendance at the parking lot from 10:00 a.m. to 5:00 p.m. in the summer months; phone ahead.

Location: Accessible off Highway 31, north of Ainsworth. Follow the signs on the rough logging road for 15 km (9 mi.). From Cody Caves rough parking lot, the entrance to the cave is a 20-minute walk.

Information: B.C. Parks West Kootenay District, 825-4421, FAX: 825-9505; Nelson InfoCentre, 352-3433. For details on rentals: Hi-Adventure Corp. Cave-guides, Box 338, Kaslo, V0G 1M0. Phone: 353-7425 or 299-5497.

■ **Kokanee Creek Spawning Channel:** Late each August, the saga of the returning salmon begins anew with the return of landlocked kokanee to the creek where they were born. The park features outdoor interpretive displays on the life cycle of the salmon.

Location: 19 km (12 mi.) east of Nelson. Ask for exact directions at the InfoCentre.

Information: Nelson InfoCentre, 352-3433.

■ **Chamber of Mines Eastern B.C. Museum:** Admission by donation. Here visitors will find a year-round display of local minerals as well as historic photos and maps from the frenzy of exploration at the turn of the century. At present, mineral mining has slowed. Limited

opening hours. Guided tours may be available; phone ahead.
Location: 215 Hall St.
Information: 352-5242.

■ **Nelson Museum:** Small admission fee. On display here are artifacts, photographic records, and archives. In 1887, the founder of Nelson, B.C. Gold Commissioner Gilbert Malcolm Sproat, hoped the town would have the foresight to keep out newspapers and lawyers. The museum displays a record-breaking speed boat, the *Ladybird,* has changing monthly displays of art, and interpretive displays on native people, explorers, miners, traders, and settlers. Guided tours may be available; phone ahead.
Location: 403 Anderson St.
Information: 352-9813.

■ **Walking or Motoring Tours:** The architecture of Nelson has enchanted movie-goers ever since the town was selected as the backdrop for the film *Roxanne.* Today, some 350 charming buildings have heritage status, and Nelson has restored its streetcar system so visitors can hop aboard for a scenic jaunt along the lakeshore. A heritage map highlights the steep streets, a glacial-water lake, and ornate homes. There are separate maps for motoring and walking tours. Self-guided tours anytime; guided tours are scheduled at periodic intervals in summer. Due to the steep streets, the motoring tours are inappropriate for motor homes or vehicles pulling trailers.
Location: Nelson InfoCentre, 255 Hall St.
Information: InfoCentre, 352-3433.

■ **Kootenay Canal Generating Station Tour:** The tour covers the powerhouse, and participants learn how a hydroelectric generating station works. Guided tours are available in summer; phone ahead. Allow 90 minutes.
Location: 15 km (9 mi.) south of Nelson on Highway 3A. Ask for exact start point at the time of booking a tour.
Information: 359-7287.

■ **Kokanee Creek Park Interpretive Program:** Park Interpretive programs, including nature walks and lectures, take place several times a week in the summer. The program introduces participants to local natural history and mountain safety. The park has a large Visitor Centre, ongoing displays, and a theatre; it is also home to one of the largest intact osprey populations left in the world.
Location: On Highway 3A, 21 km (13 mi.) east of Nelson.
Information: B.C. Parks West Kootenay District, 825-4421, FAX: 825-9505.

■ **Celebrations:** Yearly events include Snofest in February; Nelson Summer "Under the Big Top" Festival on the July 1 weekend; Midsummer Curling Bonspiel, the Great Plastic Canada Goose Race, Kootenay Summer School of the Arts (352-2403) in July; Cyswogun'fun Triathlon in August; Highland Games in September; the Christmas Craft Fair in December.
Location: Various venues in Nelson.
Information: InfoCentre, 352-3433.

■ **Harrop to Longbeach Cable Ferry:** This cable ferry operates 24 hours a day for 10 vehicles and 55 passengers. It crosses the Kootenay River in about 5 minutes.
Location: 24 km (15 mi.) east of Nelson.
Information: Kootenay Lake Ferry, 354-6521.

■ **Kootenay Bay to Balfour Ferry:** This car-passenger ferry, an extension of the highway, is billed as "the longest free ferry ride in the world." Around 15 runs a day through the outstanding scenery across Kootenay Lake make this 40-minute crossing worth a special trip.
Location: At Balfour on Highway 3A, 34 km (21 mi.) east of Nelson.
Information: Kootenay Lake Ferry, 354-6521. The ferry does not run 24 hours a day; phone ahead.

Kaslo and the West Shore

Information on the attractions and festivals of Kaslo:
Seasonal InfoCentre, Main Intersection, Box 329, Kaslo, V0G 1M0. Phone: 353-7323.

■ **Meadow Creek Spawning Channel:** The Fish and Wildlife Branch administrates a total of 4 spawning channels in the region, including this, one of the largest artificial channel systems ever built to enhance the survival rate of young salmon. When the building of the Duncan Dam affected the kokanee salmon runs in 1967, this channel was built to compensate. Meadow Creek features S-shaped channels more than 3.5 km (2 mi.) long. Best during the week of May 12, when the Gerrard rainbow trout from Kootenay Lake are in spawn. There is an interpretive display here.
Location: On Highway 31, 46 km (28 mi.) north of Kaslo; Follow the signs from the store.
Information: 825-4421.
Location: North end of Kootenay Lake, on Highway 31, 46 km (28 mi.) north of Kaslo; follow signs from the store. Ask for complete instructions at the InfoCentre.
Information: InfoCentre, 353-7323.

■ **SS *Moyie* Visitor Centre:** Token admission. Retired in 1957 after faithful service since 1898, the SS *Moyie* played a major role in the transportation history of the southern interior. It was a link with the prairies and eastern Canada via the Crow's Nest Pass and in season, every wharf on the lake would be piled high with apples awaiting the arrival of the sternwheeler. As well as the dry-docked vessel, there is a model of the Kaslo and Sandon Railway, which opened in 1895 and operated on 48 km (30 mi.) of narrow-gauge rail line. Guided tours may be available; phone ahead.

Location: Located on Front St. in Kaslo.
Information: 353-2525. Write for details: The Moyie Preservation Committee, Box 537, Kaslo, V0G 1M0.

■ **Kaslo Self-Guided Tour:** Tree-lined streets and vintage buildings, as well as restaurants, marinas, and commercial establishments, give little hint that the town has survived several sets of disasters. A fire broke out in 1894 at the height of the silver rush and later that same year a hurricane struck. During the storm, a log jam gave way and river waters roared through town—clearing out any unstable buildings. Self-guided tours anytime with a map, available at the InfoCentre.
Location: InfoCentre in the Fire Hall on 4th St.
Information: InfoCentre, 353-7795.

■ **Celebrations:** Yearly celebrations include Kaslo May Days Logger's Sports on Victoria Day weekend; Jazz Festival first weekend in August, Rainbow Golf Tournament in August; Kaslo on the Lake Summer Arts Festival (353-2661) in August; the Arts, Crafts Fair and Music Festival in September.
Location: Various venues in Kaslo.
Information: InfoCentre, 353-7323.

Creston and the East Shore

Information on the attractions and festivals of Creston: InfoCentre, 1711 Canyon St., Box 268, Creston, V0B 1G0. Phone: 428-4342; FAX: 428-9411.

■ **Creston Valley Management Area:** More than 6900 ha (17,050 ac.) of the wide flat valley of the Kootenay River are preserved as a bird sanctuary and outdoor edu-

cation centre. Herds of deer and elk roam here and the sky is filled with squadrons of geese in the autumn. The Visitor's Centre offers a variety of guided nature walks, marsh crawls and nature lectures in season; phone ahead. Binoculars are available, and there is a theatre and library.
Location: 10 km (6 mi.) northwest of Creston. On Highway 3.
Information: Administration, 428-3260; Visitor's Centre, 428-3259.

■ **Wayside Garden and Arboretum:** Admission by donation. Visitors can see rhododendrons in spring, roses in summer and more than 200 varieties of trees and shrubs all year round. The surrounding mountain views are especially lovely, framed by a gazebo.
Location: 2915 Highway 3 at Erickson, on the eastern outskirts of Creston.
Information: 428-2062.

■ **Creston Valley Museum:** Small admission. On display in the Stone House is a replica of a Kutenai Canoe, unusual and rare in design. A similar canoe has been preserved in Russia, suggesting a cultural link with the two peoples. Panhandle Pete, the talking mannequin, recounts the history of the Creston Valley. The museum has over 5,000 articles in its collection. Guided tours may be available; phone ahead.
Location: 219 Devon St., near Highway 3A north.
Information: 428-9262.

■ **Glass House:** Small admission. This circular glass free-form castle was constructed by a retired funeral director from more than a half-million embalming bottles. View it as the ultimate in recycling.
Location: On Highway 3A, 37 km (23 mi.) south of Balfour Kootenay Lake Ferry Crossing. Between Boswell Lakeside Resort and Sanca Village.
Information: Curator's residence, 223-8372; no phone on-site.

■ **Old Mining Towns:** There are several old mining towns, abandoned sites, various ruins, remains of miners' camps, flumes used to divert water, graves and ghost towns waiting to be explored in the area of Kootenay Lake and Crawford Bay. The InfoCentre will supply the names of historical societies, along with more information and maps.
Location: Various locations around Creston.
Information: InfoCentre, 428-4342.

■ **Cottage Industries:** North Woven Broom Co., the only broom-maker in western Canada, holds demonstrations and is near the Kootenay Forge, a traditional blacksmith shop that also offers demonstrations. Can be seen June through September; phone ahead for times.
Location: Highway 3A, 3 km (1.8 mi.) from the ferry terminal at Crawford Bay.
Information: Kootenay Forge, 227-9466; North Woven Broom Co., 227-9245.

■ **Ranch Visit:** This ranch breeds the small sturdy Norwegian fjord horse. Probably related to the wild Asian horse, these dun-coloured animals with black-streaked manes number only about 500 in all of Canada. The mane is cut into a traditional crescent shape. Guided tours may be available; phone ahead.
Location: Bo-Fjords Ranch: west of Highway 3A just outside Creston. Ask for exact directions when phoning.
Information: 428-2181.

■ **Candlemaking Demonstration:** Visitors can see candles manufactured in antique glass moulds, just as they were a century ago. The process involves beeswax candles that are dipped and spun into the final product. Guided tours are available; phone ahead.
Location: Kootenay Candles, 1511 Northwest Blvd.
Information: 428-9785.

■ **Celebrations:** Valentine Bonspiel in February; Butterfly Curling Bonspiel in March; Windup Bonspiel in April; Blossom Festival and Demolition Derby on Victoria Day; Creston Valley Annual Horse Show in July; Fall Fair in September; the Harvest Bonspiel in October; Craft Fair in December.
Location: Various venues in and around Creston.
Information: InfoCentre, 428-4342.

THE CARIBOO-CHILCOTIN

The aura of the 1860s Cariboo gold rush is still alive in the interior of British Columbia. The lure of gold that attracted prospectors to B.C. was the same glint that caused eastern politicians to push a railway across the nation to unite the country. Dreams of western riches drove men and women to endure exceptional hardships for the slim chance of striking it rich. Those who lived off the prospectors—the delivery companies, stage lines, madames, blacksmiths, store keepers, hotel owners, the dentist and the Assay Office employees—often prospered more than the hard-working miners. These rugged fellows had a tendency to go from rags

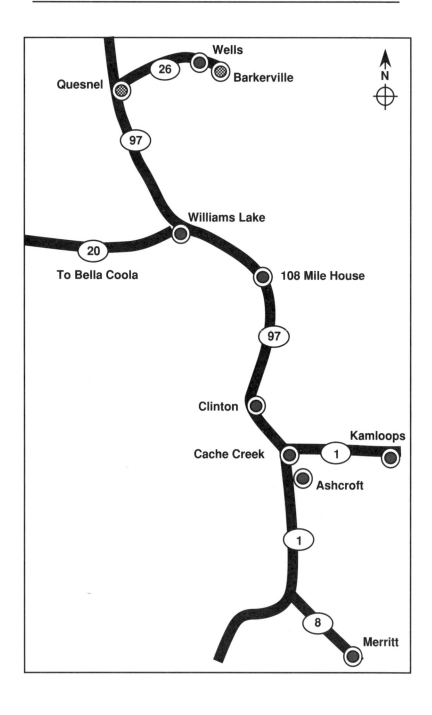

to riches and back again with frightening regularity.

By modern highway, visitors can trace the route of the Cariboo Wagon (or, more properly, "Waggon") Road to the site of this historic frenzy. Today cattle have the right of way in this dry country, where the sky is a piercing blue and rolling hills of dry grass alternate with stands of parkland trees. In places where the land forms a depression, the ground water leaches bicarbonates from the soil, resulting in numerous "soda" pools encrusted with white crystals.

This chapter begins in the honey-coloured grassy hills of Merritt and includes the highways crossroad of Kamloops, then continues northward along Highway 97 through the historic Cariboo to Barkerville, a restored gold-mining town that was once the largest city north of San Francisco. There is a side trip along Highway 20—sometimes called the "great freedom" highway as there are no traffic lights or stop signs for hundreds of kilometres. Surveyed and started for military purposes in the 1800s, the road was completed only in the 1960s and some sections are still unpaved. To the present day, horses outnumber cars and ranches are barely past the "pioneer" state. Along the route, rolling hills backed by the long lakes of the Chilcotin plateau give way to the spectacular Coast Mountains. Highway 20 terminates at the "home of the mountain gods," Bella Coola, 465 km (288 mi.) due west of Williams Lake.

General Information

Information on the attractions and festivals of the Cariboo-Chilcotin: Cariboo Tourist Association, 190 Yorkston Ave., P.O. Box 4900, Williams Lake, B.C. V2G 2V8. Phone: 392-2226; from the western U.S.A.: 1-800-663-5885; FAX: 392-2838. Ask about sports-fishing maps, cross-country skiing, horseback riding, guide maps, gold towns, adventure vacations, guest ranches, river rafting, historic sites, and the gold rush trail.

Information and maps on B.C. parks in the Cariboo-Chilcotin district: Ministry of Parks, Cariboo District, 540 Borland St., Williams Lake, V2G 1R8. Phone: 398-4414, FAX: 398-4686.

Information on touring the Cariboo by train: B.C. Rail, P.O. Box 8770, Vancouver, V6B 4X6. Phone: 984-5246 or 631-3500; from the Western U.S.A.,1-800-663-5885; FAX: 984-5505.

Information on programs, tours, and educational publications on the Cariboo forests: British Columbia Forestry Association, Cariboo Region, 72 South Seventh Ave., Williams Lake, V2G 4N5. Phone: 392-2544, FAX: 398-5708.

List of guest ranches and dude ranches: Ministry of Tourism, Parliament Buildings, Victoria, V8V 1X4. Phone: 1-800-663-6000.

List of rodeo and stampede entertainment, barn dances, and casinos: Williams Lake Stampede Association, P.O. Box 4076, Williams Lake, V2G 2V2. Phone: 392-6585.

Merritt and Area

Information on the attractions and festivals of Merritt: InfoCentre, Box 189, Merritt, V0K 2B0. Phone: 378-2281, FAX: 378-6485.

 ■ **Spius Creek Fish Hatchery:** This hatchery enhances steelhead, chinook, and coho stocks. Best viewing: coho adults from August to December; juveniles from January to May; steelhead adults from April to May; juveniles from June to September. Guided tours may be available; phone ahead. **Location:** Take Highway 8 west of Lower Nicola. Cross the Nicola River Bridge at Spius about 16 km (10 mi.) along. Follow signs to the hatchery.
Information: 378-2992.

■ **Nicola Valley Museum:** Admission by donation. Photographs and artifacts on cattle ranching, mining, and tourism depict the vast empire of grass. Craigmont Mines made a large donation to the museum, and its

archives contain a comprehensive selection of *British Columbia Gazettes* dating back to 1887; the museum association also publishes a popular historical newsletter called the *Quarterly*. Limited opening hours. Guided tours may be available; phone ahead.
Location: 2202 Jackson Ave.
Information: 378-4145.

■ **Quilchena Hotel and General Store:** This operating hotel features an authentic saloon complete with spittoon, brass foot rail, and long bar. The 16 quaint rooms of the 1908 Quilchena Hotel, with iron beds, wash stands, and shared bathrooms, have survived the pace of progress. Adjacent is the Quilchena General Store, built in 1912 and today selling canned goods and western paraphernalia. The town of Quilchena has a population of about 75 people and is located on Quilchena Cattle Company land.
Location: 22 km (14 mi.) east of Merritt, on Highway 5A.
Information: 378-2611, FAX: 378-6091.

■ **Kane Valley Demonstration Forest:** Interpretive signs point out special trees, undergrowth, and other features of interest along a nature trail in this peaceful valley; total length of walk, 2.5 km (1.5 mi.). Operated by the B.C. Forest Service.
Location: Ask for start point and map at the Merritt InfoCentre.
Information: InfoCentre, 378-2281, FAX: 378-6485; B.C. Forest Service, 378-9311, FAX: 378-9320.

■ **Open-Pit Copper Mine Tours:** Vast open pits are mined by the conventional "truck and shovel" method on a 24-hour-a-day basis; approximately 275,000 tonnes (300,000 tons) of ore and waste are mined each day, yielding about 133,000 tonnes (147,000 tons) of ore. All ore is trucked to one of two in-pit moveable crushers. The conveying system of each crusher is capable of handling 6,000 tonnes (6,600 tons) per hour. The concentrates grade out at 40 percent copper and some molybdenum. Copper is used for the transmission of electricity, particularly in small motors, and molybdenum is essential in the hardening of steel. Phone ahead for guided tours.

Location: Highland Valley Copper, approximately 60 km (37 mi.) north of Merritt. Ask for start point at the time of booking. **Information:** The Merritt Chamber of Commerce will book tours, 378-5634; Highland Valley Copper in Logan Lake, 575-2443. Not suitable for persons under the age of 12. For safety, no open-toed footwear or shorts are allowed, and participants should wear clothing that covers the arms.

■ **Monck Park Indian Digs, Petroglyphs, and Interpretive Program:** Around these beaches, park naturalists are periodically available to explain an archaeological dig, native petroglyphs, and natural features of the area. Interpretive presentations are held in the summer; phone ahead. **Location:** Nicola Lake, 22 km (14 mi.) east of Merritt, northeast of Highway 5A. The location of petroglyphs and pictographs throughout B.C. is protected due to vandalism; for exact directions, inquire of the park attendant. **Information:** B.C. Parks, Thompson River District, 828-4494, FAX: 828-4633.

■ **Celebrations:** Yearly events include Curling Bonspiel in January; Ice Fishing Derby, Indoor Rodeo in February; Multicultural Celebration in May; Williams Lake Stampede Festival, Kinsmen Day in June; Nicola Valley Rodeo and Fair Days on Labour Day Weekend. The rodeo features a parade, pancake breakfast, and old-time fiddlers' contest. **Location:** Various venues, Merritt and area. **Information:** InfoCentre, 378-2281, FAX: 378-6485.

Kamloops and Area

Information on the attractions and festivals of Kamloops: InfoCentre, 10 - 10th Ave., Kamloops, V2C 5L2. Phone: 374-3377, FAX: 828-9500.

Information and maps on B.C. parks in the Kamloops district: Ministry of Parks, Southern Interior Region, #101 - 1050 West Columbia St., Kamloops, V2C 1L2. Phone: 828-4501, FAX: 828-4737.

■ **Tranquille Marsh Waterfowl Habitat:** Whistler and trumpeter swans and snow geese periodically pass through this marsh in migration, and wildlife, from rabbits to bighorn sheep, is frequently sighted along the trails. Best times: spring and fall migrations.
Location: The marsh is located on Tranquille Rd., 10 km (6 mi.) north of Kamloops. The best place for wildlife viewing is a short distance farther north on Red Lake Rd. Inquire at the InfoCentre for exact locations and backroads directions.
Information: InfoCentre, 374-3377.

■ **Kamloops Museum and Art Gallery:** Small admission. Museum displays cover the native history of the region, the transition period when furtraders established a post here, the days of the gold rush, and the coming of the transcontinental railway. The art gallery in the same building features periodic photographic exhibitions, sometimes by international organizations, as well as regional and local artists. Guided tours may be available; phone ahead.
Location: 207 Seymour St.
Information: 828-3576.

■ **Rocky Mountain Rangers Museum:** Admission by donation. This museum chronicles the military history of the area. Kamloops was first established because of its geographic position, which was of interest to military strategists. Younger sons of British titled families were sometimes sent to the colonies on an allowance. Because their upper-class background often included military training, their presence here served to enhance the role of the military. Guided tours are scheduled; phone ahead.

Location: 1221 McGill Rd. in the J.R. Vicars Armoury.
Information: 372-7424.

■ **Train Robbery Site:** Near Kamloops is the unmarked site of Bill Miner's 1906 train robbery. With gold, minerals, and valuables coming from the mineral-laden interior and salary payrolls being delivered northward to miners, the area was a natural for a professional thief. Bill Miner, reputedly a polite robber, was caught after an exceptionally long horse chase and sentenced to life imprisonment in New Westminster. Somehow he escaped—probably back to the United States. Speculation says he carried on with his chosen occupation. The movie *Grey Fox* chronicles his exploits.
Location: The approximate site is beside Highway 1, near the Monte Creek Train Station, 24 km (15 mi.) east of Kamloops. Ask for exact directions at the InfoCentre.
Information: InfoCentre, 374-3377.

■ **Pulp Mill or Sawmill Tour:** Separate guided tours are available. The pulp mill tour covers the production of pulp that is later made into high-grade papers; the sawmill tour covers a facility that produces finished lumber mainly used in new-home building; the forest tour takes participants into the woods to review forest management operations. Guided tours are available in summer; phone ahead. Ask about the duration of each tour.
Location: Weyerhauser Canada, various start points, as arranged.
Information: Public affairs department at the pulp mill, 828-7389; InfoCentre, 374-3377. Not suitable for persons under the age of 13. For safety, no open-toed footwear or shorts are allowed, and participants should wear clothing that covers the arms.

■ **Secwepemc Native Centre and Museum:** Small admission. The rich mythology of the Shuswap people is explored at a museum which features archaeological materials and has a traditional Shuswap canoe on display. An adjoining gift shop offers native handicrafts. Several times a year special

events are held at the centre. Phone for the times of the Kamloopa
Pow-Wow Days, dramatizations of native "coyote" stories, or
Shuswap native gatherings to which the public are invited.
Location: 345 Yellowhead Highway, in the residential school.
Information: 828-9779. Write: Kamloops Indian Nations, 315 Yel-
lowhead Highway, Kamloops, V2H 1H1.

■ **Celebrations:** Yearly events include Penguin
Challenge in January; Grand Mariner Cup in February;
Bull Sale in March; Kamloops Professional Indoor Rodeo,
Bantam Hockey Tournament in April; Sky-Diving Meet, Annual
Coin Show in May; Sagebrush Downs Horse Racing, June through
September; High School Rodeo in July; Kamloops Country
Bluegrass, Folkfest Music Festival in late July; Sunfest Celebra-
tions, July through August; Kamloops International Air Show,
International Baseball Tournament, Kamloopa Native Pow Wow
in August; Coquihalla Challenge Bike Race on the Labour Day
weekend; Provincial Fall-Winter Fair in autumn.
Location: Various venues in and around Kamloops.
Information: InfoCentre, 374-3377.

Cache Creek and Ashcroft

Information on the attractions and festivals of Ashcroft:
Seasonal InfoCentre, Junction of Highway 1 South and
Highway 97C, Box 183, Ashcroft, V0K 1A0. Phone: 453-9434.

**Information on the attractions and festivals of Cache
Creek:** Seasonal InfoCentre, Highway 97 North, Box 460,
Cache Creek, V0K 1H0. Phone: 457-5306.

■ **Ashcroft Manor:** Historic Ashcroft Manor was
a roadhouse complex and gristmill, established in 1862,
at the height of the Barkerville rush. Miners on their
way to the gold fields were said to have eaten from a table laden

with three kinds of meat, vegetables, and home baking. At night they slept in bedrooms, on the floor, or on the kitchen counters. Now it is an active tea house, restaurant, museum, and craft store. The desertlike surroundings feature tumbleweed and cactus. Visitors are welcome to browse the complex.
Location: Along Highway 1 at the turnoff to Ashcroft, 10 km (6 mi.) south of Cache Creek.
Information: 453-9983.

■ **Ashcroft Museum:** Admission by donation. The lower floor of this 1916 federal building features a display on aboriginal peoples and the "glory days," at the turn of the century, when Ashcroft was a rest-stop for stagecoach passengers. Upstairs are displays on the history of farming and ranching in the area sometimes known as the "Arizona of Canada." Guided tours may be available; phone ahead.
Location: 404 Brink St.
Information: 453-9232.

■ **Ghost of Walhachin:** This undeveloped panoramic viewpoint features the crumbling remains of roads and nearby irrigation flumes baking in the sun, testimony to the efforts of English settlers to transform the desert into fertile orchards. After making an enthusiastic start, the settlers somewhat reluctantly returned to help Britain in World War I. During their absence, a storm ripped out the flumes and the trees withered in the blazing sun. The once-flourishing remnants of a green dream are now called the Ghost of Walhachin.
Location: Viewed from Highway 1, 16 km (10 mi.) east of Cache Creek. Ask for exact directions at the InfoCentre.
Information: InfoCentre, 457-5306, FAX: 457-9669.

■ **Hat Creek Heritage Ranch:** Admission by donation. The centrepiece of this ranch is Hat Creek House, established in 1861 by colourful Donald McLean, a trouble-shooter for the Hudson's Bay Co. His 3 sons became notorious for stealing horses and later for murdering a policeman. Donald himself, who was reputed to have killed 19 people during his lifetime, was killed in the Chilcotin Wars, in spite of the fact that he reportedly wore a bullet-proof vest made of buckskin. At the site is the last remaining intact Cariboo Waggon road-house, a large structure of 24 rooms. Stagecoaches are also on display. Wagon rides are included in the visit; guided tours of the buildings are held every day in summer. Operated by the B.C. Ministry of Recreation and Culture. **Location:** Upper Hat Creek Rd., 11 km (7 mi.) north of Cache Creek, near the junctions of Highways 12 and 97. **Information:** 457-9722. Write: Heritage Properties Branch, 333 Quebec St., Victoria, V8V 1X4.

■ **Jade Shop Demonstration:** B.C. jade was formed deep in the earth's crust over millions of years and is technically known as nephrite or silicate of magnesium. The milky green substance is 4 times harder than marble and prized as having the mysterious powers of restoring good health and bringing good fortune. At this shop visitors can watch the ongoing process of polishing, cutting, and mounting B.C. jade and other semi-precious stones. **Location:** Cariboo Jade Shop, 1093 Todd Rd., Cache Creek. **Information:** 457-9566.

■ **Celebrations:** Yearly events include Ashcroft Curling Bonspiels from January to March; Ashcroft Rodeo Stampede in mid-May; Graffiti Weekend and Old-Time Drag (Cache Creek), in June; Hang-Gliding Competition (Cache Creek), Gold Rush Trail Ride in July; Bar BX Days (Cache Creek) in August and Ashcroft Fall Fair in September. **Location:** Various venues, Cache Creek and Ashcroft. **Information:** InfoCentre, 457-5306, FAX: 457-9669.

Clinton

Information on the attractions and festivals of Clinton: Seasonal InfoCentre, 1400 Cariboo Highway, Box 256, Clinton, V0K 1K0. Phone: 459-2640.

■ **False-Front Buildings:** The town of Clinton is located at "47 mile" on the old stage-coach road. The streets of Clinton today vividly illustrate its not-so-distant "wild western" past. False-front buildings in the commercial centre of town are still in active use. Groups can sometimes book a guided tour; write ahead.
Location: Main street of Clinton.
Information: Museum, 459-2442. Historical information or group visits: South Cariboo Historical Museum Society, P.O. Box 75, Clinton, V0K 1K0.

■ **South Cariboo Museum:** Admission by donation. This museum features a scale model of the historic Clinton Hotel, constructed in 1862 and the original home of the annual Clinton Ball, first held in 1868 and continuing to the present. The hand-made brick building was a schoolhouse and part-time courthouse for Judge Matthew Begbie; his original chair is still here. Sheltered behind the museum is a blacksmith shop and horse-drawn sleighs. While here, ask directions to the historic Pioneer Cemetery, circa 1861. The InfoCentre is housed in the same building as the museum.
Location: 1419 Cariboo Highway.
Information: Museum, 429-2442; InfoCentre, 459-2640.

■ **Celebrations:** Yearly events include Ice Carnival in February; Spring Fling Cabaret in March; May Ball and Ride in late May; Men's Fastball Tournament in June; United Nations Non-status Rodeo and 4H Beef Club Show Day in August; Octoberfest, Hallowe'en Party and Fireworks in late October.
Location: Various venues in and around Clinton.
Information: Museum, 429-2442; InfoCentre, 459-2640.

100 Mile House and Area

Guided tours of the forestry industry in the Cariboo:
Cariboo Lumber Manufacturer's Association, #301 - 197 North 2nd Ave., Williams Lake, V2G 1Z5.

Information on the attractions and festivals of South Cariboo: InfoCentre, 422 Cariboo Highway, 97 South, Box 2312, 100 Mile House, V0K 2E0. Phone: 395-5353, FAX: 395-4085.

■ **Bird Sanctuary Walk:** This short stroll features many bird species that inhabit this zone of hot summers and cold winters. Short trails lead around a slough.
Location: Just off Highway 97, behind the log-cabin InfoCentre, at 100 Mile House.
Information: InfoCentre, 395-5353, FAX: 395-4085.

■ **108 Mile Heritage Site:** Admission by donation. Behind an ingenious gate designed to let people out and keep horses in are several outbuildings taken from the 105 Mile Ranch. The main house was briefly used as a roadhouse circa 1906, and other outbuildings include a post office dating from the 1860s, an ice-house, a small barn, and the Watson Barn, a gigantic log structure built by a British nobleman to house Clydesdale horses. Ask about the old 108 Roadhouse and its infamous owner who eventually murdered her husband. The pair was probably responsible for the murders of up to 50 prospectors and women who passed this way. Guided tours are available periodically in the summer; phone ahead.
Location: Log barns, roadhouse, north of the Mile 108 Resort, beside Highway 97.
Information: InfoCentre, 395-5353, FAX: 395-4085. Historical information: 100 Mile and District Historical Society, Box 2002, 100 Mile House, V0K 2E0. Phone: 791-5288 (seasonal).

■ **Red or Black Stagecoach:** These two original 1860 stagecoaches were first used to transport passengers from the last boat-accessible point on the Fraser River into gold country. The red stagecoach, now housed outdoors under a roof, was part of the famous Barnard Express (BX) fleet. The chinked-log building immediately behind the red coach is still in use. Both primitive-looking vehicles, with even more primitive suspension systems, are now restored. Women passengers, when they made the gruelling journey, were allowed to ride on the outside, so they could void their stomach contents more gracefully out the open windows. After a night's sleep at the roadhouse, drivers would serve warning they were about to hitch up the horses. Since animals were hard to come by, any horse that could walk on four legs was pressed into service. When the last horse was hitched, the animals invariably bolted and refused to stop until they were winded. Tardy passengers were left behind.

Location: Red stagecoach is found outside the Red Coach Inn, along the Highway, Village of 100 Mile House; black stagecoach is in front of the Mile 108 Resort's main lobby.

Information: Red Coach Inn, 395-2266; Mile 108 Resort, 791-5211.

■ **Village of 100 Mile House Demonstration Forest:** Set aside to illustrate current forestry practises, this forest focuses on multiple-use management. Visitors can see examples of silviculture, points of historical interest such as the Old Cariboo Waggon Road, selective logging and clear-cut areas, cattle grazing and wildlife management areas. Self-guided tours anytime with a map available from the local InfoCentre. Guided tours may be available; phone ahead.

Location: Access road on the south side of the railway overpass on the 99 Mile Hill; 1 km (.6 mi.) west of Highway 97. Pick up a map at the local InfoCentre.

Information: Guided tours may be booked through B.C. Forest Service, 395-3812; Weldwood of Canada, 395-2285; Ainsworth Lumber, 395-2222; or the InfoCentre, 395-5353.

■ **Celebrations:** Yearly events include Cariboo Nordic Ski Society Marathon, an event in which thousands participate, the first weekend in February; Ogden Music and Drama Festival in April; Old-Time Fiddlers and Little Britches Rodeo in May; Square Dance Jamboree, Championship Cutting-Horse Show in June; Logger's Sports, The Great Cariboo Horse Ride (791-6662, 791-6305) in July; Fishing Derby in July and August; I.R.A. Rodeo and Motor X Races in August; Open Golf Tournament, South Cariboo Fall Fair in September; the Arts and Crafts Fair in November.
Location: Various venues in and around Mile 100 and Mile 108.
Information: InfoCentre, 395-5353, FAX: 395-4085.

Williams Lake and Area

Information on the attractions and festivals of Williams Lake: InfoCentre, 1148 Broadway South, Junction of Highway 97 and 20, Williams Lake, V2G 1A2. Phone: 392-5025, FAX: 392-4214.

■ **Scout Island Nature Centre:** The nature house has several "hands-on" exhibits and a rooftop observation deck designed to view birds and wildlife. Raised walkways penetrate the wet marshland and there are interpretive signs indicating native B.C. trees and shrubs. Open from May to September. Presentations are held in the summer. Allow 2 hours.
Location: West end of lake, on Highway 20 at the south end of town.
Information: 398-8532.

■ **Station House Art Gallery:** Found in the old B.C. Rail station, this gallery features presentations by regional and local artists who interpret the rural and

ranching spirit of the area. Presentations are held at regular intervals; phone to inquire.
Location: 1 North MacKenzie Ave.
Information: 392-6113.

■ **Williams Lake Museum:** Admission by donation. Photographs and pioneer artifacts illustrate life from the gold-rush days of the 1860s to the era of the 1920s; the collection includes Interior Salish artifacts and a printing press. Guided tours may be available; phone ahead.
Location: 113 - North 4th Ave., near City Hall.
Information: Museum and Historical Society, 392-7404.

■ **Mill and Forestry Tours:** Five companies in the area provide separate tours of their facilities or a look at forestry operations: West Fraser Mills, Weldwood of Canada, Fletcher Challenge Canada, Jacobsen Bros. Forest Products, and Lignum all provide a guided look at their operations subject to safety restrictions. Approximately two-thirds of all employment in the region is attributable directly or indirectly to forest industry activity. Guided tours are available in summer; phone ahead. Ask about the duration of each tour.
Location: Various, as arranged.
Information: InfoCentre, 392-5025 for reservations. Not suitable for persons under the age of 12. For safety, no open-toed footwear or shorts are allowed, and participants should wear clothing that covers the arms.

■ **Open-Pit Copper Mine Tour:** This huge open-pit copper mine was first opened in 1917. In a 24-hour-a-day operation, the ore is removed by truck, then processed in crushers to yield high-grade copper ore. Guided tours are available in summer; phone ahead. Allow 1 hour.
Location: Gibraltar Mines, 18 km (11 mi.) east of Highway 97, north of Soda Creek. Ask for exact directions when an appointment is accepted.
Information: 297-6211, FAX: 297-6536. Write: Gibraltar Mines, P.O. Box 130, McCleese Lake, V0L 1P0. Not suitable for persons

under the age of 12. For safety, no open-toed footwear or shorts are allowed, and participants should wear clothing that covers the arms.

■ **Cariboo Friendship Society Craft Shop:** The centre is a unique building depicting a modern interpretation of an Indian pit house and providing a variety of social services to the native community. Visitors can browse among the native arts and crafts, moccasins, jewellery, and gloves. Ask about the occasional native dance nights.
Location: 99 South Third Ave.
Information: 398-6831, FAX: 398-6115.

■ **Celebrations:** Yearly events include the Annual Snowball Tournament in January; Cariboo Carnival in February; Curling Bonspiels from February to March; Trailride Gymkhana, Trade Fair, Musical Theatre Society, Annual Bull Sale in April; Trail Rider Spring Horse Show in May; World-Famous Professional Rodeo, Stampede in June-July; Senior Horseshoe Tournament, Laketown Horse and Rider Endurance Race in July; Nemaiah Valley Rodeo in August; C.H.S.A. Fall Horseshow, Sugarcane Finals Rodeo, Cariboo Fall Fair, Open Golf Tournament, Lifetime Sports Triathlon in September; Medieval Fair in November.
Location: Various venues, Williams Lake.
Information: 392-5025, FAX: 392-4214.

■ **Williams Lake Stampede:** The blockbuster stampede in Williams Lake is world famous, and features bronco busters, bull riders, calf-roping contests, barrel racing, and chuckwagon races. Held around July first.
Location: Various venues, Williams Lake.
Information: 392-4422. Write for information: Williams Lake Stampede Association, Box 4060, Williams Lake, V2G 1L9.

The Chilcotin—Side Trip on Highway 20

Highways Department: 398-4510, FAX: 398-4454.

Information on Tweedsmuir Park: Ministry of Parks, Cariboo District, 540 Borland St., Williams Lake, V2G 1R8. Phone: 398-4414; FAX: 398-4686.

Information on the attractions and festivals of Bella Coola: Seasonal InfoCentre, P.O. Box 670, Bella Coola, V0T 1C0. Phone: 799-5919.

Information on hiking Alexander MacKenzie Heritage Trail: Alexander MacKenzie Trail Association, 242 Reid St., Quesnel, V2J 2M2; phone: 992-7111. Ask for general information. Or write: P.O. Box 425, Station A, Kelowna, V1Y 7P1. Phone: 398-2409, 398-4250. Maps available from Visitor Services Coordinator, B.C. Parks, 640 Borland St., Williams Lake, V2G 1R8. Allow 24 days on foot to traverse. Experienced hikers only; partial-trail guided walks available.

■ **Snootli Creek Hatchery:** This remote facility is designed to enhance the runs of chum and chinook salmon in the Bella Coola River systems. Best viewing times: chum in July and August; chinook and pink from August to September; steelhead in June; juveniles from February through June. Phone ahead to be certain that hatchery personnel are on the site. **Location:** 4 km (2.5 mi.) beyond Hagensborg. **Information:** 982-2522.

■ **Bella Coola Museum:** Admission by donation. The museum is housed in a school house and surveyor's cabin dating from the last century. On display are items brought from Norway by a community of Norwegians attracted to the area by its resemblance to the fjords. Relics from the Hudson's Bay fur-trading days indicate that this outpost represented the long-sought, but too-far-north, link with the Pacific. Open by appointment.

Location: Town centre.
Information: 982-2328.

■ **Commemorative Plaque of the Chilcotin War:**
Believing that they had been given blankets contaminated with small pox, threatened by the arrival of gold prospectors, and disturbed by the building of a road through their territory, Chilcotin natives murdered a team of road surveyors in a series of ambushes. The colonial governor dispatched troops and Chief Alexis helped bring the warriors to justice. Five men were hung in New Westminster. Peace was restored, but the road was never properly finished.
Location: 5 km (3 mi.) west of Nimpo Lake.
Information: InfoCentre at Bella Coola, 799-5919; Williams Lake InfoCentre, 392-5025, FAX: 392-4214.

■ **Sir Alexander MacKenzie's Inscription:** Canada's most historic graffiti is a rock bearing an inscription that marks the arrival of explorer Alexander MacKenzie "by land, the 22 of July, 1793." Today, his diaries are studied to match his descriptions to present terrain, and to retrace his largely unsung journey overland across Canada.
Location: Specifics on location from the Bella Coola InfoCentre.
Information: InfoCentre, 799-5919.

■ **Bella Coola Forestry Tour:** On this tour visitors see a western red cedar 4.5-m (15-ft.) in diameter, second-growth management techniques, an interpretive trail system, the Nusatsum Valley alpine forest and glaciers, and logging operations on South Bentinck Arm. Guided tours are available in summer; phone ahead. Allow 4 hours.
Location: Fletcher Challenge Canada, Bella Coola Division Office. Ask for specific directions when booking.
Information: 982-2323.

■ **Long-Range Marine Navigation Visit:** A huge inland tower is part of the marine navigational system that tracks tankers, ships, and boats traversing the waters between Alaska and the lower states. Ships from all parts of the world ply the coastal waters of

British Columbia and all are tracked for safety reasons and for verification of position in the event of an environmental mishap. This navigation system can pinpoint marine traffic within a 4,000-km (2,500-mi.) range. Visitors are welcome to drop in and visit the station with a phone call in advance. Guided tours may be available; phone ahead.
Location: Loran C Tower, 36 km (22 mi.) west of Williams Lake, at Riske Creek. Ask for exact directions before starting out.
Information: 659-5611.

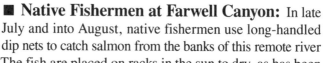

■ **Native Fishermen at Farwell Canyon:** In late July and into August, native fishermen use long-handled dip nets to catch salmon from the banks of this remote river canyon. The fish are placed on racks in the sun to dry, as has been done for centuries. Native rock paintings can still be seen on the overhang south of the bridge.
Location: 45 km (28 mi.) offroad from Highway 20. The junction to the canyon is 49 km (30 mi.) from Williams Lake. Ask for exact location at the Williams Lake InfoCentre.
Information: Williams Lake InfoCentre, 392-5025, FAX: 392-4214.

■ **Pictographs:** More than a hundred native rock paintings can still be seen at this site. Pictographs fade over time. Do not disturb the site.
Location: Thorsen Creek, 10 km (6 mi.) beyond Hagensborg towards Bella Coola. The location of petroglyphs and pictographs throughout B.C. is protected due to vandalism; for exact directions, inquire at the local InfoCentre or ask knowledgeable locals.
Information: InfoCentre at Bella Coola, 799-5919. Write: The Archaeological Society of B.C., P.O. Box 520, Station A, Vancouver, V6C 2N3. Phone: 464-1984.

■ **Traditional Native Meeting Place:** This undeveloped site was the historic meeting place for coastal and interior natives who travelled along "grease" trails—so-called because one of the trading items, the eulachon (or oolichan) was so oily its body was used as a candle. Coastal people traded cedar bark strips, dried sea weed, dried-berry cakes, dried salmon, shells and eulachon for moosehide, doeskin, furs, and tools from the peoples of the interior. At the site there are an unexcavated smoke house, pictographs, and ancient burial grounds. Do not disturb this site.

Location: Stuie, in the Atnarko Valley, 14 km (9 mi.) west of the Tweedsmuir Provincial Park headquarters. Ask for exact directions before setting out.

Information: Park Supervisor, at Tweedsmuir Provincial Park by remote phone. Use the Williams Lake operator, Tweedsmuir Park N692224 Hagensborg Channel YS.

Quesnel and District

Information on the attractions and festivals of Quesnel: Seasonal InfoCentre, 705 Carson Ave., Quesnel, V2J 2A8. Phone: 992-8716, FAX: 992-9606, year-round.

Information on the Billy Barker Festival: 150 Event Festival, P.O. Box 4441, Quesnel, V2J 3J4. Phone: 992-1234.

Travel-the-backroads maps: Specify the Cariboo Explorer Scenic Circle Tour Map; Quesnel Area Scenic Circle Tours. Write: Quesnel Chamber of Commerce, 703 Carson Ave., Quesnel, V2J 2B6. Phone: 992-8716, FAX: 992-9606.

■ **Recreational Gold Panning:** Bring a gold pan, master a few simple techniques and find a few flecks, some colour, or at least gold flour. When the waters swell in the springtime, new gold deposits wash down. There are more than 114 historically productive creeks, canyons and gulches in the Quesnel Highlands; casual panners prefer the Quesnel River where it joins the Fraser River inside Quesnel city limits. This zone is set aside for free public panning.

Location: Inquire at the InfoCentre. The Gold Commissioner's office is for serious hobbyists.

Information: Chamber of Commerce, 992-8716. Write: Gold Commissioner's Office, #102 - 350 Barlow St., Quesnel, V2J 2C1. Phone: 992-4301; FAX: 992-4314.

■ **Cottonwood House Park:** Small admission. In pioneering times a horse-drawn BX stagecoach bounced passengers along a section of the original Cariboo Waggon Road. The 1864 house and outbuildings bought by the pioneering Boyd family in 1874 and are now restored. Operated by the Ministry of Recreation and Culture.
Location: 28 km (17 mi.) east of Highway 97 on Highway 26, on the historic Cariboo Waggon Rd.
Information: 992-9598.

■ **Heritage Corner:** Here stand the remains of a Hudson's Bay Building circa 1882, the river steamer Enterprise and a giant Cornish waterwheel used for sluicing gold. There is a commemoration to the Overland Telegraph Line, an ambitious scheme to string a telegraph wire from New York to Europe via northern Canada, Alaska, and Siberia. Many kilometres of wire had been strung in northern B.C. when the trans-Atlantic telephone cable instantly outmoded the scheme and left many an investor broke. Guided tours may be available; phone ahead.
Location: Carson Ave. and Front St. along Highway 97.
Information: Book a tour through the Chamber of Commerce, 992-8716, FAX: 992-9606.

■ **Quesnel and District Historic Museum:** Small admission. This comprehensive collection of small artifacts includes the equipment used by Chinese prospectors who reworked many of the tailings left by others. There is also a collection of instruments used in a pioneer doctor's clinic, prospector's paraphernalia, and native relics.
Location: 707 Carson at Lebourdais Park.
Information: 992-9580.

■ **Forest Industry Tours:** Four companies in the area provide separate tours of their facilities or a look at forestry operations within the Cariboo region: West Fraser Mills,

Weldwood of Canada, Quesnel Forest Products, and Quesnel River Pulp Mill. Guided tours are available in summer; phone ahead. Some of these tours may be booked through the InfoCentre. Ask about the duration of each tour when booking.

Information: InfoCentre, 992-8716; West Fraser Mills, 992-9244; Weldwood of Canada, 992-5511; Quesnel Forest Products, 992-5581; Quesnel River Pulp, 992-8919. Not suitable for persons under the age of 12. For safety, no open-toed footwear or shorts are allowed, and participants should wear clothing that covers the arms.

■ **Celebrations:** Yearly celebrations include the Legion Trade Fair in May; Billy Barker Days in July; Fall Trade Fair in September.
Location: Various venues, Quesnel.
Information: 922-8716 or 992-1234.

Barkerville and Wells

Visitor and historic information for Barkerville: Barkerville Historic Town, Visitor Services Manager, Barkerville, V0K 1B0. Phone: 994-3332, FAX: 994-3435. Public tours, courses, and workshops are available.

Information and maps on Bowron Lakes and other B.C. parks in the area: Ministry of Environment, B.C. Parks, Cariboo District, 540 Borland St., Williams Lake, V2G 1R8.

■ **Wells:** This town was established in the 1930s as a gold-mining centre and the community is in the process of restoring many of the historical buildings. Three places of special interest are the Hard Rock Mining Museum, the Wells Historical Museum (994-3422), and the Island Mountain Art Gallery (994-3466). Also stop by the old Wells Hotel and Gallery (994-3427), a functioning historic wooden hotel or the Jack of Clubs Hotel (594-3412), which gives a glimpse of life in a bygone era. Those who enjoy historic explorations can ask about Blessing's Grave Historic Park or the Stanley Cemetery where the open pits of 36 Chinese graves are evidence of bones sent back to China for proper burial.

Location: Wells is 80 km (50 mi.) east of Quesnel on Highway 26. Drive along Pooley Street, the town's main historical street.

Information: Wells Seasonal InfoCentre, 994-3237; Barkerville information, 994-3332, in the off-season.

■ **Barkerville Heritage Town:** Outstanding value at around $5; admission is valid for 2 days and is charged the third weekend in June until Labour Day. Barkerville is a restored historic goldmining city complete with animators who assume roles typical of the 1870s. They immerse themselves in history, dress in authentic clothes and then act out their role for the summer. Visitors find a teacher at work, a blacksmith musing about metal supply problems, and a slick gold promoter. There is "Hanging" Judge Begbie himself, who holds court twice a day down the path at the Richfield courthouse. Guided tours of the town are held regularly throughout the summer. Visitors are advised to take the time to walk over to the graveyard, where the average age of death is 31 years, and to walk the "last mile from Richfield." Even in Judge Begbie's day, everyone walked to court to catch the eloquent antics of this charismatic dispenser of justice. The town consists of a church, a Chinese community, a hotel, a school, a bakery, the printer's shop, a Cornish wheel, the dentist's office, and the famous "Billy Barker" claim. The Theatre Royal produces original plays every summer day except Friday. Allow 1 or 2 full days to visit. Public tours, courses, and workshops are available; call for times.

Location: 70 km (43 mi.) along Highway 26 east of Quesnel.

Information: 994-3332 for visitor services; Theatre Royal, 994-3232, for the current program.

■ **Celebrations:** Yearly events include Dominion Day on July 1; Island Mountain Arts Festival (Wells) in July and August; St. Savior's Church concerts in August;

Invitational Horse-Carriage Races, the Wells Heritage Festival on Labour Day weekend; Victorian Christmas on the weekend before Christmas.
Location: Various venues in Wells and Barkerville.
Information: Wells InfoCentre, 994-3237; Barkerville Information, 994-3332, FAX: 994-3435.

■ **Eldorado Gold-Panning Concession:** Small fee, but visitors are assured of striking gold; a bargain price for a guaranteed strike. Participants are provided with a pan and small sack of black dirt guaranteed to contain gold flecks; under the guidance of a real prospector, they are instructed in gold-panning techniques. After a few minutes of work, the gold is separated from the slurry and the flecks placed in a tiny vial.
Location: Just inside the main gates at Barkerville.
Information: 994-3474.

THE YELLOWHEAD HIGHWAY

Highway 16, the Yellowhead route, is located along a network of gentle mountain passes roughly at the latitude of 54 degrees, starting in the Rocky Mountains and forking westward to the Pacific. The highway boasts lower gradients, fewer vehicles, and less stressful contours than any other pass through British Columbia's mountains. In the area between McBride and Prince George, the highway consists of long unbroken stretches with almost no signs of habitation. Between Prince George and Houston, the parkland terrain is punctuated by hundreds of fishing lakes—the proverbial "moose country" for which Canada is

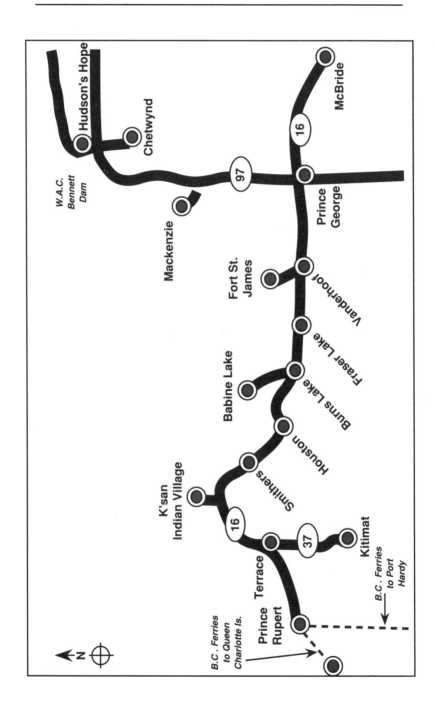

famed. At Houston, the highway enters the Bulkley Valley, a spectacular area of deep blue skies, a few snow-capped mountains, and valleys wide enough to permit farming. The country changes as the highway continues westward; more conifers appear, the rivers become more turbulent, the land folds into deeper canyons and more rugged mountains. The narrow road between Terrace and Prince Rupert has been blasted through stubborn rock and precipitation is a frequent occurrence. Prince Rupert features modern tourist accommodation, fishing fleets, shipping facilities, cruise ships, and the best Alaska king crab dinners anywhere in Canada.

Highway 16 continues on the Queen Charlotte Islands. Visible from the top of Prince Rupert's mountains, these isolated islands are a place of tall cedar trees and abundant wildlife. Fog hangs in the lush valleys and the weather is temperate year-round. The islands are the ancestral home of the Haida nation, who refer to their homeland as Haida Gwaii. Several wilderness-tour companies provide enthusiasts with sea kayaking or fly-in fishing expeditions, and those interested in the cultural and natural history of these unique islands will find plenty to do, but there is little of an organized nature that is free for the casual visitor.

Modern accommodations are available in every major centre in the region. The exception is the Queen Charlotte Islands, where advance reservations are required and facilities are spartan.

General Information

Information on the attractions of the Yellowhead Highway and the Queen Charlotte Islands: North-by-Northwest Tourism Association, 3840 Alfred Ave., P.O. Box 1030, Smithers, V0J 2N0. Phone: 847-5227, FAX: 847-7585.

Information and maps on B.C. parks in the northern interior: Ministry of the Environment and Parks, Outdoor Recreation Division, Regional Office, #430 - 1011 Fourth Ave., Prince George, V2L 3H9. Phone: 565-6270, FAX: 565-6429.

Information on programs, tours, educational publications on northern interior regional forests: British Columbia

Forestry Association, #4 - 556 Nechako Rd., Prince George,
V2K 1A1. Phone: 563-0427.

**Information on guided forestry tours in the northern
interior:** Northern Interior Lumber Section, #400 - 1488
Fourth Ave., Prince George, V2L 4Y2. Phone: 564-5136,
FAX: 564-3588.

**Information on northern interior B.C. salmon-spawning
facilities:** Salmonid Enhancement Program, Department of
Fisheries and Oceans, 4721B Lazelle Ave., Terrace, V9G 1R6;
phone: 635-2206. Or Fort Babine Enterprises, Box 2292,
Smithers, V0J 2N0.

Map of the Yellowhead Highway: Yellowhead Highway
Association, 614 McLeod Building, Edmonton, Alberta,
T5J 0P1. Phone: (403) 429-0444; FAX: (403) 426-5078.

Mount Robson Provincial Park

Map and information on Mount Robson Provincial Park:
Ministry of Parks, Park Supervisor, Box 579, Valemount,
V0E 2Z0. Phone: 566-4325, FAX: 566-9777.

■ **Mount Robson Interpretive Program:** The
Visitor's Centre here features displays of natural history typical of high mountain areas. Mount Robson, at 3,954 m (12,972 ft.)
is the highest peak in the Canadian Rockies and creates its own
weather systems. The natives call it *yuh hai has hun,* meaning "the
mountain of the spiral road." While Robson's summit can only be
climbed by experienced mountaineers, there are some nature trails
on the lower slopes for casual walkers. Watch for dippers—small
birds that walk on the bottom of the stream to catch their lunch.
Check the notice boards for times of nature walks. Presentations
are held in the summer; inquire in advance. Interpretive programs
can range from the identification of edible wild plants to discus-
sions on grizzly bears. The Visitor's Centre is open daily during
July and August; park interpreters are in attendance from June
through September.
Location: Robson Meadows Campground, near the western boundary of the park.

Information: Provincial Park Area Supervisor, Mount Robson Park, 566-4325.

Prince George and Area

Information on the attractions and festivals of Prince George: InfoCentre, 1198 Victoria St., Prince George, V2L 2L2. Phone: 562-3700, FAX: 563-3584.

■ **Forests for the World:** In 1986, Prince George residents and visitors planted trees on a 65-ha (160-ac.) site to celebrate the visit of the Prince and Princess of Wales. The park has an educational trail system, arboretum, and a lake. Those who wish to plant a tree for a small fee can write in advance to the address below and a tree will be planted. Each tree planter receives a commemorative pin.
Location: Located on Cranbrook Hill, overlooking downtown Prince George.
Information: InfoCentre, 562-3700, FAX: 563-3584. Write: Forests for the World, 1198 Victoria St., Prince George, V2L 2L2.

■ **Moose-Viewing Platform:** Moose can often be seen from the vantage point of a raised platform near the roadside. Good moose habitat is flat, watery, grassy, and often found in previously burned-out areas. Best viewing is during the long northern summer evenings, but wildlife sightings are never guaranteed.
Location: 5 minutes walk from the north side of Highway 16, about 33.5 km (21 mi.) east of Prince George.
Information: InfoCentre, 562-3700; B.C. Parks, northern region headquarters, 565-6270, FAX: 565-6429.

■ **Fraser-Fort George Regional Museum:** Admission by donation. Built to Class A standards of environment and security control to house important pieces of Canadian cultural property, displays include the area's

cultural and natural history, pioneer artifacts, an overview of the Carrier-Sekani natives of the region, and interpretive signs that detail the "tale of transportation" in the region. Guided tours may be available; phone ahead.
Location: 20th Ave. and Gorse St.
Information: 562-1612.

■ **Heritage River Trails:** Early settlements were based on river transport—first by cottonwood dugout canoes and then via the birchbark canoes of fur traders. Later, paddlewheel steamers arrived, and today jet boats skim the waves. This self-guided walking tour is a journey into the history of Prince George along an 11-km (6-mi.) trail that includes a fish hatchery, railway museum, historic cemetery, and waterfowl viewing area. Sponsored by the Rivers Committee.
Location: Access off the end of the Cameron Bridge or start from Carrie Jane Gray Park. Maps available at the local InfoCentre.
Information: InfoCentre, 562-3700, FAX: 563-3584.

■ **Railway and Forest Industry Museum:** Admission by donation. The building itself is an original Grand Trunk Pacific Railway Station, circa 1900, now restored. Recalling the days when steam was king, it houses a variety of locomotives and rail cars, vintage logging, agricultural, and fire-fighting equipment. Guided tours may be available; phone ahead.
Location: 850 River Rd.
Information: 563-7351.

■ **Prince George Art Gallery:** A regional centre for the arts, this facility promotes the works of up-and-coming artists, or presents thematic displays and travelling exhibits.
Location: 2820 - 15th Ave.
Information: 563-6447.

■ **Log Home Manufacturer's Tour:** Logs are skidded in from the woods, hand-peeled, scribe-fitted, and handcrafted to exact specifications. Each prefabricated log home is assembled, numbered, and then dismantled for shipment. Interior

finishing touches are left to the owners. Guided tours are available year-round; phone ahead. Allow 30 minutes.
Location: Nordic Log Homes, 615 Richard Rd.
Information: 562-1811.

■ **Tree Nursery and Pulp Mill Tour:** This popular tour covers the combined operations of a large industrial concern. In the nursery greenhouse, where millions of seedlings are raised for reforestation, guides explain how seedlings are toughened to ensure their survival. Visitors are then bussed to a pulp operation where huge trucks are emptied by a mechanism that inverts the entire vehicle. After a safety orientation, visitors quickly pass through a mill where huge chemical vats process wood chips into pulp. Guided tours are available in summer; phone ahead. Consideration is given on a first-come, first-served basis without reservations. Allow 3 hours. Tours conducted by Tourism Prince George.
Location: Start point: Prince George Tourist InfoCentre, 1198 Victoria St. The guided tour is of Northwood Industries.
Information: InfoCentre, 562-3700, FAX: 563-3584. Not suitable for persons under the age of 12. For safety, no open-toed footwear or shorts are allowed, and participants should wear clothing that covers the arms. Be prepared to climb stairs.

■ **Purden Lake Provincial Park Interpretive Program:** Nestled in the foothills of the Rocky Mountains, the park contains vegetation typical of the central interior region. White spruce and lodgepole pine are found at lower elevations, with Douglas fir and balsam higher up. Wildlife is abundant. A park interpreter is in attendance during the summer months to assist visitors, lead nature walks, and conduct evening programs; inquire in advance.
Location: On Highway 16, 64 km (40 mi.) east of Prince George.
Information: B.C. Parks, northern region headquarters, 565-6270, FAX: 565-6429.

■ **Willow River Demonstration Forest:** The 1.9-km (1-mi.) easy-to-walk trail illustrates ecological principles and forest management practises in a mixed hardwood and softwood area. The tour map points out various ecosystems, and identifies exam-

ples of trees and their pests, "succession," and a "productive" forest.
Location: 34 km (21 mi.) east of Prince George on Highway 16.
Descriptive maps are available at the Prince George InfoCentre.
Information: InfoCentre, 562-3700, FAX: 563-3584.

■ **Prince George Friendship Centre & Native Art Gallery:** Featuring the art of Glen Wade or other up-and-coming native artists, the works vary from original prints, wood carvings, bent boxes, gold and silver jewellery, and limited edition prints, to examples of "birchbark-biting" art, which is formed with the teeth. Dance nights, to which the public is invited, are held from time to time; inquire in advance.
Location: Prince George Native Art Gallery, 144 George St.
Information: Art Gallery, 563-7385.

■ **Celebrations:** Yearly events include the Dogsled Races at nearby Tabor Lake in January; Winter Mardi Gras and famous "Snow Golf" Game in early February; Prince George Region Forestry Exhibition, Elks May Day Celebrations, Canadian Northern Children's Festival in May; Prince George Rodeo in mid-June; Folkfest and International Food Festival in July; Salmon Valley Country Music Festival, Dakeh'l Pow-wow, Prince George Exhibition, Sandblast Sand-Skiing Competition in August; Octoberfest in October; Studiofair Arts and Crafts Fair in November.
Location: Various venues in and around Prince George.
Information: InfoCentre, 562-3700, FAX: 563-3584.

Side Trip to Mackenzie, Chetwynd, and Hudson's Hope

Information on the attractions and festivals of Mackenzie, Chetwynd and Hudson's Hope: Chetwynd InfoCentre, 5217 North Access Rd., Box 1000, Chetwynd, V0C 1J0. Phone: 788-3655; FAX: 788-7843.

■ **Chetwynd Caboose Museum:** Admission by donation. This museum features a small collection of railway artifacts. At Chetwynd, the freight-only (no passenger) railway service divides; one line heads to Dawson Creek, the other to Fort St. John.
Location: 5217 North Access Rd., adjacent to the Chetwynd InfoCentre.
Information: Museum, 788-3345; InfoCentre, 788-3655.

■ **Hudson's Hope Museum:** Admission by donation. This collection of artifacts is housed on the site of the first parcel of land surveyed here in 1899; the museum building overlooks the place where Northwest Company explorer Simon Fraser wintered during 1805 while looking for trading routes. Next to the museum, visitors can see a log church built in 1938, and still in use. Guided tours may be available; phone ahead.
Location: 10506 - 105th Ave., near the InfoCentre.
Information: Museum, 783-5735; seasonal InfoCentre at Hudson's Hope, 783-9154.

■ **Williston Lake Reservoir:** Williston Lake, an enormous man-made lake formed by the W.A.C. Bennett Dam, was created during the 1960s as a result of a project that established British Columbia as a hydroelectric producer of considerable note. The reservoir has over 1,200 km (745 mi.) of shoreline, is 362 km (225 mi.) long, and is the largest man-made lake in Canada. It took 5 years to fill, and the surface area would drown the island of Hokkaido, Japan.
Location: Williston Lake is best viewed from Morfee Mountain. Travel north off Highway 97 about 3 km (1.8 mi.) on a side road. Get exact directions at the InfoCentre.
Information: Seasonal InfoCentre at Mackenzie, 997-5459.

■ **World's Largest Tree Crusher:** This gigantic mechanism weighs in at more than 161 tonnes (177 tons) and was used to remove noncommercial forests prior to the flooding of the

Williston reservoir; the machine dwarfs any human who stands beside it.

Location: On display on Mackenzie Blvd., Mackenzie.

Information: Seasonal InfoCentre at Mackenzie, 997-5459.

■ **W.A.C. Bennett Dam Tour, and Peace Canyon Visitor's Centre:** The Bennett Dam, almost 2 km (1.2 mi.) across, was constructed from glacial moraine left over from the last Ice Age. Guided tours of the dam include an audio-visual theatre presentation and a visit to the powerhouse, 152 m (500 ft.) underground. Approximately 23 km (14 mi.) downstream, a display centre is located at the Peace Canyon generating station. This second visitor's centre features a review of dinosaur evidence, natural history, and the pioneering history of the area. Guided tours are available in summer; phone ahead. Tours can be arranged year-round for groups only.

Location: W.A.C. Bennett Dam: 24 km (15 mi.) along Dam Access Rd. on the eastern tip of Williston Lake. Peace Canyon Visitor's Centre: east side of Highway 29, 7 km (4 mi.) from Hudson's Hope.

Information: W.A.C. Bennett Dam Tours, 783-5211; Peace Canyon Generating Station, 783-9943. Write: Public Relations Department, B.C. Hydro, 970 Burrard St., Vancouver, V6Z 1Y3. Phone: 663-2212.

■ **Celebrations:** Yearly events include the Chinook Winter Carnival (Chetwynd) in February; Winter Carnival (Mackenzie) in early March; Dinosaur Daze (Hudson's Hope) in July; West Moberly Native Dancing Days (Chetwynd) near the end of July; Explorer Days and Raft Race on the Labour Day weekend.

Location: Various venues in and around Chetwynd, Mackenzie, and Hudson's Hope.

Information: InfoCentre at Chetwynd, 788-3655.

Vanderhoof

Information on the attractions and festivals of Vanderhoof:
InfoCentre, 2353 Burrard Ave., Box 126, Vanderhoof,
V0J 3A0. Phone: 567-2124, FAX: 567-3316.

■ **Nechako Valley Historical Site and Museum:** Admission by donation. This townsite, originally founded by a man named Vanderhoof, was intended to be a "haven for retired authors." The site features 11 pioneer buildings, 2 of which are fully restored. The Board of Trade Building and the Reimer-Redmond House are fully furnished, and the Royal Bank Building is under restoration. Guided tours may be available; phone ahead. After a visit, enjoy hearty home-made fare in the restored OK Café.
Location: Highway 16, 478 West 1st St.
Information: 567-2991.

■ **Celebrations:** Yearly events include the Grand Indoor Rodeo in June; Canada's largest International "Camp In" Air Show (567-3144) in July or August; Nechako Summer School of the Arts (567-3030), Ball Tournament, Annual Fall Fair and Rodeo, Heavy Pull and Horse Show in August.
Location: Various venues in and around Vanderhoof.
Information: InfoCentre, 567-2124, FAX: 567-3316.

Side Trip to Fort St. James

Historical and visitor information on Fort St. James:
InfoCentre, 115 Douglas Ave., Box 1164, Fort St. James,
V0J 1P0. Phone: 996-7023, FAX: 996-7047.

■ **Fort St. James National Historic Park and Museum:** Originally an 1806 North-West Company fur-trading post, this site has been restored to the year 1896. From mid-May through June and in September, staff guide participants through the fur warehouse, fish cache, men's house, trade store and officer's home. In July and August "Living History" is featured, when staff in period costume spin stories and demonstrate activities of another era. This outpost, once considered the Siberia of the fur-trading empire, was accessible in summer by canoe, riverboat, sternwheeler, horses, mules, wagon trail, and strong backs and legs. News arrived from the outside world once each year. Winters were harsh and the traders complained bitterly about the diet consisting almost exclusively of dried salmon.
Location: On Kwah Rd.; follow the signs to the national site.
Information: National Historic Site, 996-7191, FAX: 996-8566.

■ **Historic Catholic Church, Russ Baker Memorial, and Junkers Replica:** Our Lady of Good Hope, one of the oldest Roman Catholic churches in British Columbia, was built of logs on the banks of this northern lake to serve the needs of the native population and traders. The memorial is a tribute to hometown citizen and founder of Pacific Western Airlines, Russ Baker. The company later became known as Canadian Airlines International and this small community is proud of its link to aviation history. A permanent replica of a "Junkers" aircraft flown in this area was unveiled in 1991 and is located in the park.
Location: Cottonwood Park and along Lakeshore Dr.
Information: InfoCentre, 996-7023.

■ **Celebrations:** Yearly events include the Murray Ridge Bathtub Races in February; Canada Day Birthday Celebrations, Dominion Day on July 1; Fort St. James Family Fishing Derby in July; Fall Fair, Craft Fair in November.

Location: In and around Fort St. James.
Information: InfoCentre, 996-7023.

Fraser Lake

Information on the attractions and festivals of Fraser Lake: Seasonal InfoCentre, Highway 16, Box 430, Fraser Lake, V0J 1S0. Phone: 699-8941, FAX: 699-6469.
Planning guide to semi-wilderness family holiday or fishing resorts: Village of Fraser Lake, Box 430, Fraser Lake, V0J 1S0. Phone: 699-8941.

■ **Molybdenum Mine Tour:** Molybdenum, a metallic element bound up in ores, is used in making steel to enable it to withstand higher temperatures and pressures; molybdenum-steel alloy is used extensively in aircraft parts, and forged automobile components. Participants on this tour see the open pit, a grinding operation, a flotation separation unit, and the active operation of the mill. Guided tours are available in summer; phone ahead. Allow 60 minutes.
Information: Placer Dome Mine, Endako Division, 699-6211. Not suitable for persons under the age of 12. For safety, no open-toed footwear or shorts are allowed, and participants should wear clothing that covers the arms.

■ **Celebrations:** Yearly events include the Ice Carnival in March; Mouse-Mountain Festival in June; Fort Fraser Fun Festival in July; Endako Days in late August.
Location: Various venues in and around Fraser Lake.
Information: InfoCentre, 699-8941.

Burns Lake and Area

Information on the attractions and festivals of Burns Lake: InfoCentre, Highway 16, Box 339, Burns Lake, V0J 1E0. Phone: 692-3773, FAX: 692-3493.

■ **Opal and Agate Hunt:** Canadian opals are little known, but are found quite frequently along with white and amber agates around Eagle Creek. Scenic trails crisscross the park.
Location: Eagle Creek, about 3 km (2 mi.) from junction 16-35; turn west on Eagle Creek Rd. Ask for exact directions at the InfoCentre before venturing out.
Information: InfoCentre, 692-3773; Public Information Unit of Energy and Mines, 356-2824, for rock-hounding information.

■ **Pinkut Artificial Spawning Channel:** This project is a spawning channel designed to enhance the run of sockeye, which do poorly in hatchery situations. Gravel is cleaned and water oxygenation levels monitored closely in season. Best viewing: adult spawn in September. Nearby are ancient petroglyphs carved into rock cliffs, across from the Pinkut Creek Fisheries Camp.
Location: 50 km (30 mi.) north of Burns Lake. Take Highway 16 and turn north on the secondary road at Burns Lake. It is paved for the first 10 km (6 mi.). Follow the gravel road and the signs for the next 40 km (24 mi.). The location of petroglyphs and pictographs throughout B.C. is protected due to vandalism; for exact directions, inquire at the local InfoCentre or ask knowledgeable locals.
Information: Hatchery, Radiophone Burns Lake J-K, N622989; InfoCentre, 692-3773.

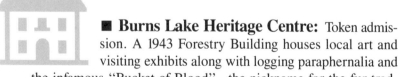 ■ **Burns Lake Heritage Centre:** Token admission. A 1943 Forestry Building houses local art and visiting exhibits along with logging paraphernalia and the infamous "Bucket of Blood"—the nickname for the fur trading office and gambling den that was the scene of a gruesome shooting. In the museum, rooms are refurbished to appear as in pioneer times at the turn of the century. The devices from a hospital operating room and Burns Lake's first X-ray machine are on

display along with picaroons, broadaxes, and snab saws—reminders of the depression era, as during those hard times, sawing railway ties was an important stop-gap industry. Guided tours may be available; phone ahead.
Location: Highway 16, in the town.
Information: Museum, 692-7450.

■ **Quarter-Horse Ranch Visit:** Wander around the barns, talk about racing, and walk out to see the gentle horses during an informal visit to the largest quarter-horse ranch in B.C. The stables here have won many trophies. Mrs. Holder breeds tiny poodles, pomeranians, and Siamese cats. All are welcome to drop by; phone ahead. Allow 1 hour.
Location: Holder's Quarter-Horse Ranch, 5 km (3 mi.) south of Burns Lake on Highway 35, on the lakeshore.
Information: Residence, 692-3722.

■ **Tintagel Cairn:** A 45-kg (99-lb.) stone here, by the side of the road, was once part of the ramparts of Tintagel Castle in Cornwall, England, reputed to be the birthplace of the legendary King Arthur. Sealed within the cairn is a time capsule to be opened in 2067 A.D.
Location: 12 km (7 mi.) east of Burns Lake. Ask for exact directions at the InfoCentre.
Information: InfoCentre, 692-3773.

■ **Celebrations:** Yearly events include the Winter Carnival in February; Bavarian Beer Festival, Kinsmen Bike Rodeo in June; Annual Blue Grass and Western Swing Music Festival in early July; Tweedsmuir Park Days, Burns Lake Fall Fair, Loggers' Sport Festival, Lakes District Music Festival in August.
Location: Various venues in and around Burns Lake.
Information: InfoCentre, 692-3773.

■ **François Lake Ferry:** The François Lake 35-vehicle ferry crosses to rolling ranchlands on the south bank, giving access to several fishing lakes and Tweedsmuir Wilderness Park. Wildlife viewing is best early in the morning and in the evening. Although there are about 20 sailings a day, with a 25-minute turnaround time, those who intend to go exploring on the other side should allow a day and bring a lunch.
Location: Highway 35, 29 km (18 mi.) south of Burns Lake.
Information: InfoCentre, 692-3773; François Lake Ferry, 692-7161.

Houston and Side Trip to Babine Lake

Information on the attractions and festivals of Houston: InfoCentre, 3289 Highway 16, Box 396, Houston, V0J 1Z0. Phone: 845-7640, FAX: 845-3682.

■ **Fulton River Project:** This spawning channel is the largest of its kind in the world. The facility includes an S-shaped spawning channel that provides ideal conditions for sockeye salmon, and a special machine that cleans the gravel between spawns. The oxygenation level of the running water is closely monitored and shade trees have been planted along the banks to provide ideal temperature conditions for the fish. This project has been studied by the Japanese. Best viewing: August and September. Explanatory pamphlets are available on the site.
Location: Babine Lake is 48 km (30 mi.) north of Highway 16 via Topley Landing on an all-weather paved road. The Fulton River fish hatchery is 10 km (6 mi.) south of Granisle.
Information: 697-2314.

■ **Forest or Sawmill Tour:** Choose between modern forest management practises and logging operations, or the operations of a sawmill that produces finished lumber. The guide is an experienced forester, now retired. Participants travel by van into the woods. Ask about the duration of each tour when booking. Guided tours are available May through August; phone ahead. Sponsored by the Ministry of Forests, Houston and District Chamber of Commerce, and Northwood Pulp and Timber. **Location:** Ask for the start point at the time of booking. **Information:** InfoCentre, 845-7640, FAX: 845-3682, for a booking. The forestry tour is accessible to children. The sawmill tour is not suitable for persons under the age of 12. For safety on both tours, no open-toed footwear or shorts are allowed, and participants should wear clothing that covers the arms.

■ **Celebrations:** Yearly events include the Winterfest in February; Shamrock Pageant, Figure-Skating Carnival in March; Pleasant Valley Days, Dog Show in May; Canada Day Celebrations on July 1; Annual Fly In, Open Golf Tournament in July; Competition Trail Riding in October. **Location:** Various venues in and around Houston. **Information:** InfoCentre, 845-7640, FAX: 845-3682.

Smithers and Area

Information on the attractions and festivals of Smithers: InfoCentre, 1425 Main St., Box 2379, Smithers, V0J 2N0. Phone: 847-9854; FAX: 847-3337.

Information and maps on B.C. parks in the region: Ministry of Parks, Skeena District, Bag 5000, 3790 Alfred Ave., Smithers, V0J 2N0. Phone: 847-7320, FAX: 847-7659.

■ **Toboggan Creek Hatchery:** This hatchery is accessible by a road through spectacular scenery. The hatchery fosters the enhancement of salmon and steelhead stocks. Best viewing: adult chinook mid-August; adult coho, October and November; juvenile fish April to June. Guided tours may be available; phone ahead.

Location: Drive west on Highway 16 for 13 km (8 mi.) to Toboggan Creek.
Information: 847-4458.

■ **Big Game Display:** Small admission. As well as examples of 9 trophy-class big-game animals, including moose, stone sheep, cougar, and buffalo, this wildlife museum reportedly contains the largest collection of grizzly bears in the world. Guided tours may be available; phone ahead.
Location: Adam's Igloo, 10 km (6 mi.) west of Smithers on Highway 16.
Information: 847-3188.

■ **Bulkley Valley Museum:** Admission by donation. The old Central Park Building features a partial reconstruction of a pioneer store, a blacksmith shop, and a tribute to local native peoples. While here, visit the art gallery next door. Guided tours may be available; phone ahead.
Location: 1425 Main St.
Information: 847-5322.

■ **Native Fishing at Moricetown Canyon:** During late July and early August, from strategic places along the canyon walls, Carrier Wet'suwet'en natives gaff salmon using long poles. As they have done for centuries, native women camp onshore, while the men take turns spearing fish. The river suddenly narrows from about 700 m (2,300 ft.) to a 15-m (49-ft.) opening, and salmon are hurled into the canyon. The natives call this place *kyah wiget,* meaning "old village." A privately run guided tour of the canyon, for a small fee, originates at the Moricetown Campground and RV Park during July and August.
Location: Take the side road to Moricetown Canyon, 37 km (23 mi.) from Smithers, off Highway 16. Obtain exact directions at the Smithers Travel InfoCentre.

Information: Smithers InfoCentre, 847-9854; RV Park, 847-2133 for times of guided tours.

■ **Celebrations:** Yearly events include the Bulkley Valley Cross-Country Ski Marathon in January; Winterfest Winter Carnival, Steelhead Bonspiel in February; Ski Smithers, Mountain Celebration in April, Midsummer Festival and Rodeo in late June; Canada Day Celebrations on July 1; Midnight Mardi Gras in July; Draft Horse Championships and Valley Exhibition in late August; Bulkley Valley Fall Fair on Labour Day weekend; Telkwa Barbecue in September.
Location: In and around Smithers.
Information: InfoCentre, 847-9854.

Villages of New Hazelton and K'san

Information on the attractions and festivals of K'san and the New Hazelton area: Seasonal InfoCentre, Junction Highways 16 and 62, Box 340, District of New Hazelton, New Hazelton, V0J 2J0. Phone: 842-6071, FAX: 842-6077. Winter: District of New Hazelton, 3026 Bowser St., New Hazelton. Phone: 842-6571.

■ **Hagwilet Suspension Bridge:** Set against the looming background of 1000-m (3,280-ft.) imposing Rocher de Boule, this highway bridge swings where an earlier cedar-rope bridge formed a defendable fortification for the natives who inhabited this fertile valley. The gorge is 79 m (260 ft.) below. Bring a camera and photograph the bridge on the approach.
Location: Turn off Highway 16, for 2 km (1.2 mi.). Follow signs.
Information: Seasonal InfoCentre, 842-6071. District of New Hazelton, 842-6571.

■ **Hands of History Self-Guided Tour:** There is much evidence of a rich native heritage in the Upper Skeena Region, which has B.C.'s largest collection of old totem poles still in their original positions. The bleached white poles are found along backroads and represent the heritage of three ancient clans: Frog, Wolf and Fireweed. Other highlights include "old town" Hazelton, a pioneer community served by steamboats on the Skeena River; the present-day Kispiox Indian village that contains 15 unique poles erected in the 1800s; and a salmon hatchery constructed of logs. Battle Hill is a simple mound that represents the remains of a native fortification designed to roll logs onto approaching enemies; it was unique among native building structures.

Location: As indicated on local maps. To put together a self-guided tour, obtain a map and instructions at the summer Travel InfoCentre at the junction of Highway 16 and 62.

Information: InfoCentre, 842-6571 (winter), 842-6071 (summer); Kispiox salmon hatchery, 842-6384; Kispiox Band Council, 842-5248. Write for historic information: Kitwanga Community Association, Box 98, Kitwanga, V0J 2A0.

■ **K'san Indian Village and Museum:** Admission is free; guided tour is extra. This traditional native village stands on the site of an original Gitk'san village at the confluence of two rivers—the Kispiox and the Skeena. Seven restored longhouses, each with their own totem, have various functions today. The museum, carving centre, and building exteriors are free to visit, but two buildings with special furnishings are entered only in the company of a guide. One is outfitted in the manner of a native longhouse before contact with whites, and the second is an example of a native longhouse circa 1920. The tour leader provides a wealth of details on pre-contact and post-contact lifestyles. Dance presentations (extra fee) are held one evening a week in the summer; inquire in advance. Guided tours are held on the hour in summer; phone ahead.

Location: 4 km (2.5 mi.) from Hazelton.
Information: 842-5544. Write for historic or visitor information: K'san Indian Village Museum, Box 326, Hazelton, V0J 1Y0.

■ **Celebrations:** Yearly events include the Ice Carnival in February; Indian Sports Day in May; Kispiox Country Rodeo in early June; Hazelton Sports Day in July; Hazelton Pioneer Days in August; Kispiox Soccer Tournament in September; Steelhead Fishing Days from September to November.
Location: Various venues in and around the Hazeltons.
Information: InfoCentre, 842-6071 (summer) or 842-6571 (winter), or Village of Hazelton, 842-5991.

Terrace and Area

Information on the attractions and festivals of Terrace: InfoCentre, 4511 Keith Ave., Box 107, Terrace, V8G 4A2. Phone: 635-4689, FAX: 638-2573.

Information and maps on B.C. parks in the region: Ministry of Environment, Lands and Parks, Skeena-Charlottes District, c/o #101 - 3220 Eby St., Terrace, V8G 5K8. Phone: 798-2277, FAX: 798-2476.

■ **Deep Creek Fish Hatchery:** This hatchery raises chinook and coho salmon for release into the Skeena River system. Best viewing: chinook in August and September; coho from October through November. There is a nature trail nearby. Guided tours may be available; phone ahead.
Location: Drive 2 km (1.2 mi.) north of Terrace, past Northwest College and watch for signs. The hatchery is 8 km (5 mi.) from Terrace on Kalum Lake Dr.
Information: 635-3471.

■ **Hot Springs Mother Pool:** The fenced-in area near the

main pool building encloses the steaming mother-pool. There are green algae filament clusters growing in the near-boiling water, although technically no plant should be able to live at such temperatures. According to a UBC analysis, this particular algae is not a commonly recognizable plant, leading to the speculation that this small pool may be the only place it grows. In the 1920s these hot springs were briefly visited by the American gangster Al Capone. At that time, there were no roads in the area, so Capone may have been hiding or he may have been seeking a cure—his unpleasant demise caught up with him shortly after he was jailed for tax evasion. The original owner's son, now in his eighties, has memories of one prospector who was pulled in by dog-sled, in the cold of winter. The man was crippled, his hands were like claws, and his dogged determination to soak in hot mud for 3 hours at a time frightened the 8-year-old boy. After the miner was moved in and out of the muds for several weeks, he snowshoed out. The waters and the special muds in the area (not used now) were long known to native people. Admission is charged to use the resort pool, but visitors can see the mother-pool for no charge. Do not enter the cordoned-off compound; stay outside the fence as there is extreme danger from eroding banks and scalding hot water. **Location:** Mount Layton Hot Springs, 15 minutes south of Terrace on Highway 37.
Information: 798-2214, FAX: 798-2478.

■ **Nisga'a Memorial Lava Bed Park:** The Nisga'a Tribal Council and B.C. Parks have established an 18,000 ha (44,000 ac.) provincial park encompassing the Tseax Lava Flow. This is Canada's youngest lava flow, possibly occurring as late as 1750, and covering an area 18 km (11 mi.) long and 3 km (1.8 mi.) wide. The park commemorates the destruction of two Nisga'a villages by the lava flow, and the deaths of 2000 Nisga'a ancestors. A variety of features are found in the park, including ridges; lava tubes, or caves; tree moulds; and subterranean streams. Facilities include a picnic site at Lava Lake, a temporary campsite on the Vetter River, and information pullouts along the highway. A handout is available in the park.
Location: 100 km (60 mi.) north of Terrace. Take West Kalum

Lake Rd. (gravel), also known as Nass Rd., to the site. Logging trucks have the right of way.
Information: B.C. Parks, 798-2277, FAX: 798-2476.

 ■ **B.C. Police Building:** This tiny building had a big job to perform in earlier days. It was the police building, courthouse, and jail in pioneer times.
Location: Northeast corner, main intersection, Kalum and Lakelse roads.
Information: InfoCentre, 635-2063, FAX: 635-2573.

■ **Raw Gold Nugget Jewellery:** While many search for gold in the north, the only way to be assured of finding it is to browse in this art studio. Jewellery made of raw gold nuggets, and special pieces carved from pink B.C. rhodonite, the "stone of love," and green B.C. nephrite jade bring out the best in local materials. Ask to stroll through the small Japanese gardens on-site.
Location: Northern Light Studios, 4820 Halliwell Ave.
Information: 638-1403.

■ **Heritage Park:** Small admission. Nine pioneer buildings have been reassembled here to demonstrate the look of earlier days in the isolated north. Each building, from the hotel, dance hall, barn and homestead house to the trapper's cabin and miner's cabin, is representative of one aspect of pioneer life. Special events are held in season. Guided tours may be available; phone ahead.
Location: On Kerby St.
Information: 635-2508. Write for historical information: Terrace Regional Museum Society, Box 246, Terrace, V8G 4A6. Phone: 635-2508.

■ **Kermodei Bear:** For many years, there were native legends of a "magical" white bear that lived in these parts. This mounted specimen is proof of its existence. It is not an albino or a polar bear, but a unique form of black bear, rarely seen.
Location: 3250 Eby St. at the City Hall.
Information: City Hall, 635-6311.

■ **Painted Longhouse and Totem:** This longhouse, used as a shop, carries an excellent selection of Tsimshian native arts, crafts and jewellery, beads, leatherwork, and hand-made moccasins. Operated by the Kitsumkalum Indian Band.
Location: Sim-Oi-Ghets House of Native Arts and Crafts, next to Highway 16.
Information: Band Council, 635-6177.

■ **Celebrations:** Yearly events include Arts and Craft Show, Northwest Music Festival in April; Trade Fair in May; Children's Festival (798-2535) in July; Riverboat Days in late July; stock-car racing in July and August; Fall Fair in September.
Location: Various venues in and around Terrace.
Information: InfoCentre, 635 2063, FAX: 635-2573.

■ **Usk Ferry:** This free ferry crosses the Skeena River carrying two vehicles. It is available on demand during select hours. On the other side is forested wilderness. Allow 5 minutes for the crossing.
Location: 20 km (12 mi.) east of Terrace on Highway 16.
Information: Skeena District Highway Office, 635-3687.

Kitimat

Information on the attractions and festivals of Kitimat:
InfoCentre, 2109 Forest Ave., Box 214, Kitimat, V8C 2G7.
Phone: 632-6294, FAX: 632-4685.

■ **Kitimat Fish Hatchery:** The work of this federally administered salmon and trout enhancement program has greatly improved salmon and trout yields. Since the town of Kitimat was carved out of the wilderness about 40 years ago, the fervor of local fishermen challenged the reproductive capac-

ity of the local streams until this facility was established. Best times to view: chum and chinook, August; coho from October to November; juveniles, February to June. Guided tours are available; phone ahead.
Location: 2 km (1.2 mi.) from the city. Cross Kitimat River Bridge and go south for 1 km (.6 mi.).
Information: 639-9616.

■ **Largest Living Sitka Spruce:** Sitka wood is so light and strong that it was used to construct airplanes in the early days of aviation. It was culled from old-growth forests until few living specimens remain. Today the wood is prized for guitars or specialty pianos and this towering giant sitka and its companions are rarities. This tree is the thickest spruce in B.C., over 50 m (164 ft.) tall, 11 m (36 ft.) in circumference and 3 m (10 ft.) in diameter; it would provide enough wood to frame 9 average-sized homes. It is estimated to be more than 500 years old and is registered as the oldest living organism in the Kitimat Valley.
Location: Radley Park. Ask at the local InfoCentre for detailed instructions.
Information: InfoCentre, 632-6294, FAX: 632-4685.

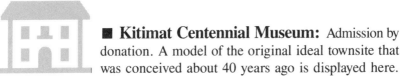

■ **Kitimat Centennial Museum:** Admission by donation. A model of the original ideal townsite that was conceived about 40 years ago is displayed here. Farming implements from the late 1800s are all that is left of white settlers who first attempted to farm the area. A few small petroglyphs have been moved here for preservation and to complement the native display of handicrafts and photographs. Guided tours may be available; phone ahead. Ask for directions to visit the nearby native community village.
Location: 293 City Centre.
Information: 632-7022.

■ **Aluminum Smelter Tour:** Raw bauxite comes from elsewhere, but it requires great amounts of electricity to liberate alumina from its ore. The massive hydroelectric power potential of northern B.C. attracted the founders of Kitimat and this plant. Most of the final product, in the form of extrusion ingots, is exported to Pacific Rim countries. The tour starts with an audio-visual presentation and continues with a bus tour through the compound, one of the largest aluminum-producing facilities in the world. Allow 90 minutes. Scheduled tours are held in the summer; phone ahead.

Location: Alcan Aluminum, situated at the head of the Douglas Channel. Follow the signs in Kitimat on Smelter Site Rd.

Information: 639-8259, FAX: 632-2260. Contact the InfoCentre for reservations and coordination with other guided tours; phone: 632-6294, FAX: 632-4685. Not suitable for those with pacemakers due to extreme magnetic fields. For a set of handouts suitable for classrooms: Alcan Public Relations, P.O. Box 1800, Kitimat, V2C 2H2.

■ **Industrial Chemical Plant Tour:** This plant seems like a space-station movie set. Huge coloured pipes connect like geometric puzzles, each containing extremes of temperature—either very hot or very cold and all under great pressure. Visitors see the mechanized production of methanol and ammonia, building blocks in the worldwide petrochemical and plastics industry. All systems are controlled by computer. Allow 60 to 90 minutes. Scheduled tours are held in the summer; phone ahead.

Location: Methaney Corporation. Follow the signs in Kitimat.

Information: 639-9292. Contact the InfoCentre for reservations and coordination with other guided tours; phone: 632-6294, FAX: 632-4685. For a set of handouts suitable for classrooms: Methaney Corporation, Kitimat Plant, P.O. Box 176, Kitimat, V8C 2G7.

■ **Pulp and Paper Mill Tour:** Participants view the manufacture of liner board, cardboard, and heavy papers in this large facility at the head of the Douglas Channel. Eurocan is Canada's number one exporter of unbleached packaging products. More than 350,000 tonnes (385,000 tons) of heavy paper products are manufactured here annually. Allow 60 to 90 minutes. Scheduled tours are held in the summer; phone ahead. **Location:** Eurocan Pulp and Paper; follow the signs to the centre of Kitimat. **Information:** 632-6111, local 409. Contact the InfoCentre for reservations and coordination with other guided tours; phone: 632-6294, FAX: 632-4685. For a set of free handouts suitable for classrooms: Eurocan Pulp and Paper, Box 1400, Kitimat, V8C 2H1.

■ **Celebrations:** Yearly events include the Craft Festival in spring; Canada Day Celebrations on July 1; Annual Coho and Fish Derby on Labour Day weekend; Canada Day celebrations and International Hill Climb on July 1 weekend; Craft Festival in autumn. **Location:** Various venues in and around Kitimat. **Information:** InfoCentre, 632-6294, FAX: 632-4685.

Prince Rupert

B.C. Ferries through the Inside Passage: The ferry, *Queen of the North,* runs year-round between Prince Rupert and Port Hardy on Vancouver Island. In the winter there is one sailing a week; in the summer, the ship leaves Port Hardy one day and Prince Rupert the next. Vehicle reservations are essential in summer; cabin reservations are optional. Write: B.C. Ferry Corporation, 1112 Fort St., Victoria, V8V 4V2. Phone: 669-1211, 386-3431; FAX: 381-5452.

Ferry travel from Prince Rupert, north to Alaska: Alaska Marine Highway System, Pouch R, Juneau, Alaska, 99811. Phone: (907) 465-3941 or 1-800-642-0066 (U.S.A.), 1-800-665-6414 (Canada). Or write: Alaska Marine Highway, P.O. Box 458, Prince Rupert, V8J 3R2. Phone: 627-1774. Note: Alaska Ferries dock side by side with B.C. Ferries in Prince Rupert. Reservations on the Alaska Marine Highway Ferry System and B.C. Ferries must be made separately. Note that ferry schedules do not necessarily connect. Leave at least a day between reservations to be sure of making connections.

Information on the attractions and festivals of Prince Rupert:
InfoCentre, 100 - 1st Ave East, Box 669, Prince Rupert, V8J 3S1.
Phone: 624-5637, FAX: 627-8009.

■ **Butze Rapids:** Called *kaien* in a local native language meaning "foam floating on the water," the city of Prince Rupert is in fact located on Kaien Island. These rapids churn, boil, and swirl ominously at the turning of the tides. The phenomenon is best on the falling tide; check the tide tables. Add an hour to the official tide tables for daylight saving time in the summer and an additional half hour for prime viewing. Then head out for a look at the water coursing over the lip of Morse Basin. **Location:** Roadside lookout, 5 km (3 mi.) from downtown Prince Rupert.
Information: InfoCentre, 624-5637, FAX: 627-8009.

■ **Natural Bonsai Trees:** Bonsai is a technique of gardening brought to perfection by the Japanese from a method originally developed in China. It involves the artificial dwarfing of plants through a method by which the tree is starved of food, deprived of root movement, the branches pruned and trained to gain the appearance of a gnarled miniature tree. At this site, nature's own "bonsai" trees have been shaped by the climate and the muskeg in which they grow. Estimated to be 125 years old, these miniature trees, *pinus contorta,* are larger than the potted variety, but very small for their age. There are also insect-eating plants around the lake, a beaver dam, and deer that wander down to the lakeside. **Location:** East to Oliver Lake. Ask for exact directions at the InfoCentre.
Information: 624-5637. Do not remove any of the laboriously growing specimens.

■ **Oldfield Fish Hatchery:** This facility raises fish for release into the wild. The life cycle of the salmon is well explained through interpretive signs and the staff will answer questions about salmon.

Best viewing: pink salmon in the creek in September; adult coho late October and early November; juveniles, year-round.
Location: Take Highway 16 past the McDonald's restaurant and onto Wantage Rd. The sign is on the building.
Information: 624-6733.

■ **Kwinitsa Railway Station Museum:** Admission by donation. The building was originally a Grand Trunk Pacific rail station moved here from a site east of Prince Rupert on the Skeena River. Inside are exhibits covering regional rail history. Allow 30 minutes. Guided tours for groups only may be available; phone ahead.
Location: On Waterfront Road, by the Via Rail station. The museum has no official street address.
Information: Summer phone, 627-1915; winter phone, 624-3207.

■ **Museum of Northern British Columbia:** Admission by donation. Praised as one of the finest small museums in B.C., the collection focuses mainly on the history of northern natives. The exhibit areas are connected in theme and portray 10,000 years of settlement on the north coast. Outside the museum are pictographs moved here for preservation, an old caboose of historical interest, and an early double-ended Skeena River cannery boat. Allow 2 hours. Guided tours may be available with prior notice; phone ahead.
Location: 100 1st Ave. East.
Information: 624-3207.

■ **Prince Rupert Firehall Museum:** Admission by donation. Prince Rupert's first fire engine was famous in its day for its electric lights and air tires. The museum houses other related artifacts. Allow 30 minutes. Guided tours may be available; phone ahead.
Location: 200 1st Ave.
Information: 627-1248.

■ **Coal Terminals Tour:** Millions of tonnes of coal from northeastern B.C. are shipped from here, mainly to Japan. This facility represents part of a large capital investment that included building a challenging rail line and a modern town (Tumbler Ridge) in the wilderness, all constructed to move coal in the early 1980s. The tour covers the modern facilities and coal-handling procedures. Of note is a northwest native carving by Dempsey Bob, *Trade and the Sharing of Ideas,* displayed in the terminal office. Mr. Bob is a master Yahltan Tlingit carver with major works in London, Tokyo, Ottawa and Victoria. Groups only, by appointment. Allow 60 minutes.
Location: Ridley Coal Terminals: Ridley Access Rd., 15 km (9 mi.) from the city centre.
Information: 624-9511.

■ **Grain Terminal Tour:** This computer-driven terminal has brought Canada to the forefront of grain and oilseed export technology. As a joint effort of 6 of Canada's largest grain companies and farmer-owned cooperatives, these terminals clean and ship many grades of grain. Over 30 percent of Canada's west-coast grain exports pass through this terminal with a capacity in excess of 4 million tonnes (4.4 million tons). At the entrance is a native carving entitled *Traders from the Sea* by Dempsey Bob. Scheduled tours are held in the summer; phone ahead. Allow 60 minutes.
Location: On Ridley Island, 15 km (9 mi.) from Prince Rupert near the Oliver Lake turnoff.
Information: 627-8777, FAX: 627-8541. Contact the InfoCentre for reservations; phone: 624-5637, FAX: 627-8009. There are many stairs to climb during this tour.

■ **Heritage Self-Guided Tour:** Token fee. To tour the downtown commercial centre, visitors can rent a cassette player and tape. The tour covers authentic reproductions of ancient totem poles as well as others commissioned to record important events in recent times. The self-guided tour also provides informed commentary on the fishing industry, shipping activity from this year-round ice-free port and information on the Presbyterian Church Heritage Site.

Location: Start point: Prince Rupert Visitor's Bureau, 1st Ave. and McBride St.
Information: InfoCentre, 624-5637, FAX: 627-8009.

■ **Celebrations:** Yearly events include the All Native Basketball Tournament in February; Wine Festival in May; Prince Rupert Seafest (627-1781), Salmon Festival and Native Indian Gathering, Kinsmen Trade Fair, Folk Fest in June.
Location: Various venues in and around Prince Rupert.
Information: InfoCentre, 624-5637, FAX: 627-8009.

The Queen Charlotte Islands, or Haida Gwaii

B.C. Ferries to the Queen Charlotte Islands: Reservations are essential for ferry service between Prince Rupert and Skidegate Landing on Graham Island in the Queen Charlottes. There are 3 sailings per day in the winter and 6 sailings per day in the summer. Allow 6 hours for the crossing. A smaller ferry, MV *Kwuna* connects Skidegate Landing to Alliford Bay on Moresby Island. About 12 sailings a day. Allow 20 minutes between the north and south Islands. Write: B.C. Ferry Corporation, 1112 Fort St., Victoria, V8V 4V2. Phone: 669-1211, 386-3431. From Seattle: (206) 624-6663.

Information on the attractions of the Queen Charlotte Islands: Queen Charlotte Islands Chamber of Commerce, Box 38, Masset, V0T 1M0. Phone: 626-5211. For comprehensive information on the Queen Charlotte Islands, send $7 to cover handling and printing charges.

Information on the attractions of Graham Island and the Queen Charlotte Islands: Seasonal InfoCentre, Village of Masset, 1455 Old Beach Rd., Box 68, Masset, V0T 1M0. Phone and FAX: 626-3995.

Information and map on Naikoon Provincial Park: Ministry of Parks, Area Supervisor, Box 19, Tlell, Queen Charlotte Islands, V0T 1Y0. Phone and FAX: 557-4390.

■ **Delkatla Wildlife and Bird Sanctuary:** The Charlottes are a major resting point on the Pacific migration routes, and more than 115 species of birds have been identified here. In addition, local species such as the Peale's peregrine falcon are abundant. Tufted puffins, sandhill cranes, trumpeter swans, seabirds, and numerous species of eagles are frequently sighted. Out at sea are killer whales, dolphins, seals, and sea lions. Between late April and May, gray whales can be seen pausing in migration. There is a bird walk trail and a viewing tower on-site. **Location:** The sanctuary is located in Masset. More of the sanctuary may be seen by driving along Tow Hill Road towards Naikoon Provincial Park. Turn left at the sanctuary sign on Masset Cemetery Rd. The "Bird Walk Trail" is posted and farther along is the Simpson Viewing Tower. Ask for exact directions at the InfoCentre. **Information:** Masset InfoCentre, 626-3995 in summer; Queen Charlotte InfoCentre, 559-4747, year round.

■ **Golden Spruce Tree:** The Charlottes are sometimes referred to as the "Galapagos of the North" owing to the unique species found here. This genetically unusual spruce tree is 50 m (164 ft.) tall. The needles, bleached to a bright yellow colour by the sun, are still living. Scientists have attempted to grow new specimens without success. Some say the best photographs are taken before noon, when the tree is back-lit. **Location:** Pull-out on the road 5.5 km (3.5 mi.) south of Port Clements on Juskatla Rd. Walk 10 minutes along a trail. The spruce is on the opposite bank of the river. Ask for exact directions at the InfoCentre. **Information:** Masset InfoCentre, 626-3995 in summer; Queen Charlotte InfoCentre, 559-4747, year round.

■ **Skidegate Band Salmon Project:** This salmon enhancement facility is run by the Haida natives, a natural extension of their traditional link to the salmon cycle. Best viewing times: late summer when the coho and chum return.

Location: Take the road west from Queen Charlotte City. The hatchery is located about 5 km (3 mi.) along Honna Forest Service Rd., next to the river.
Information: 559-4496.

■ **Tow Hill Ecological Reserve:** The drive from Masset along Tow Hill Road features a deep forest draped in bearded moss, the forest floor cushioned in spongy material, on one side and far-reaching ocean views on the other. Agate Beach is strewn with shiny, smooth, sea-worn pebbles and pieces of driftwood. A walk along the short Heillen riverside trail leads to splendid views from the top of Tow Hill.
Location: From Masset to Agate Beach is about 15 to 20 km (12 mi.). Obtain exact directions from the InfoCentre.
Information: Masset InfoCentre, 626-3995 in summer; Queen Charlotte InfoCentre, 559-4747, year round.

■ **Port Clements Museum:** Admission by donation. This museum features black and white photographs of logging camp life, and artifacts from early fishing and mining days on the isolated Charlottes. The first European contact occurred in 1774, when Juan Perez encountered the islands, but the name was bestowed in 1787 by an officer on Captain Cook's voyage. The islands were named after the wife of George III, a British monarch. The museum is open periodically.
Location: 45 Bayview Dr., Port Clements.
Information: 557-4576, to see if it is staffed.

■ **Abandoned Haida Canoe:** The largest Haida canoes ever built could carry some 40 people. This old cedar dugout canoe was partially completed, then abandoned; the bow points to the tree from which it was cut. It now provides valuable information on the traditional building methods of the Haida. Several other unfinished canoes lie in the forest, but this is the only one readily accessible. A Haida canoe, commis-

sioned in 1986, is now used by a native tour company for wilderness adventure tours.
Location: On the east side of Juskatla Rd., 13 km (8 mi.) from Port Clements. Ask for exact directions at the InfoCentre or from knowledgeable locals.
Information: Masset InfoCentre, 626-3995 in summer; Queen Charlotte InfoCentre, 559-4747, year round.

■ **Haida Longhouse Exterior:** This Haida longhouse, headquarters of the Skidegate Band Council, is fronted by a new pole designed by famous artist and native son Bill Reid. About 1 km (.6 mi.) away is a natural wonder known as "balancing rock," a boulder deposited by ice sheets. Those who wish to visit protected native villages on South Moresby must apply for a permit at the longhouse. The protected World Heritage site of Ninstints, an abandoned village with picturesque decaying totems, is located on Anthony Island off the coast of South Moresby Island. All protected areas are water or air-accessible only and require a permit to visit them.
Location: Skidegate Haida community on Rooney Bay, 2 km (1 mi.) north of Skidegate Landing.
Information: Skidegate Band Council, 559-4496; Canadian Parks Service, 559-8818.

■ **Old Masset Village, Galleries, and Museum:** Admission by donation. With a population of 800, this is the largest Haida native village in the Charlottes. Several home-based native artist studios are open to the public; watch for roadside signs. Hanging rather unobtrusively over the door of the old Masset museum is a copy of a 1912 Emily Carr painting, *Chaatl*. The museum is located in the old schoolhouse and has a map of chiefs' and artists' homes.
Location: 2 km (1 mi.) north of Masset at the entrance to the harbour.
Information: Old Masset Band Council, 626-3337.

■ **Queen Charlotte Islands Museum:** Admission by donation. Argillite, discovered in the 1820s at Slatechuck Mountain, is unique to the Charlottes, and the quarry is licensed to the Haida, the only official carvers of the material. Prized by collectors throughout the world, the blackish slate-like stone is used to create intricate pipes, totem replicas, and boxes. Excellent examples of argillite, as well as interpretive displays of pioneer history, Haida history and art are featured here. Whale watching can sometimes be very productive from this location. Open periodically from June to September.

Location: East off Highway 16 at Second Beach, Queen Charlotte City.

Information: 559-4643.

■ **Forestry Tour:** Groups of visitors to the Charlottes can arrange a group tour of a forestry operation. Ask for the duration of the tour. Forestry companies also provide the best maps of backroads on the islands.

Location: MacMillan Bloedel Ltd. Inquire about the start point when a booking is accepted.

Information: 557-4212. Write for forestry maps: MacMillan Bloedel, Box 10, Juskatla, V0T 1J0.

■ **Sandspit Timber Tour:** This is the only free conducted tour available on Moresby Island, the southern island of the Queen Charlottes. Participants see an active logging operation, yarding, loading, and hauling, an eagle-nesting site, enjoy a beach walk, and catch a glimpse of west-coast wildlife. The guide discusses the partnership of forestry and fisheries as well as the impact of forestry on the Haida people. Allow 4 hours. Scheduled tours are held in the summer; phone ahead.

Location: Start point: Sandspit Tourist Information Centre, Moresby Island, or as arranged.

Information: Fletcher Challenge Canada, 637-5323.

INDEX

Abbotsford, 88
Able Walker Museum, 44
Adams Igloo, 318
Adams River sockeye run, 226
Addington Marsh, 49
Agassiz, 98
Agate hunting, 77, 103, 188, 219, 314
Agricultural Research Station tours, 89, 100, 205
Ainu Poles and Totem Poles, 45
Air-force history, 162, 180
Airport tour, 62
Airshows, 90, 165, 310
Alberni Valley Art Gallery, Quay and Museum, 152
Albion ferry, 63
Alcan Aluminum, 326
Alert Bay, 176
Alexander Mackenzie Heritage Trail, 292
Alexandra Bridge, 109
Alice Lake, 69
Alpine garden, 17
Alpine meadows, 74, 107, 172
Aluminum smelter tour, 326
Ammonia production tour, 326
Angus Creek, 81
Anthropological museums/sites, 19, 45, 91
Antique Row, 56, 116
Anvil salute, 48
Apples and apple products, 95, 190, 196, 213
Arboretums, 54, 100, 271, 302, 305
Archaeological sites, 216, 262, 280
Archaeological Society, 217
Argillite carving, 19, 333
Armstrong Cheese, 219
Armstrong, 218
Arrow Park ferry, 266
Art festivals, 37, 47, 53, 58, 90, 101, 163, 164, 193, 200, 271
Art galleries, 21, 24, 34, 35, 43, 45, 50, 53, 89, 118, 123, 144, 152, 160, 163, 193, 201, 210
Art studios and centres, 24, 25,

45, 47, 68, 82
Ashcroft, 283
Association of Professional Foresters of B.C., 24
Aviation museum, 126

B.C. Agricultural Museum, 58
B.C. and Yukon Chamber of Mines, 18
B.C. Aviation Museum, 126
B.C. Fruit Growers Association, 209
B.C. Hydro tours, 92
B.C. Orchard Industry Museum, 209
B.C. Place Stadium tour, 22
B.C. scale-model map, 44
Babine Lake, 316
Bakeries, 24, 244
Balfour ferry, 269, 272
Ball mill, 105
Bamfield, 153
Banana farm, 191
Banners and flag sewing, 24
Barkerville, 297
Barkley Sound cruise, 151
Barnston Island ferry, 55
Barrowtown Pump Station, 89
Basset House Museum, 197
Bastion, military, 143
Beachcombing, 135, 148, 333
Beacon Hill Park, 116
Beaver Cove, 175
Beaver habitat, 107, 139, 142, 144, 248
Beaver Harbour, 181
Bee hive tours, 144, 213
Beer-making tours, 22, 216
Bell-Irving Fish Hatchery, 60
Bella Coola, 292
Bennett Dam, 310
Benvoulin Church, 210
BHP Minerals Canada, 181
Bicycling routes, 16, 36, 39, 41, 55, 60, 143, 203, 212, 252
Big Qualicum Hatchery, 159
Big Qualicum River, 159
Bighorn sheep, 194, 226, 238, 294
Bill Reid, 333

British Columbia Gazette, 279
"Bucket of Blood," 314
Birchbark-biting art, 308
Bird rescue society, 244
Bird watching, 39, 49, 52, 56, 60,
   81, 107, 122, 135, 149, 179, 192,
   194, 228, 271, 287, 289, 332
Black Nugget Museum, 141
Black stagecoach, 288
Black Tusk, 72
Blackcomb ski orientation, 73
Blackcomb-Whistler, 71
Blacksmiths, 43, 95, 220, 273, 286,
   318
Blakeburn, 187
Blessings Grave historic park, 298
Blue whale jawbones, 126, 180
Boar-raising ranch, 202
Bonfires on the beach, 38, 156
Boston Bar, 110
Boundary Museum, 253
Bowron Lakes, 297
Brackendale Gallery, 68
Breakwater structures, 86, 119
Brewery tours, 22, 216
Brick-manufacturing tour, 89
Bridal Falls, 103
Bridge Lake, 76
Bridge of the 23 Camels, 79
Bright Wines, 195
Broom-making tour, 273
Buddhist temple visit, 41
Budget cruising, 151, 171, 179
Bulkley Valley, 318
Burgess shales, 235
Burl, large, 175
Burnaby Lake Regional Park, 43
Burnaby Mountain Park, 45
Burning coal mine, 245
Burns Lake, 313
Burrvilla Victorian house, 56
Butterflies, mounted, 20
Butterfly World, live, 148
Butze Rapids, 328

Cable ferry, 269
Cable wrapped restaurant, 173
Caboose Museum, Chetwynd, 309
Cache Creek, 283

Cactus, 192
Calona Wines, 210
Campbell River, 165
Campbell Valley Regional Park, 57
Campfires, 38, 156
Campsites for groups, 56, 58
Campus tours, 27, 45, 123, 129
Can Can dancers, 80, 255
Canada Place tour, 23
Canadian Coast Guard hovercraft,
   40, 135, 149
Canadian Coast Guard traffic serv-
   ices, 35
Canadian Craft Museum, 18
Canadian Forces Base tour, 120
Canadian Lacrosse Hall of Fame,
   47
Canadian Memorial Church tour,
   23
Canadian Military Engineers
   Museum, 94
Canadian Occidental industrial
   chemicals, 36
Canadian Pacific Railway, 18, 50,
   231
Canadian Princess hotel lobby, 154
Canadian Professional Rodeo Cir-
   cuit Association, 291
Candlemaking demonstration, 273
Canoe Beach, 229
Canyon Hot Springs, 232
Cape Mudge, 169
Capilano Fish Hatchery, 32
Cariboo-Chilcotin, 277
Cariboo Friendship Society, 291
Cariboo regional forests, 278
Cariboo Wagon Road, 109, 283,
   284, 296
Carr House, 117
Carrot Park, 180
Cartier Wines, 202
Cascade Falls Regional Park, 91
Castlegar, 259
Castles, 117, 128
Cathedral Grove, 147
Cave parks, 159, 170, 172, 174,
   267
Cayoosh Creek, 77
Cedar Creek Estate Winery, 211

Cedar forests, 16, 33, 121, 164
Cedar seedlings, 54
Cement factory remains, 187
Cemeteries, 121, 263, 286, 306, 332
Centennial Fountain, 119
Challenger Relief Map, 44
Chamber of Mines Eastern B.C. Museum, 267
Champion Lakes Provincial Park, 257
Chase, 226
Chateau St. Claire Winery, 206
Chateau Whistler lobby, 73
Cheese making, 219, 229
Chemainus, 140
Chemical plant tours, 36, 326
Cherries, 190, 195
Cherry blossoms, 17, 47
Cherryville, 217
Chetwynd, 308
Chilcotin Wars memorial plaque, 293
Children's petting zoos, 33, 47, 84, 215, 232
Chilko Lake, 292
Chilliwack, 94
Chinatown, 28, 92, 128, 163
Chinese gold mining, 78, 79, 110, 188, 217
Chinese graves, 298
Chinook project, 172
Chocolate demonstrations, 23, 24
Chuckwagon races, 291
Church visits, 23, 41, 93, 106, 119, 177, 210, 239
Cleveland Dam, 32
Cliffs, 150, 219
Clinton, 285
Clock tower, 152
CNR Superintendent's House, 243
Coal Harbour whaling station, 180
Coal-mining museum, 163
Coal-terminal tours, 26, 330
Coalmont Hotel, 187
Coast Guard station visit, 158
Cody Caves Provincial Park, 267
Columbia River steamboat story, 266

Colwood-Langford, 128
Combers Beach, 155
Cominco Gardens, 240
Commercial wineries, 50, 195, 202, 207, 210
Comox, 161
Compost garden demo site, 44
Continental Divide, 237
Coombs, 148
Copper mines, 181, 279, 290
Coquitlam, 49
Cornish waterwheels, 296, 297
Cottonwood House Historic Park, 296
Cougar habitat, 212
Courtenay, 162
Cowichan Valley, 136
Cows, 27, 168, 229
Crafts, 18, 24, 82, 105, 135, 160, 161, 163, 174, 200, 247, 273, 291
Craig Heritage Museum and Park, 148
Craigdarroch Castle, 117
Craigellachie Last Spike, 231
Craigflower Farmhouse and Schoolhouse, 117
Cranberry Lake sanctuary, 84
Cranbrook, 242
Crawford Bay, 272, 273
Creston, 271
Crofton, 140
Cruise ships, 23, 34
Cruising, 179. *See Lady Rose* and *Uchuck*
Cultus Lake, 96, 97
Cumberland, 161
Cusheon Creek Hatchery, 134
Cyclotron tour, 26
Cypress Provincial Park, 34

Dutchman dairy, 231
Dairy barns, 27, 168, 229, 231
Dam tours, 92, 233, 258, 261, 268, 310
Deep Creek Tool Museum, 220
Deep Creek, 321
Deer, 87, 271
Delkatla Wildlife and Bird Sanctuary, 332

Delta, 55
Demonstration forests, 36, 62, 139,
   279, 288, 307
Denman Island, 161
Desert, pocket size, 192
Dewdney-Alouette Parks, 60
Dinosaurs, 20, 310
Discovery fishing pier, 166
Distillery tour, 212
Dog training demonstration, 50
Doll collection, 162
Dominion Astrophysical
   Observatory, 126
Douglas firs, 54, 121
Doukhobor heritage, 253, 262
Duncan, 136
Dyke trails, 39, 40, 41, 56, 88

Eagle Aerie Gallery, 158
Eagle River Salmon Hatchery, 230
Eagles, 68, 85, 100, 135, 151, 168,
   179, 244, 332, 335
Earthquake research, 126
East Kootenay Hunters
   Association, 242
Eco-Museum, 137
Elk, 248
Elk Falls Pulp and Paper Mill, 167
Elk Valley Educational Forest
   Trail, 248
Ellison Park Interpretive Program,
   216
Elphinstone Pioneer Museum, 82
Emily Carr, 21, 24, 117, 118, 121,
   334
Empress Hotel lobby, 118
Enderby, 219
Engineers, military, 94
Englishman River Falls, 149
Esquimalt, 120
Estate wineries, 163, 190, 196, 198,
   206, 208, 211

Fairmont Hot Springs, 240
Fanny Bay Ferry, 161
Farm-gate wineries, 59, 195, 199,
   202, 205
Farmers markets, 24, 135, 161, 233
Farming, historic, 58, 162, 177,

217, 284
Farwell Canyon, 294
Farwell Canyon, 294
Father Pandosy Mission, 210
Fauquier, 266
Federal Parks Service, 234
Fernandes Banana Farm, 191
Fernie, 245
Ferries to Salt Spring Island, 134
Ferries, free, 11, 55, 63, 266, 269,
   316, 324
Ferry Building Art Gallery, 34
Ferry to Alaska, 327
Ferry to Queen Charlotte Islands,
   331
Ferry to Sunshine Coast, 80
Ferry to Victoria, 115
Field, 235
Filburg Art Gallery and Lodge,
   163
Finnish community, 177
Fire-fighting planes, 149
Fire Hall tour, 24
Fireworks displays, 31, 75, 124,
   146
Fisgard Lighthouse National
   Historic Park, 128
Fish cannery museum, 41
Fish farm research, 144
Fish hatcheries. See Hatcheries.
Fisheries and Oceans tour, 36, 126
Fishing history, 41, 129, 167
Fishing pier, 166
Flag Shop, 24
Floating bridge, 211
Floating hotel, 154
Floating museum, 48
Flower-growers' auction, 45
Food processing lab, 205
Footbridge, 144, 263
Forest in Action tours, 96, 101, 139
Forestry centres, 175, 204
Forestry tours, 24, 106, 110, 139,
   153, 158, 167, 175, 188, 290,
   293, 295, 316, 335
Forests for the World Park, 305
Fort Langley, 57
Fort Rodd Hill National Historic
   Park, 128

Fort Rupert native village, 181
Fort Rupert, 182
Fort St. James, 311
Fort Steele, 244
Fort Victoria, 122
Fossils, 99, 235
Frances Barkley, 151
Francois Lake ferry, 316
Fraser Canyon, 103, 108
Fraser-Fort George Regional
    Museum, 305
Fraser Lake, 313
Fraser River Heritage Park, 93
Fraser Valley, 88
French Canadian festival, 30
Friendly Cove, 171
Fruit candy, 207
Fruit juice plant tour, 213
Fruit leather tour, 199
Fruit-packing museum, 209
Fruit-packing tour, 196
Fruit research, 205
Fulton River Project, 316
Fur-trade era, 58, 105, 312

Galena, 266
Galiano Island, 135
Ganges, 135
Gardens, 16, 34, 43, 116, 119, 125,
    128, 129, 205, 240
Garibaldi mountain, 72
Garry Point Park, 39
Gastown walking tour, 25
Gate of Harmonious Interest, 123
Gator Gardens ecological park,
    176
Gehringer Brothers Estate Winery,
    195
Gem displays, 18, 20, 103
General stores, 19, 100, 244
Geological museum, 20
George C. Reifel Waterfowl
    Refuge, 56
German community events, 28
Ghost of Margaret Falls, 228
Ghost of Walachin, 284
Ghost town ruins, 187, 188, 232,
    264
Ghosts of Hosmer mountain, 245

Giants Head Park, 204
Gibraltar Mines, 290
Gibsons, 80
Gitskan native village, 320
Glacier National Park, 234
Glacier walk, 74
Glaciers, 234
Glass house, 272
Goats, 148
Gobelin tapestries, 19
Gold-mine tour, 256
Gold nugget jewellery, 323
Gold ore displays, 17, 103, 267
Gold Panner Campground, 217
Gold-panning concession, 299
Gold panning, public, 77, 104,
    108, 121, 186, 295
Gold-panning tour, 217
Gold River, 170
Gold-rush era, 78, 109, 281, 297
Gold rush trail, Williams Lake,
    289
Golden, 236
Golden Ears Provincial Park, 61
Golden spruce tree, 332
Goldstream Provincial Park, 121
Gordon Southam Observatory, 17
Gort's Dairy, 299
Government House gardens, 116
Grain terminal tour, 330
Grand Forks, 253
Grand Truck Pacific Railway his-
    tory, 306, 329
Granite City ghost town, 187
Granville Island Brewing, 23
Granville Island Visitors Centre,
    23
Gray Monk Cellars, 211
Gray whales, 156, 332
Great Northern Railway, 105
Greek culture, 29
Green Lake, 198
Green Point Theatre, 156
Greenwood, 259
Grey Fox, 282
Grocery Hall of Fame, 39
Grocery store tours, 25
Group campsites, 56, 58, 63
Guisachan Heritage House, 210

Gulf Islands, 133
Gulf of Georgia Cannery, 41

Hagensborg, 294
Hagwilet suspension bridge, 319
Haida canoe and longhouse, 333
Haida Gwaii, 331
Hainle Vineyards, 206
Halcyon Hot Springs, 265
Halfway River Hot Springs, 265
Hands of History tour, 320
Haney Heritage Village, 228
Haney House, 61
Hang-gliding, 102, 285
Hanging tree, 78
Harbourside Walk, Nanaimo, 145
Hardwood forest, 307
Harrison Hot Springs, 98
Harrop Cable Ferry, 269
Harrop to Longbeach ferry, 269
Hastings Mill Store Museum, 10
Hat Creek Heritage Ranch, 284
Hatcheries, 32, 52, 60, 84, 90, 91,
    94, 96, 121, 134, 136, 143, 152,
    154, 159, 162, 166, 172, 179,
    204, 215, 230, 242, 265, 278,
    292, 306, 317, 321, 324, 328
Hatley Castle, 128
Hatzic Rock, 91
Haynes Point Provincial Park, 193
Hazelton, 319
Hedley, 186, 188
Helmcken House, 118
Herb garden, 17
Heriot Bay Inn, 168
Heriot Bay, 168, 170
Heritage Park, Terrace, 323
Heritage ranches, 215, 284
Heritage river trails, 306
Heritage roadhouse outbuildings,
    287
Heritage Walk, Nanaimo, 145
Heritage walks, 62, 79, 122, 136,
    141, 243, 247, 251, 256, 271,
    330
Heros of sports, 22, 47, 216, 241,
    256
Highest peak in Rockies, 304
Highland Valley Copper, 279

Hill Creek Hatchery, 265
Hillside Cellars Winery, 202
Hiram Walker Distillery, 212
Historic abandoned mining
    railroad, 187
Historic aircraft, 126
Historic bank, 310
Historic barn, 287
Historic boat ride, 171
Historic bridge, 109
Historic cable tramway, 188
Historic castle, 117
Historic cement factory, 187
Historic Chinatown, 163, 298
Historic churches, 106, 110, 148,
    210, 231, 243, 312
Historic coal operation, 181
Historic courthouses, 247, 251, 286
Historic dance hall, 323
Historic doctor's residence, 118
Historic farms, 40, 53, 61, 117
Historic firehall, 329
Historic fishing village, 41
Historic flour mill, 190
Historic fortifications, 128
Historic fur-trading fort, 312
Historic gardens, 88, 100
Historic general stores, 19, 100
Historic gold-mining artifacts, 190
Historic H.B.C. chimney, 181
Historic hotels, 100, 141, 164, 210
Historic houses, 20, 40, 43, 48,
    53, 56, 61, 88, 110, 117, 118, 119,
    163, 197, 210, 310
Historic hunting estate, 49
Historic jailhouse, 194
Historic lighthouses, 33, 128, 148
Historic log cabins, 86, 148
Historic medical equipment, 79,
    136
Historic miners' cabins, 144, 323
Historic minesweeper, 171
Historic police building, 323
Historic post office, 148
Historic printing presses, 144, 290
Historic railway stations, 105, 138,
    329
Historic ranch, 215
Historic roadhouses, 283, 284, 296

Historic route of Alexander
    Mackenzie, 292
Historic schoolhouses, 43, 56, 117,
    120, 129, 148
Historic smelter stack, 251
Historic sternwheelers, 48, 201,
    270
Historic trapper's cabin, 323
Historic weather station, 101
Holberg, 181
Hollow tree, 16
Honey, 144, 190, 213
Honeymoon Bay, 138
Hoodoos, 235
Hooser Weaving Centre, 53
Hope, 103
Hornby Island, 161
Horne Lake Cave Park, 159
Horse ranches, 273, 315
Horse riding school, 217
Horseback riding, 88
Horseshoe Bay, 37
Horticulture Pacific Garden
    Centre, 125
Hosmer Mountain ghosts, 245
Hotsprings source, 98, 231
Hotsprings, commercial, 98, 232,
    238, 265
Hotsprings, undeveloped, 76, 240,
    265
Houston, 316
Hovercraft tours, 40, 149
Huber Ink Studio, 85
Hudson's Bay Company, pioneer
    era, 181, 296
Hudson's Hope, 308
Hugh Keenleyside Dam tour, 261
Hummingbirds, 192
Hungarian community, 28

Illecillewaet, 235
Inch Creek Hatchery, 91
Inkameep Vineyards, 195
Insect collections, 20
Inside Passage, 179, 327
Interpretive programs, 16, 61, 96,
    101, 107, 121, 129, 143, 149,
    156, 193, 164, 212, 216, 237,
    257, 262, 271, 280, 304, 307

Interpretive trails, 34, 36, 69, 74,
    84, 86, 96, 142, 260, 289, 293
Intertidal life, 130, 149, 164
Inverholme Schoolhouse, 56
Invermere, 239
Iona Beach Regional Park, 39
Irrigation station tour, 89
Irving House Museum, 48
Island Mountain Art Gallery, 297
Italian community archives, 259
Italian culture, 29
Ivory studio, 25

Jack of Clubs Hotel, 297
Jade, 25, 285, 323
Jam-making, 207
Japanese Canadian internment,
    105, 252
Japanese cemetery, 163
Japanese culture, 17, 45
Japanese gardens, 17, 47
Japanese shrine, 117
Japantown, 28
Judge Matthew Begbie, 286, 298
Junkers Aircraft, 312

Kaatza Station Pioneer Museum,
    138
Kalamalka Lake, 216
Kamloops, 280
Kane Valley demonstration forest,
    279
Kaon atomic-particles tour, 27
Kaslo, 270
Kekuli pit house, 227, 263
Kelowna, 208
Kenny Lake, 58
Keremeos, 189
Kermode bear, 323
Kettle Valley Railway Station, 251
Kilby General Store Museum, 100
Kilby Provincial Historic Park, 100
Kimberley, 240
Kispiox, 320
Kitimat, 324
Kitsilano Showboat, 29
Kitwanga, 320
Knox Mountain Road, 209
Koi fish, 144

Kokanee Creek Provincial Park, 267, 269
Kokanee salmon, 209, 265, 267, 270
Kootenay area, 249
Kootenay Bay ferry, 269
Kootenay Canal Generating Station tour, 268
Kootenay Forge, 273
Kootenay National Park, 237
Kootenay trout hatchery, 242
K'san Indian Village, 320
Kwagiulth Museum and Cultural Centre, 169
Kwinitsa Railway Station Museum, 329

Lace exhibit, 161
Lacrosse Hall of Fame, 47
Ladner, 55
Lady Franklin Rock, 109
Lady Rose, 151, 153
Ladysmith, 140
Lake Cowichan, 138
Lakelse Lake, 322
Lamb-bake, Saturna Island, 135
Lang Creek Hatchery, 84
Lang Winery, 202
Langley, 57
Last Spike, 231
Laurel Packing House, 210
Lava Bed Park, 322
Le Compte Estate Winery, 198
Le Roi Gold Mine tour, 256
Lead smelter tour, 258
Legends of B.C., 68, 69, 92, 134, 192, 198, 200, 245, 251, 284, 288, 298, 322, 323
Legislative buildings tour, 121
Legislative sitting, historic re-creation, 58
Leir House Cultural Centre, 200
Lighthouses, 33, 154, 169
Lillooet, 77
Lime quarry tour, 87
Link and Pin Museum, 173
Lions Great Bridge, 144
Little Greece, 29
Little Hustan Cave Park, 174

Little Italy, 29
Little Mountain Dropoff, 150
Little Qualicum Hatchery, 159
Little Qualicum River, 149
Lobby walking 73, 118
Log church, 309
Logging railroad, 175
Log-home manufacturers' tours, 74, 306
Log lodge, 76
London Farm, 40
Long Beach, 155
Long-range marine navigation visit, 293
Longhouses, 158, 178, 182, 320, 324, 333
Loran C. Tower, 293
Lorne Hotel, 164
Lucky Jim Mine, 169
Lumby, 214
Lund, 83
Lussier Hot Springs, 240
Lynn Canyon Suspension Bridge, 33
Lytton, 109

M. Y. Williams Geological Museum, 20
Ma Murray, 79
Mabel Lake pictographs, 197
Mabel Lake, 220
McIntyre Bluffs, 197
Mackenzie, 308
MacMillan Bloedel Visitors Centre, 153
Malaspina College, 144
Manning Park, 107
Manus Enterprises, 26
Maple Ridge, 59
Maplewood Farm, 33
Marble Canyon, 237, 238
Margaret Falls, 228
Marine biology, 36, 153
Maritime navigational tower, 293
Marshall Steven Wildlife Preserve, 160
Marshes, 16, 49, 56, 57, 60, 81, 121, 134, 160, 179, 215, 271, 281, 289

Martin Flying Tanks, 145
Masset Village, 334
Mastodon jewellery, 25
Matsqui Trail Regional Park, 88
Matsqui, 88
Meadow Creek Spawning Channel, 270
Meagre Creek Hot Springs, 76
Medieval garden, 17
Medieval re-enactments, 30
Mel DeAnna Nature Walk, 260
Memorial poles, 178
Merritt, 278
Merry Creek Nature Walk, 260
Metchosin Schoolhouse, 129
Methanol production tour, 326
Mica Dam tour, 233
Midway, 249
Migrating birds, 39, 43, 49, 56, 194, 260, 271, 281, 332
Mile 108 Heritage Site, 287
Mile O Cairn, Lillooet, 78
Military history, 48, 94, 128, 143, 163, 180, 190, 201, 281
Military training, 128
Mill lookout, 86
Milltown history, 35
Mine-shaft model, 163
Mine-shaft tour, 256
Miner's union hall, 255
Mineral displays, 18, 20, 92, 103, 265
Miniature apples, 96
Ministry of Forests nursery, 54
Minnekhada Regional Park, 49
Miracle Beach Provincial Park, 164
Mission, 91
Mission Hill Wines, 207
Mission of Father Pandosy, 210
Miyazaki Heritage House, 79
Moccasin factory, 89
Molybdenum mine tour, 313
Monck Park, 280
Moodyville history, 35
Moose-viewing, 305
Moricetown Canyon, native fishing, 318
Morrell Wildlife Sanctuary, 142

Mother Lode Mine, 252
Mount Kobau, 192
Mount Robson, 304
Mount Seymour Provincial Park, 33
Mountain Ash Farm Petting Zoo, 84
Mountain View Museum, 253
Movie Stars' footsteps tour, 106
Munson's Mountain, 200
Murals, large, 140, 181, 248
Museum of Northern British Columbia, 329
Museum of the Exotic World, 20
Museum Society Activity Centre, 161

Nakusp, 264
Nanaimo, 142
Nancy Green Lake, 255
Nancy Green's trophies, 73
Naramata, 202, 203
National historic sites, 41, 58, 128, 312
Native artifacts, 19, 21, 45, 53, 56, 58, 61, 76, 82, 99, 120, 126, 152, 158, 161, 162, 166, 169, 177, 178, 181, 190, 193, 201, 253, 266, 268, 272, 290, 305, 318
Native arts, 19, 53, 83, 89, 152, 158, 182, 191, 282, 291, 308
Native carvers, 182, 320, 330
Native carvings, 19, 45, 86
Native ceremonial regalia, 169, 178
Native community, 325
Native cultural centres, 83, 243, 291, 308
Native dancing, 291, 308, 310, 320
Native fish-drying, 79
Native fortification, 320
Native legend, 245
Native lore, 89
Native pictographs, 197, 220, 294
Native pit house, 227
Native silver, 19, 182
Native sites, 79, 91, 192, 237, 238
Native talking sticks, 169
Native traditional fishing, 294, 318

Native traditional habitations, 227
Native villages, 157, 320
Native war canoes, 97
Natural disaster, 103
Natural History club, 170
Nature houses, 33, 41, 43, 122,
    129, 149, 289
Nature trails, 52, 57, 122
Naval artifacts, 21
Naval history, 117, 120, 155
Nechako Valley Historical Site, 311
Needles ferry, 266
Nelson, 267
Never-ending fountain, 174
New Denver, 264
New Hazelton, 319
New Westminster, 47
New-Small and Sterling Studio
    Glass, 22
Newcastle Island, 143
Nicola Lake, 280
Nicola Valley Museum, 278
Nimpkish Burial Grounds, 178
Nimpkish Valley, 174
Nimpo Lake, 293
Nisga'a Memorial Lava Bed Park,
    322
Nitobe Memorial Gardens, 17
Nootka Sound, 171
North American Guard Dog Train-
    ing Academy, 50
North Island Forestry Centre, 175
North Vancouver, 32
North Woven Broom Co., 273
Northern Lights Studio, 323
Norwegian community artifacts,
    292
Norwegian fjord horses, 273
Nuatsum Valley Forestry tour, 293
Nuggets, gold, 217
Nut Farm, 96

O'Keefe Historic Ranch, 215
O.K. Dried Fruit Ltd., 199
Observatories, 17, 125
Ocean rapids, 81, 328
Ocean Sciences tour, 126
Ochre Beds, native, 237
Ogden Point Breakwater, 119

Ogopogo, 199
Oil rig, 246
Okanagan Art Gallery, 201
Okanagan Cooperative Growers
    Packing House, 196
Okanagan Falls, 197
Okanagan Mountain Provincial
    Park, 212
Okanagan Valley, 186
Okanagan Vineyards Estate
    Winery, 196
Old-growth forests, 16, 54, 62, 96,
    101, 121, 142, 147
Old Hastings Mill store, 19
Old Masset Village Museum, 334
Old School House Gallery, 160
Old Wells Hotel and Gallery, 297
Oldest Anglican church in B.C.,
    100
Oldest building in Vancouver, 19
Oldest schoolhouse in Canada, 118
Oldfield Fish Hatchery, 328
Oliver, 194
Olympic champion medals, 73,
    256
100 Mile House, 287
108 Mile Heritage Site, 287
Open-pit copper mines, 181, 279,
    290
Orpheum Theatre tour, 26
Osoyoos, 191
Ospreys, 244, 26
Othello tunnels, 105
Overland Telegraph, 296
Oyster cultivation, 85

Pacific Garden Centre, 125
Pacific Institute of Aquaculture and
    Fisheries, 144
Pacific Rim National Park, 155
Pacific Rim Whale Festival, 157
Pacific Spirit Regional Park, 16
Packaging products tour, 326
Paint Pots ochre beds, 237
Painter's Lodge, 167
Pandosy Mission, 210
Park and Tilford Gardens, 34
Park Interpreter Programs, 96, 101,
    107, 121, 129, 149, 156, 164,

193, 212, 216, 234, 235, 237,
  257, 262, 269, 304, 307
Parksville, 147
Paydirt tour, 217
Peace Canyon Dam, 310
Peace Memorial, 263
Peachland, 203
Pearson College of the Pacific, 129
Pemberton, 76
Pender Island, 135
Pentiction, 199
Petrochemical tour, 326
Petroglyphs, 134, 146, 150, 169,
  170, 189, 322
Phoenix Mine Site, 252
Photographic displays, historical,
  35, 48, 73, 86, 136, 181, 190,
  193, 195, 204, 205, 236, 259,
  266, 268, 278
Pictographs, 197, 220, 294, 329
Pier for fishing, 166
Pinkut Creek Artificial Spawning
  Channel, 314
Pioneer artifacts, 82, 96, 95, 126,
  148, 152, 166, 181, 190, 201,
  216, 220, 229, 239, 272, 289,
  305
Pioneer cemetery, 286
Pioneer fire-fighting, 253, 306,
  329
Pioneer forestry, 204
Pioneer logging, 173
Pioneer oil search, 246
Pioneer printship, 244
Pioneer rectory, 246
Pioneer store, 318
Pioneer villages, 43, 228, 231
Pit houses, native, 227, 263
Pitt Meadows, 59
Place Des Arts Gallery, 50
Placer Dome Mine, 313
Platzl, 241
Plywood plant tour, 229
Pocket Desert Ecological Reserve,
  192
PoCo Walking Trail, 49
Point Ellice House, 119
Police artifacts, 190
Police history, 21, 163, 193, 323

Porpoise Bay Park, 81
Port Alberni, 151
Port Alice, 176
Port Clements, 333
Port Coquitlam, 49
Port Hardy, 179
Port McNeill, 173, 175
Port Moody, 49
Port of Vancouver tour, 26
Potlatch, 178
Powell River, 83
Powerland farm machinery, 95
Presbyterian church, 210
Prince George, 305
Prince Rupert, 327
Princeton, 186
Provincial assembly, 58
Provincial library, 121
Pulp and paper mill tours, 70, 86,
  145, 153, 167, 176, 282, 307,
  326
Punjabi market, 30
Puntledge hatchery, 162
Purden Lake Provincial Park, 307
Purdy's Chocolates, 24

Quadra Island ferry, 168
Quail's Gate winery, 208
Qualicum Beach, 159
Quatse River hatchery, tidal
  marsh, 179
Queen Charlotte City, 332
Queen Charlotte Islands, 331
Queen Elizabeth Park, 16
Queen of the North ferry, 179
Queen's Park, 47
Quesnel, 295
Quilchena Cattle Co., 279
Quilchena Hotel, 279
Quinsam River hatchery, 166

R. N. Atkinson Museum, 201
Radar Hill, 155
Radio telescopes, 198
Radium Hot Springs, 238
Railway history, 50, 61, 218, 231,
  232, 242, 281, 306
Railway models, 209, 270
Railway stations, historic, 101, 105,

138, 205, 251, 261, 329
Railway tunnels, 105
Rainbow Junction Art Centre,105
Rainbow trout, 270
Ralph River, 172
Ranch visits, 273, 315
Ranching history, 284
Rathtrevor Provincial Park, 149
Rattlesnake habitat, 192, 212
RCAF history, 163, 180
Reaction ferry, 111
Red stagecoach, 288
Reimer-Redmond House, 311
Revelstoke, 232
Reversing rapids, 81
Rhododendron gardens, 123, 125
Rhododendron Lake, 148
Rhododendrons, wild, 107
Rhodonite, 323
Richmond, 39
Rick Hansen, 22, 137
Ripple Rock, 155, 165
Robert Held Art Glass, 22
Roberts Bank tour, 26
Robertson Creek, 152
Robson Square Media Centre, 30
Rockhounding, 77, 99, 103, 188,
    189, 219
Rocky Mountain Rangers Museum,
    281
Roedde House, 20
Rodeos, 278, 291
Rogers Pass, 234
Rogers Sugar Museum, 20
Roosevelt elk, 171
Rose gardens, 17, 34, 47, 125, 201,
    271
Rossland, 255
Royal British Columbia Museum,
    120
Royal Hudson steam train, 71
Royal Roads Military College, 128
Royal Westminster Regiment
    Museum, 48
Ruby hunt, 99
Ruskin Generating Station, 92
Russ Baker Memorial, 312
S.S. *Movie*, 270
S.S. *Samson*, floating museum, 48

S.S. *Sicamous*, 201
Saanich Peninsula, 125
Sagebrush, 188, 193
St. Ann's Academy Schoolhouse,
    120
St. Eugene Mission Church, 243
St. Lazlo Estate Winery, 190
St. Peter's Stolen Church, 239
Salmon Arm, 228
Salmon enhancement facilities, 32,
    52, 60, 68, 84, 94, 104, 121,
    134, 136, 143, 152, 154, 159,
    162, 166, 172, 179, 215, 230,
    279, 292, 317, 321, 324, 328,
    332
Salmon research, 36, 144
Salt Spring Island, 135
Sam Kee Building, 28
Samson V, 48
Sandcastle competitions, 102, 150,
    151, 164
Sandon ghost town, 264
Sandspit timber tour, 335
Sandstone Mineral Museum, 103
Sandy beaches, 129, 149, 216, 262
Sasquatch Provincial Park, 101
Saturna Island, 135
Sawmill tours, 51, 62, 70, 86, 106,
    110, 139, 153, 188, 212, 282,
    290, 316
Sayward, 173
Schoolhouses, 43, 56, 117, 118, 120,
    129, 228, 231, 286
Scientific tours, 27, 36, 144, 198,
    205, 213, 326
Scout Island Nature Centre, 289
SeaBus, 31
Seal Bay Regional Park, 162
Seal viewing, 129, 135, 161
Seashell exhibits, 82, 161, 164
Seawall promenade, 34
Sechelt Nation Cultural Complex,
    83
Sechelt, 80
Second-growth forests, 52, 54, 57,
    62, 96, 101, 139, 167, 175
Secwepemc Native Centre, 282
Seedling nursery, 307
Serpentine Fen, 52

Seven Mile Generating Station tour, 258
Seymour Demonstration Forest, 36
Shakeside House, 69
Shannon Falls, 69
Shelter Bay, 266
Shuswap Area, 225
Shuswap Lake Provincial Park, 227
Sicamous, 230
Sidney, 126
Silver Lake Forestry Centre, 204
Silver smelter tour, 258
Similkameen Region, 186
Simon Fraser University campus tour, 45
Sinclair Canyon, 238
Sitka spruce, 25, 33,
Skaha Lake, 200
Skaha-Okanagan Lake Channel, 199
Ski hill orientations, 73, 75
Skookumchuck Narrows, 81
Sliammon Hatchery, 85
Slocan, 264
Smelter model, 253
Smelter tour, 258
Smithers, 317
Snootli Creek Hatchery, 292
Society for Creative Anachronism, 30
Sointula, 176
Sooke, 129
South Cariboo Museum, 286
South Okanagan Art Gallery, 201
Spallumcheen Region, 218
Sparwood, 248
Spawning channels, 81, 104, 209, 226, 265, 267, 270, 314, 316
Spenser Mansion, 117
Spius Creek Fish Hatchery, 278
Sports Hall of Fame, 22, 47, 216, 241, 256, 257
Spotted Lake, 192
Sproat Lake, 149
Spruce seedlings, 54
Squamish, 67
Squamish Spit, 69
Stadium tour, 22

Stagecoaches, 44, 288, 296
Stained-glass windows, 23, 93, 160, 177, 243
Stamp Falls Fishway, 152
Stampede, Williams Lake, 291
Stanley Park, 16
Star-gazing, 17, 125, 192
Station Art Gallery, 247
Station House Art Gallery, 289
Stave Falls, 92
Stave Lake group lodge and camp, 63
Stawamus Chief, 68
Steam engine models, 152
Steve Kulash Taxidermy, 45
Steveston Village, 40
Stewart Farmhouse, 53
Sto:Lo Bigfoot Moccasin Factory, 89
Stock Exchange tour, 27
Storm-watching, 235, 155
Strathcona Park, 170
Sucker Creek salmon-spawning area, 104
Sugar museum, 20
Sumac Ridge winery, 206
Summer School of the Arts, 200, 205, 269
Summerland, 204
Sun-Rype juices, 213
Sun Yat Sen Gardens, 28
Sunshine Coast, 80
Surprise Ranch, 202
Surrey, 51
Suspension bridges, 33, 55, 319
Swan Lake Bird Sanctuary, 122, 215
Swans, 281
Syringa Creek Provincial Park, 261, 262

Tahsis, 172
Tasting tours, 207, 213, 219
Taxidermy display, 20, 45, 201, 242, 243, 318
Tea ceremony, 17
Telegraph Cove, 174
Tenderfoot fish hatchery, 68
Terrace, 321

Texada Island, 87
Thornton hatchery, 154
Three Valley Gap Pioneer Village, 231
Tidal flats, 39, 60, 179
Tidal pools, 155, 164, 182
Tintagel Cairn, 315
Tlupana-Conuma hatchery, 172
Toboggan Creek hatchery, 317
Toboggan runs, 33, 72
Tofino, 155, 158
Totem poles, 16, 19, 45, 116, 118, 120, 137, 178, 181, 182, 320, 324, 333
Tow Hill Ecological Reserve, 333
Trail, 257
Tranquille Marsh waterfowl habitat, 281
Trans-Canada Railway Museum, 50
Transportation history, 44, 48, 306
Tree art gallery, 173
Tree nurseries, 96, 307
Tree safaris, 81, 116
Trethewey House, 88
TRIUMF tour, 26
Trounce Alley, 122
Trout hatcheries, 204, 242, 257, 270
Truck-manufacturing tour, 213
Trumpeter swans, 60, 162
Tsawwassen, 55
Tweedsmuir Provincial Park, 292
Tyax Mountain Lodge, 76
Tynehead Regional Park, 52

UBC Animal Science dairy barn, 27
UBC Botanical Gardens, 17
UBC campus tour, 27
UBC experimental farm tour, 168
Uchuck II, 171
Ucluelet, 154
Union Steamship Co., 143
United Flower Growers auction, 45
United World College, 129
University of Victoria campus tour, 123

University tours, 27, 45
Upana Caves, 172
Upper Arrow Lakes ferry, 266
Usk ferry, 324

Valley of One Thousand Faces, 173
Vancouver Island, 131
Vancouver Stock Exchange Visitor Centre, 27
Vancouver, 15
Vanderhoof, 311
Vaseux Lake Wildlife Sanctuary, 194
Veneer plant tour, 217
Vernon, 214
Victoria, 115
Victorian houses, 20, 56, 58
Volksmarch routes, 97, 241
Voodoo fighter, 163

W.A.C. Bennett Dam, 310
Wagon rides, 215, 285
Walking trails, 39, 49, 50, 52, 57, 60, 61, 62, 71, 81, 96, 149, 155, 159, 166, 170, 171, 179, 187, 212, 243, 255, 279, 294, 306
Waneta Dam Tour, 258
Water transportation museum, 210
Waterfalls, 69, 91, 103, 129, 149, 151, 171, 228, 235
Waterfowl viewing, 39, 43, 49, 52, 56, 60, 84, 129, 215, 228, 306
Waterwheel Park, 139
Weaver Creek Spawning Channel, 99
Weaving, 53, 89, 163
Wells, 297
Westbank, 207
West Coast Railway Association, 19
Western Canadian Universities Marine Biology Station, 153
West Kootenay National Exhibition Centre, 261
Westmin Resources, 172
Westminster Abbey, 93
Whale-spotting, 156, 157
West Vancouver, 32
Whaling station, 180

Whippletree Junction, 137
Whistler, 71
White Lake, 198, 203
White Rock, 51
Wickaninnish Visitor Centre, 156
Wild Goose farm-gate winery, 199
Wildflowers, 16, 96, 107, 147, 264
Wildlife, 52, 56, 60, 84, 87, 96,
    137, 143, 160, 162, 179, 226,
    243, 248, 255, 260, 264, 281,
    289, 332, 333
Williams Lake, 289
Williston Lake Reservoir, 309
Willow River Demonstration
    Forest, 307
Witty's Lagoon, 129
Windermere Valley Pioneer
    Museum, 239

Windsurfers, 69
Winery tours, 190, 195, 196, 198,
    199, 212, 205, 206, 208, 210,
    211
Winfield, 212
Wood manufacturer's tours, 217
Woss Junction, 174

Yale, 110
Yarrow, 96
Yellow Pine Interpretive Trail, 260
Yellowhead Highway, 303
Yew Lake Trail, 34
Yoho National Park, 235

Zeballos, 174
Zinc smelter tour, 258
Zuckerburg Island Heritage Park,
    263